Guide to Decision:
The Royal Commission

Charles J. Hanser

Guide to Decision:
The Royal Commission

The Bedminster Press   1965

Copyright © 1965, The Bedminster Press, Incorporated,
Totowa, New Jersey
Library of Congress Catalogue Card Number: 65–24957
Manufactured in the United States of America by H. Wolff, N. Y.
Designed by Adrianne Onderdonk

Readers of this book are invited to send their names and addresses
to The Bedminster Press, Vreeland Avenue, Totowa, New Jersey,
U.S.A., to receive announcements and literature about other books
in the social sciences published by The Bedminster Press.

JN
407
H3

50791

O.K.K.P.

Preface

Decision-making in societies has a unique fascination. The exercise, even the observation, of leadership has always been intriguing in itself; and the results of ultimate decisions are fateful beyond measure.

We recognize the hazard and turmoil of our age. Groups dispute not simply the application of rules but the rightness and justice of the rules themselves. Changes in beliefs, in customs, in the very face of the earth seem to leave nothing stable, nothing certain. The world presents us with choices whose outcome can mean survival or disintegration. What persons, then, and what processes can be most trusted to make decisions that look to the best interests of all?

That question, with the peril that makes it so momentous,

has challenged other societies in the past. Yet it has probably never been more crucial than it is today.

The better the decisional process and the more inclusive and accurate the information fed into it, the more valid the final decisions. Just as obviously, the more valid the decisions the greater the well-being of the members of the society.

A democracy imposes high standards. Decisions not only must be right; they cannot be handed down from above—no matter how kindly the dictator. Not only must they be accepted; with important qualifications, as many citizens as possible must help make them. Final decisions are entrusted to legislative, executive, and judicial leaders, but they must be responsive to the pressures of the national life. No one association, not even the sovereign State, can be all-inclusive, for freedom lies in a pluralist society, in the very play of power of different groups.

But we must recognize here certain dangers. Almost all statements of fact, analyses of controversial problems, and recommended policies come from groups competing for power, material goods, or freedom to do what they want. They come, that is, from sources whose interests or perspectives are less than that of the total population. Or, in any particular instance, are they less? Who can tell, and how? In either event the "facts" and judgments are usually contradicted, with an all-too-familiar dismal cycle of arguments, charges, claims, counter-claims, and counter-counter-claims.

If on one problem after another there is no standard of reference, no set of facts that can be taken as authoritative, no yardstick that can be accepted as impartial—if there is not even a judge to winnow or sum up—the public becomes increasingly confused, with cynicism not far behind. Who could measure the resultant harm to the society from lowered morale, lessened respect for leaders, the doubt that gradually undermines the sense of what is right or good?

Even that corrosion may be less damaging than the consequences if a significant proportion of final decisions are only
the unwilled result of a trial by strength of opposing vested-
interest blocs. From that trial it may be thought that leaders
and citizens will be able to determine Right, much as a jury is
presumed to cull Truth from the clash of prosecuting and defense attorneys. Do they? Do policies shaped by such pressures achieve the best interests of the total society? Is there a
necessary, even a usual, correlation between validity of policy
and political or economic or propagandist strength, or a balance of such strengths? If not, who could tell to what level the
well-being of the society may not be depressed?

We need make no invidious comparisons of the damage,
up to civil war, caused by these impairments in existing and
would-be democratic societies. Note only that the United
States, for instance, has a marked disposition to accept such
controversy and "resolution" as inevitable. There is a unanimous sentiment for a written instrument, the Constitution,
but a widespread distrust of political agencies. In any controversial problem, from medical care to divorce, from agricultural surpluses to automation to integration, the country
shows no comparable respect for any human instrument that
is presumed to lead—be it church, court, government, press,
or university.

Are these impairments unavoidable; could they be minimized? Not by one dictatorial voice nor by bland conformity,
for diversity and competition in ideas are indispensable. But
would it be possible to find a source of judgment that could
be relied on for integrity, intellectual competence, the broad-
est possible viewpoint on problems, and the least personal or
group interest in particular resolutions? In an imperfect
world, power realities may usually determine final decisions.
But among the forces taken into account, as antecedents to
decision, could judgments that derived their strength from

such a source be included—might they even sometimes be determinative?

Put in that form the question seems to invite an answer from utopia. But ask instead: Have such judgments ever been systematically secured and become operative in ultimate decisions? We may then look for possible precedents in the real world, even though they be outside our national borders.

For it is no idle fancy to regard civilization as one vast counter on which are spread out for view all the ways of organized life ever devised. Here are innumerable varieties of decisional processes. They range from the custom of static, communal societies, through councils of elders, to absolute monarchy with its divine right of kings, personal and party dictatorships, representative assemblies of all kinds.

Similarly varied are the antecedents to decision, the kinds and sources of information on which decisions have been based. These antecedents have been limited to the knowledge of a single inspired prophet, of a family or clique or minority party. They have included the findings of soothsayers, of scientific research, of public opinion polls. There have been such specific mechanisms of decision as trial by ordeal or by combat, arbitration, majority vote, proportional representation.

This display-counter is open to any country. It can be inspected at leisure, and any item can be removed for use at home. To be sure, cultural search and borrow is hardly a well-developed art. All too often national vanity or vested interest perpetuates an always depressive and sometimes fatal cultural inbreeding.

But there is in this array of decisional processes one that should make a strong enough appeal to national self-interest to overcome these obstacles—especially if inspection showed not only its great usefulness but also how easy it would be to adopt. This mechanism is not unknown; it is, in fact, recognized as the best of its kind ever developed. It is hardly untried, since it has been refined over nearly a thousand years. It is not outmoded, since it is called on constantly by probably the world's politically most sophisticated country. Its findings of fact are accepted by the knowledgeable as definitive; its policy directives almost invariably guide societal evolution. The aid it has given has been called "literally beyond estimation." Yet, paradoxically, published information about it is limited to one introductory book (25 years old now and out of print), a few articles, and brief references in works on government and history.

I refer to the Royal Commission of Great Britain. This is the ranking investigatory and advisory body of that country. It is the guide to what is and what should be; it is the implementation of the Sovereign Intent that "Right be Done." But this only identifies, it does not even suggest full significance.

What really is this decisional mechanism, this process-antecedent to ultimate decision? What services, intended and latent, can it perform for a country? How is it used in its native environment; what conditions or standards are required for its most effective use? Is it a prototype that can be fitted congenially into the political framework of other countries?

I address students of social structures and processes; citizens whose understanding is so important to the success of a Royal Commission, or its equivalent; and political leaders in whose hands lies the power to use this structure, to misuse it, or not to use it at all.

The professional concern of the student of society is with understanding. Beyond understanding lies a broader concern with possible application of any new or clearer insight. The more conscious the knowledge of all the functions of the Royal Commission and of the importance of the standards that protect it against partisan perversion and mediocre membership, the more aid the structure can give to the rational handling of a society's strategic problems. I can only hope that this equal concern will prove, like love at its best, not to have distorted understanding but to have sharpened and deepened it.

I record with gratitude the help of Hans L. Zetterberg, John C. Rees, and my wife, Johanne. Only his students can appreciate with me what is owing to William C. Casey.

C J H

May, 1965
Pacific Palisades, Calif.

Contents

Guide to Decision:
The Royal Commission

1 Liberty and order: the police

The place was Hyde Park, London. The time was April 1928. Miss Irene Savidge, age 22, a stenographer, and Sir Leo Chiozza Money, age 57, a former Member of Parliament, were seated together on a park bench, talking. Did anything else occur? Two police officers on duty in the park later testified to conduct so clearly violating certain laws of public decency that they felt it their duty to arrest the pair. The magistrate before whom the charges were brought, however, was completely dissatisfied with the testimony of the officers—so much so that he dismissed the case without even hearing all of the evidence and censured the officers in exceptionally vigorous language. To cap it all he awarded ten pounds costs against the police.

Against a backdrop of mounting public irritation with morals legislation and police attempts to enforce it, this simple incident was the opening scene in a drama that was to become known to students the world around as the Savidge Case. Its theme was the fateful efforts of a Leviathan State to remedy the grievances of citizens, to probe inward for self-diagnosis of societal illness, and then to cure itself.

Three Royal Commissions on the police, in 1906, 1928, and 1960, might at first seem of specialized interest and perhaps of secondary importance. But the preservation of order is basic in any society. Justice, obedience to law, and respect for civil liberties, on the public-police level, underlie practically all aspects of freedom in a democratic society. They directly affect the safety and well-being of every citizen, every day. And the difficulties of achieving them are never overcome once and for all time.

The Savidge Case

At this period the population of London was about 8,000,-000; the metropolitan police numbered some 20,000. Stanley Baldwin was Prime Minister in a Conservative Government.

The action of the magistrate in so reprimanding the police had its almost inevitable reaction in the House of Commons. On May 7, 1928, the Home Secretary was asked a series of questions about the case. As a result, he ordered an inquiry to determine whether the two arresting officers had been guilty of perjury before the magistrate. Here was a familiar enough development, though one might well pause to reflect on a political system that can have the governing body of an empire require a Cabinet minister to assume responsibility for the conduct of two city policemen.

The next development, however, was distinctly out of the ordinary. In the perjury inquiry all the principals were questioned as a matter of course, but it was the nature of the interrogation of Miss Savidge that touched off a crisis, one of historical importance in British public-police relations.

Thomas Johnston, a Labour Member of Parliament, described that interrogation, two days after it occurred, in a May 17 debate in the Commons on this "matter of urgent public importance."

Two police officers, one a woman, he began, had gone to Miss Savidge's place of employment, told her she was wanted to clear up certain points in the Leo Money case, and, without giving her any opportunity to communicate with her family or legal adviser, had taken her to Scotland Yard in an official car. There the woman police chaperon was dismissed, and Miss Savidge was then questioned for five consecutive hours.

In the course of this interrogation, Mr. Johnston charged, Miss Savidge was asked many improper questions—about her wages, her relations with Sir Leo Money, whether she had her legs crossed when talking with him in the park, what the color of her petticoat was—and indelicate demonstrations were made about the position of her hand. Mr. Johnston reported that Miss Savidge had become so tired at the cross-examination that she let the statements go at what the two interrogating officers had written down, statements often slanted to the desire of the police. But, he admitted, "it is to the credit of the officers—and I say this frankly—that at this period, at any rate, they offered her tea." The questioning continued for five hours, and Miss Savidge was finally taken home in a police car at 8 P.M., her mother having only been notified at 6 o'clock of her whereabouts. Once home she allegedly collapsed and asserted that the officers had repeatedly warned her not to say a word to anyone that she had been at Scotland Yard.

There was the full case against the police. Its enormity inspired Mr. Johnston to invoke the duty of Parliament "to offer a resolute and determined opposition to anything in the nature of a Cheka, or the Turkish system, or the Star Chamber method, or what is known in the United States of America as the third degree." Nor was he alone in his revulsion. There was an outburst of indignation at his account. Members threw a barrage of questions at the Home Secretary: Did he think this method of interfering with His Majesty's lieges to get evidence was one for which he had no responsibility? On what grounds did he think a citizen could be detained without warrant? Would he make it clear that it was not legal to deny access of a witness to his legal advisers?

There was no mistaking the temper of the House, which cut across party lines. Members were angry at this violation by the police of the norms of fair play against a relatively defenseless young woman. They were also afraid it represented a growing encroachment on the whole range of civil liberties. When the Home Secretary rose to answer, the House was silent but gradually warmed to him as he showed he was impressed by the seriousness of the issue.

He agreed that the matter was of "absolutely vital importance" and that "the Secretary of State himself should devote his whole time to getting at the bottom of the affair." Since he had been in office there had been no similar case, and he admitted that the accusations, if there were any truth to them at all, were "of the most damning character" to the police. He added, however, that the police denied much of what Mr. Johnston had reported.[1]

The outcome of the debate was the Home Secretary's

---

[1] For this debate see *Parliamentary Debates,* House of Commons, Vol. 217, 5/17/28, Cols. 1216-20 and 1303-39. For other Savidge Case references, see also Vol. 217, 5/23/28, Cols. 1921-31; and Vol. 220, 7/16/28, Cols. 35-36 and 7/20/28, Cols. 803-92.

agreement to appoint a Tribunal of Inquiry to investigate the circumstances of Miss Savidge's interrogation, and then to consider whether a subsequent broader inquiry into police methods was called for.

The Tribunal had a Conservative and a Labour Member of Parliament, with a retired judge as chairman. Its report[2] was split. The judge and the Conservative member accepted the police account of the interrogation and exonerated them of misconduct. The Labour member accepted Miss Savidge's account and denounced the police for improper questioning and for admitted actions like misleading the witness on the purpose of her interrogation and refusing her the right to consult her advisers. He felt an undesirable system might have developed at Scotland Yard and raised fifteen questions about procedure which he said could only be answered by a full investigation.

Public reaction was probably summed up by a publication which remarked of the majority report that "paradoxically the whitewash was laid on so thickly that everyone could see through it."

However inconclusive the Tribunal was about what had occurred at the interrogation, it did perforce dispose of the Savidge Case in itself. No disciplinary action was taken against either the two officers who had first arrested Miss Savidge and Sir Leo Money or the two who had interrogated Miss Savidge. But far from stilling public debate, the composition of the Tribunal, its narrow focus, and its divided judgment only served to fan the doubts and controversy about police procedure in general.

It was evidently not certain how typical Miss Savidge's experience had been. But it was clear from continued Parliamentary debate and press opinion that if any regularized

[2] Inquiry in Regard to the Interrogation by the Police of Miss Savidge, *Report of the Tribunal* (London, H.M.S.O., July 1928).

police practices had developed that infringed any rights of citizens they must at once be corrected. Only a definitive investigation could meet the situation. The Government agreed to appoint a Royal Commission.

The Royal Commission on Police Powers and Procedure

The stage was now set for the Commission. It was appointed on August 2, 1928, some four months after Miss Savidge and Sir Leo Money had been arrested, and it made its unanimous *Report* less than seven months later, on March 16, 1929.

The chairman of the impartial Commission of eight members was Lord Lee of Fareham, former Minister of Agriculture and highly regarded for his ability to produce a report rapidly and to get agreement among his colleagues. Lord Ebbisham was a chief magistrate, a man of "balanced judgment and strong common sense." Reginald Poole was head of a famous firm of solicitors; he "probably knows more secrets and more about the proper methods of unraveling them than most people." Frank Pick was managing director of the London traffic combine, the Underground Railways and the General Omnibus Co. The representative of labor was James T. Brownlie, president of the Amalgamated Engineering Union. There were two women members: Dame Merial Talbot and Miss Margaret Beavan, both of whom had given distinguished public service. Miss Beavan was Lord Mayor of Liverpool.

The press, with few exceptions, highly approved the Commission, echoing what appeared a general feeling in the country for the "fullest and most searching investigation."

In its report the Commission made over 100 specific recommendations on such matters as the training of police,

methods of questioning, use of plain-clothes and women police, regulation of searches, identification parades, procedure
on arrest, detention on suspicion, and rights of witnesses and
of those in custody.

The Commission's first suggestion was that one standard
Instruction Book be prepared for all police forces in the
country. This should incorporate the best features of the
different existing manuals.

For many years the chief guide of the police in interrogation had been the Judges' Rules—nine administrative directives drawn up by British jurists. The Commission found
marked divergence of opinion among the police on the mean-
ing of these Rules, and consequent variation of practice
throughout the country. It therefore made a number of recommendations to clear up ambiguities. The traditional "caution" should be retained, for instance, but, to relieve officers
of the difficult responsibility of deciding exactly when it
should be given, the Commission suggested that it be given at
the outset of any formal questioning of either a witness or a
suspect. This should be sufficient even where the personal
character of a witness was involved, as it was with Miss Savidge.

To prevent embarrassment or injury to reputation, the police should avoid visiting employees at their place of work, or
children at school; normally they should try to suit the con-
venience of witnesses. The Commission ruled against a time
limit in taking statements but advised officers to watch for
signs of fatigue and then to offer a break "with or without
refreshments." A rigid instruction should be issued forbidding
questioning of persons, once they were in custody, about any
crime or offense with which they had been charged. Noting
that the circumstances under which the police take statements
are so varied that inflexible rules would be a mistake, the
Commission laid down only broad principles. They reminded

the public that the police needed adequate powers to preserve order just as much as citizens needed safeguards against abuse of those powers. No set of regulations could prevent the possibility of an occasional abuse.

The Commission found little evidence of misconduct, no evidence of the third degree, and no evidence that the police profited by the number of convictions they secured. While bribery was not unknown, reports of it were greatly exaggerated; it was mainly associated with the enforcement of unsupported laws. No case was established against the police as a whole for improper or over-zealous interference with the public.

The Commission did, however, severely censure the Criminal Investigation Department of Scotland Yard for "a tendency . . . to regard itself as a thing above and apart, to which the restraints and limitations placed upon the ordinary police do not, or should not, apply. This error, if not checked, is bound to lead to abuses which may grow until they bring discredit upon the whole Police Force." (p.102, *Report*)

The fact that police are called on to enforce laws which are not supported by public opinion inevitably impairs their good relations with citizens, observed the Commission; and the sense of antagonism thus aroused tends to hamper the police in suppressing crime. Many of the complaints made to the Commission proved to be directed not against the police but against such laws as many felt were unnecessary interference with private conduct of no concern of the state. These were mainly laws on street betting, solicitation, lotteries, and certain phases of motoring. Authorization of on-track totalizators, for one, was logically and morally difficult to reconcile with prohibition of off-track betting. Parliament was therefore recalled to its responsibility for remedying the legislation in these fields.

To enable them to estimate the extent of police criticisms, the Commission queried all 180 forces in England and Wales

on the complaints made against them in 1927 and the first ten
months in 1928.

Astonishing as it may seem, 134 Chief Constables reported
not a single complaint in those 22 months. In the remaining
46 forces, there were 149 complaints, most of them trivial
or found on investigation to be unjustified. In only 31 of the
149 charges were the police at fault and either censured or
punished.

Press reaction to the report was uniformly favorable. The
London *Times* (2/23/29) regarded it as a

> . . . remarkable and valuable study of a question as
> complicated as it is delicate and vital. . . . The compo-
> sition of the Commission and the record of its members
> in the public service give special weight to the views and
> recommendations it expresses after a very searching and
> laborious investigation. . . . The first broad result . . .
> will certainly be welcomed by all classes with real satis-
> faction and some relief. The police are entirely freed
> from the more odious of the charges and insinuations
> lavished against them in particular quarters of late.

The *Nation and Athenaeum* (3/30/29) said, "It is a long
and careful document . . . a series of valuable recommendations, the acceptance of which would make such abuses as
are alleged less likely to occur." The conservative *Spectator*
(3/30/29) called the report "satisfactory" because "it contains a number of recommendations which arise appropri-
ately out of the evidence, are full of common sense, and
ought, if acted upon, to remove the old causes of suspicion."

The left-wing *New Statesman* (3/30/29) praised the report as, on the whole, an excellent document, "which deserves to be read from end to end" and "in nearly every
respect" supporting views advocated by this periodical, for
instance proscribing use of plain-clothes police for arrest of
persons charged with public indecency. It disagreed, however,
with the Commission's directive that the police be forbidden

to question a person in custody about the charges against him. This the *New Statesman* regarded as "absurd," hopelessly handicapping the police. "We are all supporters of the fundamental principle of the common law of England that any man must be presumed to be innocent until he is proved guilty, but that principle certainly does not imply that a suspect should not be asked questions and should not be allowed to inculpate himself, if he is stupid enough to do so."

The report of the Commission marked the end of societal diagnosis and, with the appointment of a new police commissioner, the beginning of therapy.

While the Commission was still sitting, both the Commissioner and Assistant Commissioner of the metropolitan police resigned. With critical feeling as strong as it still was then, the Home Secretary realized the new commissioner had to be exceptionally well qualified. He appointed Lord Byng, 65, who had retired after a notable military career and the governor-generalship of Canada.

When Lord Byng assumed office (about four months before the Commission reported) the press had been almost weekly headlining "Another Scotland Yard Scandal." In this atmosphere of publicity and exaggeration he found it very difficult to carry out his reforms—basically to weed out a small proportion of higher echelon officers who were unfit and to tighten the standards of the rest. Every transfer, every fresh move, was highlighted and probed for sinister significance.

Lord Byng therefore arranged a meeting with leaders of the London papers and in effect asked them to treat discipline cases with a sense of proportion. The report of the Royal Commission testifying to the general good health of the police gave impartial support to the justice of this request, and as a result the press for some two years or more avoided references to these cases.

Two months after the Commission reported a (minority)

Labour Government with Ramsay MacDonald as Prime Minister came into office and announced it would give the closest possible attention to the recommendations of the Commission. By July 1930 a Circular embodying the Commission's clarification of the ambiguities of the Judges' Rules had been issued to the police "for the purpose of removing any possibility of misunderstanding in the future."

Some feared the new rules were much too stringent. At least three times, in 1930, 1931, and 1932, Home Secretaries had to deny in Commons that they were hampering the police.

In November 1930 the single Instruction Book that the Commission had called for was being prepared for use of police officers throughout the entire country.

On May 2, 1932, a Member in the House of Commons recalled that at the time of Lord Byng's appointment there had been great discussion about the disorganized condition of Scotland Yard, that a number of persons had been dismissed and that the House had been told that a complete reorganization was taking place. The questioner sought to learn, therefore, of what the "clearing-out" had consisted and what new arrangements had been made "to prevent the kind of scandals that had happened."

Sir Herbert Samuel, the Home Secretary in the new National Government, replied that there had been a number of prosecutions. Stern action had been taken with regard to certain abuses, and day-to-day administration was continuing to prevent them. He added that "The morale of the section of the force affected by these events has improved, and everyone agrees that the situation is far better than it was a few years ago." [3]

It took Parliament over thirty years to implement the Commission's advice to remedy the legal and moral tangle of

[3] *Parliamentary Debates,* House of Commons, Vol. 265, 5/2/32, Col. 885.

laws on gambling. Two later Royal Commissions specifically set up on betting and lotteries even made similar and more detailed recommendations in 1933 and 1951. But the ironic alliance of churches and book-makers blocked reform until 1960, when a new Betting and Gaming Act was finally passed. Among other changes the Act legalized off-track betting with Government licensees.

The effects of the Commission's work can also be seen indirectly. The report of the Commission revealed that the police did generally observe the rights of citizens. This in itself allayed the fear of gross or frequent improprieties. Its recommendations looked to even further reduction of isolated instances of injustice and to further refinement of the norms of personal liberty. But the Commission could only recommend; responsibility for action rested with the Government and the police. The attitude of the public was therefore a compound of relief and alertness. It was many years before that special wariness subsided, and press and parliamentary vigilance are constant.

The fact, therefore, that since the Commission's report there was, until 1959, nothing comparable to the Savidge Case, nothing that evidenced a significant or widespread distrust of police methods, is more than suggestive. Had the police not tightened their procedures as directed by the Commission it is hardly possible that in more than a quarter of a century some scandal or crisis would not have occurred and led to reinvestigation.

The Royal Commission on the Police, 1960

The drama of the Savidge Case, and the Royal Commission which grew out of it, was not a unique episode in British history. Hence before probing its significance, a brief epilogue is in order on its antecedent and its successor. The 1906 and the 1960 Royal Commissions on the police are so similar to the 1928 one that no added insight is gained from another close view. We are concerned here with understanding a societal mechanism, not with history or current affairs.

The relatively happy state of public-police relations since 1929 does not mean, of course, that the Commission provided a guide for all time or that the record of the police has been without blemish. But what criticism of the police there has been speaks perhaps most eloquently by what it does not say.

In 1941, for example, "Solicitor" (Conway Loveridge Hodgkinson) brought out a revision of his 1932 book, *English Justice,* based on his extensive experience with courts and police. He again complained that the police were not following the directive of the Commission not to question prisoners. But he admitted his examples of this and of other charges might seem trivial, and that there was "very little inherently wrong with the police." He also feared that because he had no sensational tales to tell, the public might not be convinced of what he felt was the urgent need for reform.

That even the author found little inherently wrong with the police may have been strong evidence of their good behavior. As always, however, there is the difficulty of how to evaluate judgments of a single author or commentator, since they are made outside a frame where due process, experienced rulings of evidence, and cross-examination by peers are available as checking mechanisms. It is when criticism finds expression through many voices, over a significant time, that a society faces the necessity of making a definitive appraisal of the situation.[4]

---

[4] The Minutes of Evidence of almost any Royal Commission will show what may happen to statements made "out of frame." The London *Times* (11/21/28) reported one homely instance, which happened during the police Commission hearings. The chief magistrate of

This was what brought about the 1928 police Commission, and it was not the first time, nor the last. In 1906 a similar background of complaints and criticisms had led to a Royal Commission on the Duties of the Metropolitan Police, with consequences also similar to those of the 1928 Commission. Indeed, experienced in this field, as with the civil service as a whole, indicates that an operational audit may be required about once a generation. Over 30 years having passed since the 1928 Commission, it could have been prophesied that an-

---

an English city had charged in his original statement, "In some cases, particularly night charges and street offences, the police take no pains to represent the true facts, but tell a stereotyped story which has no relation to fact. The evidence of one police officer supporting another, in my opinion, adds little or nothing to its weight." He added that he himself had had an experience forty years prior in which the police account was quite contrary to the facts.

When the Commission chairman noted that this was a grave charge, the witness replied that he referred really to details, that in the main the police were generally right in their account, and that if he had to write his answer to the questionnaire again he would express himself differently. The chairman remarked that to state that the police tell stereotyped stories unrelated to fact seemed a large deduction to draw from an incident of forty years ago and that since the witness would now redraft his reply there was no longer any substantial value to his present statement. Another Commissioner asked the witness whether he had in mind a single specific case that would justify his further statement that most police officers are young and are brought into contact with prostitutes and loose women who establish friendly relations with them, and that "scandals occur." The witness admitted that he did not, and agreed he had better withdraw that statement also.

Compare also the charges made against the British civil service by Lord Hewart, summed up in the title of his 1929 book *The New Despotism,* with the 1932 report of the (Donoughmore) Committee on Ministers' Powers. Here is a highly significant illustration of the relative validity of the testimony of any one man, even a Lord Chief Justice, speaking unchecked to the general public, and that of several men speaking within the frame of what was a Royal Commission in all but name.

other grand inquest of the police was about due. And so it came about.

The immediate background began to take shape in 1959, when the country was shocked to learn that 23 policemen had been found guilty of indictable offenses. The Lord Chief Justice charged that the London police were 3,000 under strength because of low pay. Sentiment began building up in the press that the public was losing its traditional respect for law officers and was dissatisfied with the way they handled complaints.

All this seemed to coincide with rising crime statistics, and, with Parliament apparently unable to question police operations outside London because of the independence of local forces, the efficiency and accountability of the whole British system came under debate. What, again, were the facts? What, again, should be done? So the cycle was repeated with the creation in January 1960 of the Royal Commission on the Police.

In an *Interim Report* issued November 1960, specific pay increases were recommended and prompt action was taken to implement these, though not, unfortunately, the formula by which they were calculated. This immediately raised police morale, stimulated recruitment, and reduced resignations.

In their final *Report,* May 1962, all 14 Commissioners agreed the current police system was not as efficient as it could be and did not properly hold officers to public account. Thirteen members felt the system was basically sound. The partnership between central and local governments was a political idea of immense practical value, they explained, and one long accepted in many fields. Their recommendations therefore sought to improve effectiveness, mainly by giving the Home Secretary increased power over all local forces and by reducing the number of smaller ones through merging.

One Commissioner submitted a minority report, arguing

that the current system was hopelessly behind modern requirements. He proposed instead a national police system under the control of the Home Secretary, with administration through not more than 15 regional commissioners.

An official public opinion sample made for the Commission showed there had been no lessening of respect for the police—on the contrary. Even the number of complaints against the metropolitan police was actually less than it had been 25 years before. What had deteriorated, both public and police respondents felt, was public standards of behavior, particularly those of young people.

Recommendations were also made to improve the handling of the relatively few complaints so that it would be evident to all that justice had been done.

The 1960 Commission continued the renovating function of its predecessors, this time with respect to police effectiveness and responsibility. The Government accepted the majority's decision against a national police force at this time and for a reorganized partnership between local and central authorities. It quickly appointed a Chief Inspector of Constabulary over all forces in England and also followed the recommendation to set up a central police research and planning unit under his direction.

The core of the Commission's advice was implemented in a Police Act which received Royal Assent June 10, 1964. This seeks to increase police efficiency by giving the Home Secretary power to direct local authorities to amalgamate smaller forces and to retire their Chief Constable (i.e. Chief of Police) if he is inefficient. Broader accountability of local forces will be effected by giving the Home Secretary the right to call for reports from Chief Constables. Parliament can then exercise its right to be informed through Questions to the Home Secretary.

To allay fear that public complaints against police conduct

might not be fairly judged by the police themselves, three members of the Royal Commission had proposed a Commissioner of Rights to examine complaints in certain circumstances. The majority of the Commission, however, felt that the advantages of independent review would be more than offset by damage to police morale. The new Act follows the majority advice. It provides that Chief Constables must investigate every complaint at once and authorizes them to request a Chief Constable of another force to provide an officer to make the investigation; this second Chief Constable is then obliged to comply with the request. To back this up, the Home Secretary is empowered to direct that this be done if he sees fit. Complainants are authorized to be present at inquiries; and the central Inspectors of Constabulary are required to keep themselves informed on the manner in which complaints are handled. The Home Secretary also has reserve power to appoint someone to investigate any matter concerning the policing of an area, and his agent has authority to summon and examine witnesses. This is regarded as a last-resort power.

Finally, where there is any question of a crime having been committed by the officer, the report of the investigation has to be sent to the central, independent Director of Public Prosecutions, who will decide whether further action should be taken and if so by which division of government.

The functions of the Royal Commission

The account of the 1928 Royal Commission presented the bare facts of a single Commission in operation. While the facts undoubtedly say a great deal for themselves, they are scarcely likely, without some analytical help, to convey the full societal role of this structure. Indeed, some of the facts by themselves may even mislead judgment.

It is a fact, for instance, that this Commission made no startling or revolutionary proposals. Its recommendations dealt mostly with refinements of police practice and had that undramatic, deceptively "sensible" quality which may leave the feeling that almost any intelligent person could have made them. It is a fact that the Commission's advice to reform betting and allied laws, which went beyond refinement and represented a new approach to the problem, was not implemented for over 30 years. The conclusion from these two facts might be that the societal yield from the Commission, though useful, was rather meager for all the time and effort spent by such distinguished citizens.

The kind of summary hindsight reports that characterize the literature would not help very much to dispel this possible impression. "No legislation followed the Report; but the high court judges made new rules respecting the methods of police questioning, and a new attitude of accosting was proclaimed for London." [5] The Royal Commission "made a number of important recommendations with a view to improving matters, and it is unfortunate that few of these were implemented." [6] Or, "In the Savidge case . . . indifferently to party competition . . . the temper of the assembly was such that the [Home] Secretary had to concede the setting-up of a Royal Commission . . . which led to a significant revision of the powers assumed by police-authorities." [7]

---

[5] H. M. Clokie and J. W. Robinson, *Royal Commissions of Inquiry* (Stanford: Stanford University Press, 1937), p. 132.

[6] J. M. Hart, *The British Police* (London: Allen & Unwin, 1951), p. 47.

[7] Harold J. Laski, *Parliamentary Government in England* (New York: Viking Press, 1938), p. 120. On p. 121 Laski remarks: "The Savidge case was what the journalists call front-page news until the government had given assurance of remedy for the complaint. Can

It is not through such typical focus on the immediate legislative or administrative implementation of a Royal Commission's recommendations that insight into the nature of this structure is to be gained. Perhaps a closer look at the problem facing the society in this instance and at the Commission's functions in handling it may be more revealing.

The Commission had its origin in a Parliamentary question raised both to redress a grievance and to remedy defects in police practice which that grievance seemed to disclose. The way the police had questioned a witness was the latest and most serious of a number of actions which had greatly antagonized citizens. Public disapproval had apparently reached the point of a significant loss of confidence in the police. It had also shaken the morale of the force itself. There was thus a threat not only to fundamental rights of citizens but also to law observance and enforcement generally. For withdrawal of public confidence in the police would mean less co-operation by citizens, and lowered morale in the force would mean less efficient control of crime.[8]

The crucial importance of public approval may be more fully appreciated by a side glance at the special character of the British police. This structure was established in London in 1829 and was copied throughout the country within thirty years. And there is good evidence that it was largely respon-

---

anyone imagine a Berlin stenographer's receiving similar treatment if she had complained to a Reichstag deputy about the unwelcome attentions of the German Gestapo?"

[8] Even the cautious language of the 1928 *Annual Report* of the Commissioner of the Metropolitan Police admitted: "Another effect of the critical attitude of the Press and public has been a general reduction in the number of charges brought. For this there may be other contributory causes, but there is good reason to believe that the Constable's confidence in the public and in himself was for a time slightly shaken, and that the efficiency of the force suffered in consequence." Quoted in Sir Norwood East, *Society and the Criminal* (London: H.M.S.O., 1949), p. 245.

sible for the change from the violence and lawlessness of the golden age of gangsterism in Britain in the 18th and early 19th centuries, to a respect for law and a standard of public orderliness unequaled in any other major country of the world.[9]

The basic operational principle of the British police is to make citizens realize the personal and communal benefits of public order. Laws will then be obeyed not because of external force but because citizens themselves insist on it. Respect for the police is therefore decisive. Their efficiency is entirely dependent on their ability to maintain from day to day public approval of their actions.

The high repute in which the police have normally been held has by no means exempted them from the sharpest criticism. This in turn, paradoxically, has no doubt helped keep their standards up.

How successful this public-police relationship has been is witnessed by the level in Great Britain of police efficiency, of law observance, and of civil liberties. Scotland Yard and the London "Bobby" have long been renowned the world over, the envy of foreigners. And it is a commonplace to observe that the British people are among the most law-abiding in the world or that individual liberty is probably recognized and protected more completely in Great Britain than in any other country.

These levels point up what the country had at stake in this problem of social order and why any incipient deterioration in the quality of police operations would at once call out every remedial resource at the country's command. It was the essential task of the Royal Commission to maintain, and where possible to raise, all three levels.[10]

[9] See, for example, Charles Reith, *British Police and the Democratic Ideal* (London: Oxford University Press, 1943).

[10] Lest the Savidge Case be thought exceptional, it is pertinent

At the time of the Savidge Case charges against the police, the Conservative Party was in power. While few would argue that Conservatives are less vigilant about liberty than others, it is one of the functions of ministers to defend actions of

---

to note two other typical examples of the level of civil liberty, both from the memoirs of H. M. Howgrave-Graham, Secretary of the Metropolitan Police from 1927 to 1946: *Light and Shade at Scotland Yard* (London: John Murray, 1947), pp. 176 and 132. A constable who rebuked a woman motorist for stopping beyond the cross-walk was himself officially reprimanded for impertinence because he said to her, "Madam, if you would cast those delightful eyes of yours five yards to the rear you would observe a white line which is put there for a very definite purpose."

A citizen who was stopped for questioning by plain-clothes police late one night because his actions seemed suspicious, refused to believe they were detectives, refused to identify himself, and refused to go peaceably to the police station for interrogation. Once taken there by force, however, he quickly established a respectable identity and was, of course, at once released. At this point the author remarks that the police should have apologized, helped him find the hotel he had been seeking, and might even have taken him there in a car! But the detectives were in no such mood after having had to waste all that time, so the citizen left in great indignation, and next day complained to his Member of Parliament. The sequel was a "protracted debate" in Commons. The Home Secretary, after trying to make light of the case, found himself overborne by a "chorus of indignation" and had to promise that the Police Commissioner himself would investigate.

If it be feared that "things are different now," one need go back no farther than November 18, 1959, when Parliament spent three hours debating a Motion of Censure of the Home Secretary in a case of alleged assault by a policeman on a citizen. This brought out the whole problem of how complaints against the police were handled and was one of the factors leading to the 1960 Royal Commission on the Police.

The level of police efficiency was indicated by the Home Secretary in a 7/20/28 Commons debate. He reported that in 1926 there had been 154 murders, 28 in London, and that in the nearly four years he had been Home Secretary there had been only two or three murders unaccounted for (i.e. the murderers uncaught), except for some who committed suicide and one or two who fled the country. He added that no other police force in the world could match that.

Further evidence of police efficiency and of the level of general

their departments. Any admission of fault is always politically embarrassing, if not actually damaging. With this undeniable bias, how could the Government, by itself, be trusted with the sort of critical and comprehensive investigation of one of its own agencies that the situation so patently called for? This obvious political self-interest would disqualify any Government for this function.

Nor could the Opposition parties, Labour or Liberal, have met the requirements of the problem. With the political capital that can be made of important sins of omission or commission by any department of the party in power, the self-interest of an Opposition would similarly preclude public confidence in any investigation it might have made.

The Monarchy, above political rivalry, could have represented all conflicting interests. But its function is to lend prestige to the work of citizens and organizations, not to perform their work itself.

The civil service is nonpartisan and could be trusted to follow loyally any directives from its political chiefs. But the Home Secretary as the top police authority would fall under the same disqualification as the Government, since he is a political appointee. The permanent civil service heads of the police would find aligned against them all the deep-seated British distrust of the bureaucratic expert as policy maker.

---

law observance is supplied by comparative crime rates in 1928 as reported by Bennett Mead in the November 1929 *Annals* of the American Academy of Political and Social Science, p. 77. These show London, with an enormously greater population, having a far smaller proportion of homicides, robberies, burglaries, larceny, and auto theft than any of the cities against which it was measured—Detroit, Cleveland, Baltimore, Buffalo, and Rochester and 7 Canadian cities.

The 1931 *Report on Lawlessness in Law Enforcement* issued by the (Wickersham) National Commission on Law Observance and Enforcement, details American experience with the third degree and also gives an account of the Savidge Case.

Since, also, it was they themselves who were under suspicion, they would hardly have been able to overcome the presumption of disqualifying self-interest. As policemen doing a job they would be supposed most immediately interested in the quickest, easiest, and most successful methods. To give them the added function of publicly investigating their past methods and making an impartial decision between the rights of witnesses and suspects as citizens, and the quick apprehension of criminals, when every further regard for civil rights seems to still further complicate law enforcement, would surely be asking too much.

In this respect a Member of Parliament was beside the point when he argued, after the Tribunal Inquiry, that more investigation was hardly required: that if the third degree existed the Home Secretary could remove it simply by revising the rules for interrogation. This was of course possible. But the situation had developed to the point that what was required was a restoration of public confidence in the police. The public had to know, authoritatively, whether or not the third degree did exist in Britain; it had to know to what extent other rights of citizens were being observed; it had to be assured that current police methods or any revisions of them struck a proper balance between rights of citizens and maintenance of order. No protestations of the Home Secretary that the Savidge Case was an exception, no set of rules devised by him or his civil service heads, would ever have been sufficient to the problem.

Nor could any private or civic organization have resolved the situation. They all have a function in alerting the public and the Government to injustice and inefficiency—perhaps even in suggesting remedies. But it is unrealistic to suppose that the investigation of any newspaper, the advice of any editorial writer, or the study of any private research agency would ever have been accepted as sufficiently authoritative.

A Tribunal of Inquiry was appointed, it will be recalled. Its scope was limited, however, to the interrogation of Miss Savidge. It was nonpartisan (actually bipartisan) in its membership, and this may have been suitable for its limited function. But for any comprehensive analysis of police methods or for any reliable decision on remedial changes, the Tribunal was admittedly inadequate.

It is at this point, then, that the country faces a vital problem but has no resources left with which to handle it. If the problem continues unresolved the consequences become increasingly serious. The press will continue to headline every case of police inefficiency or corruption or violation of individual rights. Further inroads on liberty may be made, or there may be constant fear that they will be. With confidence in the police increasingly undermined, with the Government apparently unable or unwilling to remedy defects, respect for the laws decreases and less help is given the police by the public in the apprehension of criminals. The morale of the police continues to decline, their own respect for law is lowered, more are susceptible to bribery, efficiency decreases, and it becomes more difficult to attract the better qualified recruits. And on and on in a progressively vicious spiral, a social direction whose end is anarchy and disintegration, or a police state.

What, then, is the society to do? Just stand helpless watching this civic deterioration, waiting until public attention turns, in despair, to some other concern? Just hope that with the reduction of public scrutiny the problem itself will also go away? Just pray that the country can somehow tolerate or absorb this cancer, that something, sometime, will arrest the disease before it becomes completely crippling?

Fortunately a last resource was available: the Royal Commission, the highest-ranking investigatory and advisory body.

The reasons for calling on the Royal Commission can

therefore only be appreciated against this background of deficiencies, primarily of political and civil service leaders, in self-criticism and in self-correction of their governmental structures. These deficiencies constituted obstacles to the handling of this strategic problem in social order. And implicit in these deficiencies or obstacles were the functions of the Royal Commission. It remains to consider these functions.

The chief motive of the Government in appointing the police Commission could well have been the self-protective desire to counteract the partisan propaganda being made of criticisms. Such a narrowly political appraisal would be both superficial and misleading; if the analysis stopped there the significance of the mechanism would be wholly missed. For, even if the Government's concern *was* mainly partisan, there is no evidence that it impaired the public functions of the Commission.

The very first function of the Commission (as with every Royal Commission) was to supplement already functioning government personnel by bringing able outsiders into positions of responsibility. These eight persons, co-opted from diverse fields, focused on this important problem talents that otherwise would not have been used in working toward its resolution. Not only that: the very fact of the Commissioners' dissociation from police administration and from political competition enabled them to handle the problem more effectively than any persons, regardless of ability, within the standing governmental system—if only because their findings inspired more confidence.

Nor did the assemblage of knowledge and the widening of social communication stop there. The Commissioners in turn brought into the problem-solving process at a lower level (again, as does every Royal Commission) hundreds of witnesses whose factual evidence, suggestions, and expressions of attitude fed back additional intelligence. This also would otherwise have been lost to the problem, or available only within bureaucratic channels or in such relatively unfertile forms as resolutions, books, articles, or Letters to the Editor. Here, surely, is efficient extension of citizen participation in governance.[11]

With the aid of these citizens the Commission fulfilled its declared functions: to determine, first, the facts of police practice and, second, the proper balance between law enforcement and rights of citizens.

It was a relatively simple research problem to learn police procedures. The Home Office could easily have done this itself. To determine the proper balance between order and liberty was more difficult. It was not merely a matter of description, of finding "facts." What it was might be called judgment, balancing values whose objective criteria, if any, are uncertain or at least not universally accepted. It might be called "prescribing a right course of action" in view of existing facts, or of "approximating social truth"—truth here being that policy yielding simultaneously maximum order and maximum liberty.

The police Commission illustrates the function of this structure in providing a method for making value judgments. The Home Office, the police force, the press, independent liberals, opposing parties in Parliament—all saw the "social facts" of this problem from their place in the political and social scene, from their particular set of interests. Each view was therefore restricted and incomplete—much as those famous identifications of an elephant as, for example, a tree or a snake or a fan.

---

[11] No evidence is available on whether the psychological effects of such participation were to increase the self-respect and morale of citizens or to lessen what is called social distance by increasing respect for and confidence in leaders by citizens. Research might confirm these potential functions. Much depends probably on how successful a given Commission is.

The design of the Royal Commission is aimed at correcting precisely such deficiencies. Its members have minimum self-interest in the problem, though they bring understanding of important viewpoints, such as those from law, business, labor, and local and national governments. They have expert assistants; they secure facts and still other views from every relevant source. Their procedures are competent and fair. They balance conflicting and partial perspectives and thus reach a closer approximation to the truth. Though awareness of these features of the police Commission may have been limited, or taken for granted, the widespread acceptance of the Commission's findings proves the effectiveness of these structural arrangements.

By emphasizing their validity and importance, the Commission strengthened the norms of individual liberty—the right to be free from unwarranted interference, respect for individual personality, the presumption of innocence, protection of the weak, the right not to incriminate oneself. This reaffirmation was not on some abstract platitudinous level but included specific ways to secure enforcement. Even the Commission's general criticism of the Criminal Investigation Department of Scotland Yard was a deterrent to violation. For this criticism focused attention on the department's conduct, and, as Harold Laski has remarked, "A government [or any unit] that is compelled to explain itself under cross-examination will do its best to avoid the grounds of complaint." [12]

The Commission also strengthened social order, not least simply by demonstrating that effective police power and procedure was just as important for a society as individual liberty. Its balance of these twin needs also increased public understanding of the inevitability of occasional conflicts of interest.

The Commission restored public confidence in the police, a

[12] *Parliamentary Government,* p. 121.

confidence which, of course, could only be kept by continued good behavior. It did this in several ways. It approved most police practices (thus also strengthening the hands of the police in law enforcement). It placed allegations of improper conduct in better perspective by showing the impossibility of preventing isolated instances of misconduct, by showing that some cases were the result of uncertainties in the Judges' Rules (here the Commission removed the ambiguities) and by showing that other cases were not properly to be blamed on the police (here the Commission directed public criticism to Parliament). Finally, the Commission demonstrated that the police on the whole had a very good record of respecting civil liberties.

It is a reasonable hypothesis that the restoration of confidence in the police was itself an aid to social order. Without implying any one-for-one correlation, the more citizens trusted and respected the police, the more citizens would observe laws voluntarily, and the more they would be inclined to assist the police. This in turn would increase efficiency in law enforcement.

The report of the Commission also helped improve the morale of the force. With public acceptance of the Commission's favorable verdict on its record, the long debate on police practices ended. Headline stories in the press stopped. Officers were therefore less fearful that energetic performance of their duties, or some unusual incident, might bring a distorting spotlight on them to their own disservice or that of the force. The changes of the new police commissioner could also be made without sensational publicity. Both effects increased police efficiency in law enforcement.

The Commission's analysis of its complex problem, its factual report on police practices, and a good number of its recommendations were accepted by political leaders and the public generally because of the quality of the Commissioners and of their methods. The Commissioners were recognized as impartial—neither apologists for the current administration nor critics with some political or ideological axe to grind. They were similarly recognized as competent—not naive idealists or narrow specialists or hard-bitten cynics. And the traditional procedures of the Royal Commission ensured fair, comprehensive, and trustworthy handling of its subject.

Because of that acceptance, then, debate ceased and public distrust of the police abated. Thus the Commission helped stop that vicious cycle of deteriorating police standards, increasing press attacks, mounting public antagonism, lowered police morale, more violations of civil liberties, less effective law enforcement, which constituted the original basic problem. The importance of reversing this ultimately disastrous cycle could hardly be exaggerated. But one gains little appreciation of this or of the Commission's functions therein by considering only the legislative or administrative changes immediately attributable to the Commission.

The focus on the Royal Commission in this and following case studies is not in disregard of the importance of related structures and processes—here, an independent press watching the police and publicizing the Royal Commission, a Parliament sensitive to injustice and able through its Question Period to hold the executive to account, a Government with its norm of responsibility of a Minister of State for the conduct even of a police officer, a Monarchy surrogating its prestige to the Royal Commission, an honest and responsive police force, an incorruptible and efficient judicial system, a responsible legal profession.

The social sciences may one day develop measurements to establish the relative importance of such disparate elements. It is certainly not possible now, and it would be idle to try to determine any mechanical or single causal-functional relationship between the Royal Commission and the societal effects we have just considered in this public–police field.

Fortunately for understanding this structure, such refinement in measuring techniques is not needed. Even from this brief view of readily available information there can be no doubt that the Royal Commission played an indispensable role in the achievement of the high levels of police efficiency, law observance, and civil liberties that have long existed in Great Britain.

As is just about every Royal Commission in its area, the police Commissions, in sum, were a guide in social direction. Their balance of differing interests pointed the society further up and closer to the top of that bell-shaped curve, between frontier anarchy at one extreme and totalitarianism at the other, where lies the optimum attainment of freedom. In so doing they met successfully, in the field of public–police relations, one of the greatest challenges to this age: the problem of individual liberty and social order, of freedom and authority.

Royal Commissions on the civil service

To go from the police Commissions to Royal Commissions on the civil service as a whole is but to widen scope.

It would be gratuitous to demonstrate the importance to the modern state of the character and quality of its civil service. The Royal Commission has played a significant part in the development of the British service, and to confirm this through examination of the 1902, 1912, 1929, and 1953 Commissions (to note only those so far in the 20th century) would give additional evidence of the usefulness of this structure. But these Commissions reveal in their broader field no significantly different functions from those already shown by the police Commissions, though they do relate more to the strategic area of social change than of social order.

It should be made clear, however, why it has become almost constitutional practice to use Royal Commissions (or near equivalent committees) to make the major operational audits of the service. Experience has shown that these are required at least once a generation to correct the defects and abuses that seem to creep in imperceptibly over the years, and to adjust the service to changed conditions or to a more sensitized social conscience.

Civil service heads and their experts, immersed as they are in day-to-day administration, almost forfeit the ability to see these broader problems freshly and independently. Certainly the public would not trust them to be able to do this alone.

No party Government, regardless of its complexion, would be trusted even to make a comprehensive investigation of the service, let alone major changes in it. For the civil service is the impartial administrator of the policies of whatever party is in power. Any attempt by any party to modify the service in important respects would raise charges of political manipulation and would invite retaliation by the Opposition when it became the Government. This would inevitably destroy the character of the service.

A bipartisan approach, though safer, would lack the contributions of other perspectives than party members'. And extragovernmental structures—universities, private research agencies, civic organizations—would be even more inadequate for this function of social adaptation of an entire service than they were for that of the police segment of it.

Hence the recurrent use of the Royal Commission. The standards of selection enable citizens to trust any Government to appoint independent, competent and balanced Commissioners. The standards of operation enable citizens to trust those Commissioners to make authoritative analyses and prescriptions.

It may suffice, then, to observe that while the Royal Com-

50791

mission is hardly alone responsible, it certainly makes an essential contribution to a civil service that most scholars regard as one of the great achievements of the modern world.

Periods of criticism of the police or the broader civil service need not necessarily persuade us that the world's high estimation is no longer true. During such disenchantment citizens focus, rightly, on what needs to be improved; they are apt to disregard virtues and to discount praise. But, on past experience, this is simply part of a perennial cycle to maintain standards or to raise them. What is pertinent is that there exists a mechanism to evaluate the criticism and its object and then to guide any corrective action.

2 The Royal Commission in the twentieth century

The Royal Commission stands at the apex of a neatly designed set of advisory bodies.

Departments of State such as the Treasury or Home Office may have standing committees for day-to-day or periodic consultation. They may also appoint a special Departmental Committee to investigate some subject or help formulate a policy. If the problem concerns more than one department others may co-operate in setting up a joint or interdepartmental committee. Special committees may also be appointed by the Prime Minister or the Lord Chancellor to advise on problems of the whole government, such as the increased delegation of legislative and judicial functions to executive agencies. Most of the members of all these bodies are outsiders, though some government officials may be included. Some of these departmental or interdepartmental or special committees turn out to be as important as Royal Commissions. But their prestige and legal status are lower, and they can all be discharged by a succeeding Government.

There are also advisory mechanisms of Parliamentary origin. Here composition is normally limited to Members from either House. Select Committees are now used mostly to handle problems involving the House itself, for instance its relation to nationalized industries. About four or five are appointed annually, and they have compulsory powers.

Tribunals of Inquiry usually consider situations in which some wrong may have been done by a government official, but it is difficult to formulate legal charges, as in the Savidge Case. Here the misconduct is quasi-political and therefore inappropriate for a law court, yet the proof should be quasi-judicial and therefore removed from the political arena. The Tribunals have the compulsory powers of a high court. As with Select Committees, their work is confined to the period when the House by which they are appointed is sitting. Since the 1921 enabling Act, over a dozen Tribunals have so far been appointed.

Parliament may also create special bodies called Commissions, operating much as Royal Commissions but having no Royal Warrant. These usually consider more strictly political problems, such as the Dardanelles and the Mesopotamia Commissions created by statute in 1916 to investigate the conduct of the war in those areas. On the other hand the (Simon) Indian Statutory Commission, set up in 1927 to advise on the future political development of India, was also made a Royal Commission. That is, the King issued a Royal Warrant of Appointment whose authority was based on a Parliamentary Act, not on the prerogative of the Crown.

Then there are Parliamentary Conferences, of equal numbers drawn from each House, on occasion with invited non-members but based mainly on party representation. Conferences also are usually limited to more political problems, such as reform of the House of Lords. They have been likened to conferences between belligerents.

Lastly, there are Royal Commissions. These are appointed by and derive their powers from the legal center of authority, the Crown. They are the highest-ranking of all the advisory bodies and are usually reserved for the most important problems, hence their relatively infrequent use. Once created, a Royal Commission is not part of or subordinate to any other institution. It is not a committee responsible to a larger body; it has a legal status formally equal to that of the other primary institutions of the state, such as Parliament or Privy Council.

Unlike departmental or interdepartmental committees, a Royal Commission is not appointed for any specific period or at the pleasure of any minister. Unlike Parliamentary committees, it does not terminate at the end of a legislative session. It cannot be suspended by any succeeding Government, and it continues until its work is finished. Further, it does not advise any department, the cabinet, or even Parliament, therefore is not subservient to any. It reports to the Crown itself.

These formal bodies are, of course, in addition to the services of any individual on whom the Government may call, as it did on Lord Denning in the Profumo Case, or to the unofficial working groups which any party may set up to help work out a policy.

Which of this variety of instruments a Government may use depends, then, on what needs to be done. There is here a nice correspondence of tool and problem, with no need ever to use a crowbar to remove a cinder from the eye of the body politic.

Manner of appointment

A Royal Commission is technically appointed by the Crown, but, since this royal prerogative is no longer used independently of ministerial advice, it is actually the Government of the day that appoints every Commission. It may do this on its own initiative or in response to outside pressures. But however varied the originating circumstances it is the central Government, specifically the Prime Minister and his cabinet, that makes final assessment of the situation and has responsibility for the decision whether or not to create a Commission. This is true even if the Commission is created, as it may be, by an Act of Parliament. Here, however, rather than being titled "Royal Commission on . . ." (whatever the subject), it is known for example as the "Indian Statutory Commission" or the "Coal Industry Commission."

Whether authorization is based on the prerogative of the executive (i.e., of the Crown) or on Parliamentary statute, a Royal Warrant of Appointment is drawn up, generally by the Home Office. It lists the Commissioners, names their chairman, and gives their "Terms of Reference"—a statement of the problems the Commission is to consider. It also authorizes the Commission to summon witnesses and to send for evidence, but this does not confer the right to compel testimony, a power reserved for courts and Parliamentary committees. If a Commission needs subpoena powers they are conferred by Parliament, either when the Commission is created or later. But Commissions usually can secure full cooperation without resorting to compulsion.[1]

Each Commission is a separate entity in itself. Commissioners are appointed for the life of the Commission, and if a

[1] See Appendix 1 for sample Royal Warrants.

vacancy occurs a replacement may be named. Regardless of any emergency the Royal Warrant prescribes no time limit on a Commission.

Procedure

The first task facing a newly appointed Commission is to lay out its plan of procedure. This will naturally vary according to the problem set it.

First meetings of the Commission will decide the kind and amount of information needed, the best sources, and the easiest ways of getting it. The Commission may accordingly appoint special investigators for statistical or other research; it may call for documents or any other evidence, often elicited by a questionnaire. It may interrogate witnesses in public or private sessions. Or members may themselves conduct personal inquiries.

In addition to the government departments, private organizations, and individuals it has invited to testify, a Commission usually issues a public invitation to ask for a questionnaire or to submit pertinent evidence. On the basis of all this material the Commission normally selects a number of witnesses to interrogate in open hearings. The prior submission of written material gives members a background of knowledge, and cross-examinations are usually confined to the written evidence the witnesses have already submitted. Although any of the Commissioners may cross-examine, the chairman usually takes the lead in this.

When the collection of information is finished the Commission retires to consider its recommendations. The secretary prepares a summary of the evidence, and either he or the chairman then drafts a tentative report for the full Commission. Every effort is made to have the final report unanimous, as that increases its effectiveness. If any differences cannot be reconciled, there may be a majority and one or more minority reports; or individual Commissioners may add reservations. If needed, interim reports may be submitted.

When the report is in final form it is sent to the Home Office as the official channel of communication with the Sovereign. It is then by royal command laid before Parliament. The report, as "Command Paper," is printed for sale by Her Majesty's Stationery Office. Upon submission of its report the Commission dissolves.

Commissioners receive no salary, merely a nominal allowance for any night work away from home. Witnesses get the same allowance, no special fee for testifying. The Commission's secretary is on loan from some civil service department. The main expenses of the Commission are therefore the salaries of its staff, the usual office costs, and stationery and printing costs.

Numbers and composition

Although they long antedated 1800, there have been since that date nearly 600 Royal Commissions: 60 from 1800 to the reform era of 1832; 389 from 1832 to 1900; 72 from 1900 to roughly the end of World War I; and 71 from 1919 to 1965.[2]

[2] Appendix 2 gives first a chronological list of the 143 Royal Commissions created since 1900, with date of appointment and date of final report, and whether operating, semipermanent, or created by statute.

A second list classifies these Commissions by type of problem handled and gives for each Commission the year of appointment, the number of members signing the final report, the composition type

Of the 143 Commissions created since 1900, 126 have been what may loosely be called *ad hoc* advisory in character. It is this type that has distinguished the mechanism in modern times. The Royal Commission has also been used for other purposes, however. Eleven of the remaining 17 have been operating Commissions exercising executive or judicial functions, such as the 1919 and 1946 Commissions created to determine the principles on which inventors should be compensated for use of their work, in the two world wars, and on those principles to decide specific awards. The other six Commissions are semipermanent, such as the Commission on Fine Art, first set up in 1841 and renewed in 1924, to give counsel to organizations concerned with architecture and civic betterment.

The range of problems on which Royal Commissions have worked is practically as extensive as the life of the country. As might be expected, governmental and economic categories contain the largest number of Commissions, accounting for 20 per cent and 18 per cent respectively of the total. About 10 per cent of the Commissions dealt with social problems and the remaining half handled problems in the field of dominions and colonies (13%); city planning, housing, and transportation (10%); military affairs (9%); health (8%); education (6%); and art, museums, and exhibitions (6%).

Depending on its composition three types of Commissions are recognized: expert, representative, and impartial.

Problems of a more technical nature, for instance cross-river traffic, or those not provoking violent partisan controversy, such as financing of museums, are generally handled

---

(whether impartial, expert, or representative), and the type of report (unanimous, unanimous but with some reservations or dissents, majority-minority, or split into three or more divisions).

A third list gives the Governments and Prime Ministers since 1900.

by a small "expert" Commission. These members can be accepted as bringing to the problem admittedly necessary professional or other special competence. They lose no time getting acquainted with the field of their investigation; and political or partisan issues are minimized.

The proper composition of a Commission is far more difficult when the problem given it is broader, less susceptible to clear-cut solution, or complicated by strong partisan feeling. Here a representative or an impartial Commission is appointed, though either may have one or more experts on it.

A "representative" Commission may be appointed if the Government thinks it useful to expose conflicting interests to the same facts within the frame of a body with a wider joint responsibility. The consequent negotiations may secure a core of acceptable policy on which the Government can act. A representative Commission generally has a larger membership, sometimes running into the twenties. In addition to the usual qualifications required for Commissioners, members are appointed also because they are acceptable spokesmen for the special interests involved with the problem. Perhaps the best example of this type of Commission is one in 1919 on the coal industry. Three union officials represented the miners; three operators represented the mine owners; three "friends of labor" represented the workers in other industries; and three business leaders represented the employers in other industries. The chairman was a distinguished judge.

In an "impartial" Commission the effort is to select Commissioners who have no direct personal interest in the problem but who have solid reputations for integrity and good judgment. It is hoped they will weigh without prejudice the evidence presented by all interests and then come up with valid and viable recommendations. As a result of the experience with the 1919 thirteen-member representative coal Commission with its split reports, the next coal Commission, in 1925, was a small impartial one of four men, none connected in any way with the coal industry.

Impartial Commissions are the most common. They account for nearly half of all the Commissions appointed since 1900. Only one out of six Commissions was representative, and the remaining 39 per cent were expert. If correlations are made between composition type and problem areas it will be seen that in the field of education all but one of the Commissions were expert, while there was none of this composition in the field of social problems. There was also an overwhelming preference for impartial over representative Commissions for the handling of governmental problems—eighteen to one.[3]

If it is one department of state that is seeking advice, its Minister would normally select the Commissioners, with the Prime Minister's approval. If the Commission deals with a cross-department problem or one charged with special political importance, the Prime Minister himself would select its members, in consultation with his cabinet and interested parties. There are no legal restrictions on eligibility for appointment to a Commission.

All Commissions have a secretary, appointed after consultation of the Commission chairman and the political and civil service heads of the department most closely concerned. He is a higher civil servant of the administrative class and while on loan to the Commission is relieved of his regular departmental duties. The secretary is the executive director of a Com-

---

[3] To classify every Commission, in retrospect, as impartial, expert, or representative is to suggest a rigidity not inherent in the mechanism. In many instances, also, the elements of impartiality, expertise, and representation of vested interests are so mixed as to make decision a subjective estimate based on which feature is thought to predominate. Too much significance, therefore, should not be attached to compilations based on this characteristic. Obviously, however, the background and experience of the members of any particular Commission are of the greatest importance.

mission, supervising its investigative procedure. He also serves as liaison with the Treasury and often in a similar capacity between chairman and fellow Commissioners. He is no mere office manager, and, though not an official member of a Commission, an efficient and tactful secretary contributes immeasurably to its success.

On occasion "assessors" are attached to a Commission. These are specialists, usually administrative officials, with something of the function of counselors in a court of law. They have no part in the findings of a Commission but cross-examine witnesses. Because of their special knowledge they serve to bring out evidence which might otherwise be overlooked. To this end some Commissions have also permitted opposing factions to cross-examine each other's witnesses.

The average number of persons appointed to a Royal Commission is about ten. This figure is based on the number signing the final reports of the advisory Commissions appointed since 1900 (i.e., not including the operating or semi-permanent Commissions). Memberships of expert Commissions average between eight and nine, of impartial Commissions between nine and ten, and of representative Commissions between 13 and 14.

Some value judgments

The Royal Commission is a centuries-old institution dating back to the Domesday Survey, 1080-86, possibly the first Royal Commission report. In succeeding centuries this structure has been variously viewed depending on whether it was exclusively an agency of the Crown as before the rise of Parliament in the late 13th century, or whether it had Parliamentary sanction.

In the 19th century it was the reputed guiding light of the whole Victorian reform era, in many important fields "reversing every main principle, and almost every assumed chief elementary fact, on which the general public, parliamentary committees, and leading statesmen, were prepared to legislate." [4] Commission disclosures

> shocked public opinion and . . . Parliament, fortified by the reports and recommendations . . . gave a smooth passage to several controversial Bills which were in no way the product of the government machine. And so Britain got a quick and quiet revolution in the laws of factories, poor relief, municipal corporations, prisons, . . . public health, . . . civil procedure and summary jurisdiction and mitigation of savage punishments.[5]

I know of no student of the Royal Commission, in the 20th century, who does not regard it with the highest esteem. "It is probably true to say," writes Herman Finer,

> that since the early part of the 19th century hardly a social, economic, or political statute of any importance has been drafted and introduced into Parliament otherwise than as a result of recommendations of a Royal Commission. . . . This is the form of inquiry used in Great Britain to cover investigation of facts and exploration of policy in political problems of first class importance.[6]

[4] E. Chadwick, from a speech in 1859, quoted in A. Todd, *Parliamentary Government in England* (London: Longmans, Green, 1869), Vol. II, p. 346.

[5] Sir Cecil Thomas Carr, *Concerning English Administrative Law* (New York: Columbia University Press, 1941), pp. 3-4. For further evidence on the Victorian Commissions see e.g. G. M. Trevelyan, *British History in the Nineteenth Century* (Garden City: Doubleday, 1953). The best history of the Royal Commission is found in H. M. Clokie and J. W. Robinson, *Royal Commissions of Inquiry* (Stanford: Stanford University Press, 1937).

[6] Herman Finer, "The British System" in *University of Chicago Law Review,* Spring 1951, p. 554.

Sir Arthur Salter, a British expert, confirms this: "Radical changes are usually initiated from outside the Government service, and, on all the more complicated social and economic problems, exploration by a Royal Commission is the usual preliminary to legislative action." [7]

Wilhelm Dibelius writes that the Royal Commission is a typically English device "for bringing the best brains in the country to bear on great legislative tasks. . . ." [8] Harold J. Laski has written that "the aid that device has given to clarity in both policy and administration is literally beyond estimation." [9] Alan Barth observes that it is composed of "eminent men" able to give a "thorough and dispassionate survey" of major social problems.[10] Arthur Harrison Cole thinks, "Nothing quite like it exists elsewhere in the world, and no other government has an equally potent instrument for impartial, expert inquiry on broad, public questions." [11] And Felix Frankfurter believes that "the history of British democracy might in considerable measure be written in terms of the history of successive Royal Commissions." [12]

In spite of the fact that there is not a single study of the Royal Commission itself which does not praise it almost unqualifiedly, one will encounter violent criticisms of Royal Commissions. These fall into two groups.

The first and largest consists of criticisms of specific Com-

[7] Sir Arthur Salter, in *Advisory Bodies,* ed. R. V. Vernon and N. Mansergh (London: George Allen & Unwin, 1940), p. 8.

[8] Wilhelm Dibelius, *England* (New York: Harper Bros., 1930), p. 253.

[9] Harold J. Laski, *Parliamentary Government in England* (New York: Viking Press, 1938), p. 293.

[10] Alan Barth, *Government By Investigation* (New York: Viking Press, 1955), p. 212.

[11] Arthur Harrison Cole, *A Finding List of British Royal Commission Reports* (Cambridge: Harvard University Press, 1935), p. 7.

[12] Felix Frankfurter, *The Public and Its Government* (New Haven: Yale University Press, 1930), p. 162.

missions. These are almost invariably made by those who disagree with a Commission's conclusions. Here it is interesting to note that a particular Commission may be accused of an unbalanced or mediocre membership, of exhibiting class prejudice, of inadequate procedures, or of "dangerous" or "timid" or otherwise faulty recommendations—but it is never charged with dishonesty or violations of civil rights, with being composed of "front" men for an anonymous staff which does all the work, or with being subservient to the Government.

The second, and very small, group of criticisms of the Royal Commission mechanism itself is composed of incidental comments. There is no suggestion that there exists elsewhere a superior instrument for investigation or advice; usually the Royal Commission is simply compared invidiously to the presumed superiority of earlier Commissions. For instance, O. R. McGregor writes:

> Fifty years ago, in a social atmosphere less favourable to clear thinking on such issues, the problems and opposing opinions were defined, and relevant evidence was collected and sifted in the tradition of the great Victorian investigating Commissions [he is referring to the 1909 Royal Commission on Divorce]. The Morton Commission [on marriage and divorce, 1951], among the least distinguished Royal Commissions of the twentieth century, marks a further stage in the transition of the Royal Commission from an investigating and clarifying agency to a device for obfuscating socially urgent but inconvenient issues.[13]

[13] O. R. McGregor, "The Morton Commission: A Social and Historical Commentary," *British Journal of Sociology*, September 1956, p. 189. But in a book on the same subject, written a year later (*Divorce in England* [London: William Heinemann, 1957], p. 193) this general criticism is toned down to the comment that the Morton Commission "proved a device for obfuscating a socially urgent but inconvenient issue."

And Aneurin Bevan, in *Why Not Trust the Tories?* (1944), made the charge, though it is only implicit, that the Royal Commission is a political tool used by Tory Governments to delay reform.

Professor William A. Robson, praising Sir William Beveridge's report on *Social Insurance and Allied Services,* notes that Beveridge had a remarkable array of qualifications for his task: he had done original economic research of high quality, was in close touch with the wide range of social investigations conducted by universities, had extensive experience of public administration and a vital, quick and constructive mind, and represented no vested interests. Robson goes on:

> We may compare these qualities with the type of Departmental Committee and Royal Commission which is nowadays [he was writing in 1943] so frequently entrusted with the task of enquiring into difficult or controversial matters. The chairman is apt to be an aged High Court judge, ignorant of the subject or a superannuated politician—often an ex-Minister who has been elevated to the peerage. Such a chairman tends to regard a mere investigation as a matter of minor importance compared with an important lawsuit or a debate in the House.
>
> The other members of a typical . . . Royal Commission usually represent sectional interests, with a smattering of independent persons. . . . The Report, often accompanied by a Minority Report, Reservations and Notes, tends to be a demonstration of the gentle art of dodging the issue, an essay in equivocation.
>
> We have for so long become accustomed to these degraded forms of public enquiry that Parliament has forgotten what great tasks were achieved by Royal Commissions in their heyday during the nineteenth century; and the public has almost become hardened to the sense of frustration which occurs when a great opportunity for

plain speaking and the formulation of ambitious aims is thrown away.[14]

There the criticism ends; no illustrations, no substantiation, no explanation.

Anyone who tries to make his own judgment about the Royal Commission soon discovers that there are hardly any studies on which a judgment may be based. Any social structure of which it was said that its aid was "literally beyond estimation" would seem to cry for exhaustive analysis, for articulate understanding of its rationale. Yet Professor Laski himself gives no substantiating insight. His comment is typical of passing allusions found in most of the ranking texts, if, indeed, the Royal Commission as genus is mentioned at all.

So also, for another instance, Wilhelm Dibelius no more substantiates his comment that the Royal Commission brings the "best brains" to bear on great tasks than he does his immediately following charge that this is seldom done without some "admixture of politics"—that the statesman who nominates the Commission "can almost always determine the course that it is going to take, since he will have a pretty good knowledge beforehand of the minds of the experts whom he puts on it, while, of course, avoiding any appearance of 'packing' his team."

Attention to the Royal Commission of Great Britain is in fact long overdue. Very little has been written about it, even in political literature, and no attempt has been made to analyze its full societal import. There is not a single volume by a British author on this structure and only one by American scholars, the Clokie and Robinson study. True, specific Royal Commissions are usually given mention in the histories of legislative or administrative action in Britain. But one searches

[14] William A. Robson, "The Beveridge Report: An Evaluation," *Political Quarterly,* April-June, 1943, pp. 150-51.

in vain for analysis of the order that has been devoted to the
Monarchy, Parliament, or the civil service. There are only
bits and snatches widely scattered over the political and social literature.[15]

[15] So scanty is this literature that as of this writing it could be
abstracted in a dozen pages. Two articles constitute the quickest introduction to the mechanism: R. M. Jackson, "Royal Commissions
and Committees of Enquiry," *The Listener* (London: B.B.C., April
12, 1956) and Jack A. Rhodes, "Legislative Services in the British
Parliament," *The Southwestern Social Science Quarterly,* June 1952.

The most comprehensive treatment and the only book devoted
entirely to Royal Commissions is by Hugh M. Clokie and J. William
Robinson, *Royal Commissions of Inquiry* (Stanford: Stanford University Press, 1937). The two next most important sources are devoted
to advisory bodies in general: *Government by Committee: An Essay
on the British Constitution,* by Professor K. C. Wheare (Oxford:
Clarendon Press, 1955); and *Advisory Bodies: A Study of Their Uses
in Relation to [British] Central Government, 1919-1939,* ed. R. V.
Vernon and N. Mansergh (London: George Allen & Unwin, 1940).
There is only one official British study: the *Report* of the Departmental Committee on the Procedure of Royal Commissions (London:
H.M.S.O., 1910).

The most readily accessible lists of Royal Commissions are *Finding List of British Royal Commission Reports: 1860 to 1935* (Cambridge, Mass.: Harvard University Press, 1939), with Preface by
A. H. Cole; and P. and G. Ford, *A Breviate of Parliamentary Papers*
in three volumes, covering the period 1900-16, 1917-39, and 1940-54,
all published by Basil Blackwell, Oxford, in 1957, 1951, and 1961 respectively. These three volumes also give the terms of reference,
members, and summary of conclusions of the Commissions.

Four other articles nearly exhaust the main sources of information: Herman Finer, "The British System," *University of Chicago Law
Review,* Spring 1951; A. Mervyn Davies, "Brains in Government,"
Forum and Century, May 1937; Harold F. Gosnel, "British Royal
Commissions of Inquiry," *Political Science Quarterly,* March 1934;
and W. Harrison Moore, "Executive Commissions of Inquiry," *Columbia University Law Review,* Vol. 13, June 1913, pp. 500 ff.

Major references can be found, for example, in Herman Finer,
Theory and Practice of Modern Government (London: Methuen,
1961); Sidney and Beatrice Webb, *Methods of Social Study* (London:
Longmans, Green, 1932); and Wilhelm Dibelius, *England* (New
York: Harper Bros., 1930).

It is also a limitation of the literature that the Royal Commission has in effect been treated as an adjunct to Parliament and the administrative departments. Hence the emphasis has been on the immediate contributions a given Commission may make to contemporary legislative or administrative action. If no immediate action follows it, the Commission is regarded as a failure.

We have, then, a curious disparity between the testified importance of this structure, criticisms at the opposite pole, and no real attention by anyone. And it certainly leaves one both dissatisfied and suspicious—dissatisfied with a gap in our knowledge of social structures and processes, and suspicious that an approach to the Royal Commission that is limited to a political orientation, that focuses on the partisan purposes, formal organization, and manifest reasons for appointment, may be much too superficial to yield adequate understanding. Therefore my attempt here: to locate the strategic problem-areas within which the Royal Commission operates, to make a functional analysis of the structure by identifying all its political and social consequences for the larger society.

I have selected several Commissions that illustrate most clearly these various functions and kinds of consequences. The selection includes Commissions appointed by Conservative, Liberal and Labour Governments; Commissions of different composition type; Commissions dealing with a variety of economic, political, and social problems; and Commissions of different degrees of importance and success. The telescoped attention given to some of the Commissions is mainly to avoid repetition.

This cross section spans half a century. The most recent

An example of the treatment given in ordinary texts can be seen in Hiram Miller Stout, *British Government* (New York: Oxford University Press, 1953), where two paragraphs on p. 130 of a 417-page volume describe the Royal Commission.

Commissions are not necessarily the most meaningful. Not enough time may have passed either to judge results or to cool the heat of controversy. Problems and events too close to us tend to engender stronger and more extreme and more tenaciously held opinions; and these not only may cloud judgment of a particular Commission but could easily get in the way of calm appraisal of the Royal Commission itself. Understanding of this structure and of the services it can perform does not depend on being "up-to-date on the latest developments."

When I refer not to a specific Royal Commission but to the Royal Commission generically, as a societal structure or mechanism or agency, I do not mean to imply that other advisory bodies, particularly special committees set up to advise the whole Government or even departmental and interdepartmental committees, have significantly different functions or that they may not be just as impartial or competent or influential. The Royal Commission has the greater prestige mainly because it is appointed officially by the Crown, and because it cannot be discharged by a succeeding Government. Normally, therefore, the more important or controversial the problem, or the more reluctant interested parties might be to disclose vital information, the more likely a Royal Commission would be appointed rather than a committee. But differences here are more of degree than of kind; it is difficult to find any consistent pattern in the reasons for selection of one or the other. The 1917 Haldane Committee on the Machinery of Government, for instance, or the 1929 Donoughmore Committee on Ministers' Powers, or the 1961 Robbins Committee on Higher Education, might just as well have been Royal Commissions.

A study of all advisory bodies would, of course, be instructive in showing the range of instruments from which a Government should be able to choose. But I do not think attention to these far more numerous committees would have contributed substantially more understanding of a highest-level investigatory and advisory agency—whatever name it may operate under.

In describing the work of the Royal Commission in specific areas I have deliberately avoided any comparisons with how successfully or unsuccessfully countries without such a mechanism have handled similar problems. Differences in geography, population, and resources alone make meaningful cross-national comparisons very difficult. I have tried only to lay open the role of this mechanism in Great Britain; those familiar with the problems in their own country may then have some adequate basis for judging how their own leadership could use the Royal Commission.

3 Freedom and control: the press

It is certainly not only the Government and its agencies that may perform their functions inadequately or fail to adapt to changed conditions. Private structures—industrial and labor groups, professional organizations, educational and church bodies—may also fall short of justified expectancy. When this criticism is made by responsible sources the society must first learn the facts. If these disclose inadequacies in performance, the problem then becomes how to effect the necessary corrections. A third problem is how to satisfy citizens that both have, in fact, been done.

It may also be charged that the alleged faults will not be corrected by the structure itself. Here the Government, representing total interests, may intervene directly. But what if the Government be deterred by uncertainty or internal conflict or by lack of public confidence in its own impartiality? Yet some action may have to be taken. For if denial of serious charges of malfunction does not silence the critics, the work of the structure may be impaired by reduced understanding. The broader society, too, may be weakened by dissension or confusion. If the charges are true, remedies should not be delayed.

The use of the Royal Commission in such situations is probably best illustrated by the Commissions on the Press, 1947 and 1961, and on Oxford and Cambridge Universities.

Background

The National Union of Journalists, the largest professional group in British journalism, had become increasingly dissatisfied with both the organization and the performance of newspapers. At its annual conference, Easter 1946, it passed a resolution requesting a Royal Commission inquiry. The Labour Government at first rejected the proposal but later reconsidered; it announced that its final decision would be at least partly based on the sentiments expressed by the House of Commons in a free debate.

In the debate, October 29, 1946, proponents of the Motion calling for a Royal Commission sought to establish a *prima facie* case of monopoly in the press incompatible with its freedom. They cited the decrease in the number of newspapers in the preceding 25 years, with the control of the remaining newspapers coming into fewer hands. This concentration of ownership concentrated also a power, which was being used to suppress opinion, to distort news, and to subject journalists to a London-dictated uniformity of viewpoint and to commercial considerations irrelevant to the responsible distribution of serious news.

Opponents of the Motion argued that there was nothing approaching a monopoly in newspaper ownership, but rather a tendency, at least in the national press, in the opposite direction. Ownership by one man of several newspapers with a moderate circulation was no more undesirable than ownership of one newspaper with a large circulation. No evidence had been given of suppression, distortion, inaccuracy, or other alleged abuses; in fact the British press was a shining example of freedom. A Royal Commission could learn nothing new. If it found any abuses it could not correct them; if it suggested legislation it would open the way to government control. Even its mere existence would throw unjustified doubt on the integrity of the press.

On the division the Motion carried by 270 to 157 votes.

The motives of the Government in deciding to implement the Motion were the subject of heated charges, denials, and countercharges. Critics of the Government charged that while the original union proposal for an inquiry had been turned down, something happened later to cause a reverse decision. This was that the four most powerful newspaper groups, Beaverbrook, Rothermere, Kemsley, and Camrose, opposed the social and economic changes being made by the Labour Party. Hence the Government would have liked to limit their power to influence citizens.

An inquiry by Royal Commission, it might have been thought, . . . would prove to the electorate . . . that these Press combines were octupuses strangling news at its source, distorting everything to give it a party—worse, an anti-Government—bias. A Royal Commission might well build up a public demand that something should be

done about the Press. Better still, it might even discover
. . . some way in which something could be done. . . .[1]

The Government flatly denied this political motivation. It
maintained that the National Union of Journalists had, in its
opinion, established a case against the press which deserved
authoritative inquiry. Far from the Government's being thin-
skinned about press criticism, it was the press itself that appeared unduly sensitive. For surely, considering the vital institution it was, it could hardly be more immune from public
inquiry into the way it fulfilled its functions than, for example, the British Broadcasting Corporation, industry, or the
civil service.

At the other extreme, Professor K. C. Wheare suggests that
the press Commission was created because the Government
wanted to pacify those concerned with the problem. He
thinks the Government was faced with agitation on a matter
in which it was not interested and not prepared to make a
change.[2] For the Labour Government already had enough
difficulty with its extensive reform program without stirring
up still more trouble by antagonizing the press with an investigation.

Even if it were possible, there would be little point in estab-
lishing which of these alleged motivations actually inspired
the Government. None distorted the composition or the findings of the Commission. The Government did not pack the
Commission with antipress members likely to recommend
strict controls; and if, on the other hand, the Government
thought it was appointing members who would not offend
newspapers by cutting deeply or reporting boldly, the critical

[1] Ernest Watkins, *The Cautious Revolution* (London: Secker and
Warburg, 1951), p. 160.
[2] K. C. Wheare, *Government by Committee* (Oxford: Clarendon Press, 1955), p. 90.

findings of the Commission must have been quite disconcerting.

What is significant is that once the Government was accused of seeking to muzzle the press, it was obvious the public would never trust either the "facts" the Government might find or any remedies it might prescribe. But, what is equally significant, the public *would* trust the Government to name an impartial Royal Commission and would then trust that Commission for a fair and competent investigation.

The Royal Commission on the Press, 1947

The Government took considerable time to select the members, announcing their names in Parliament on March 26, 1947.[3]

[3] The chairman was Sir William Davis Ross, Provost of Oriel College, Oxford, and President of the British Academy 1936-40. There were also: the Reverend Melbourn Evans Aubrey, Moderator of the Federal Council of the Evangelical Free Churches of England 1936-38 and General Secretary of the Baptist Union of Great Britain and Ireland since 1925; Neil Scobie Beaton, chairman of the Scottish Cooperative Wholesale Society 1944-45; R. C. K. Ensor, barrister, served on several newspapers 1909-30, was member of the Royal Commission on Population and was formerly Senior Research Fellow of Corpus Christi College, Oxford; John Benstead, General Secretary of the National Union of Railwaymen and member, General Council of the Trades Union Congress; Hubert Hull, barrister, who had served in the Treasury; John B. Priestley, author and playwright; Gilbert G. Sharp, barrister, Recorder of King's Lynn since 1943, member of the Council of the Liberal Party organization 1941; Lady Violet Bonham Carter, President of the Liberal Party Organization and member of Executive of League of Nations Union until 1941; Lord Simon of Wythenshawe, chairman of the Fuel Advisory Council and of the Council of Manchester University; Sir George Alexander Waters, editor of the *Scotsman* 1924-44; Mrs. Barbara Frances Wootton, Reader in Social Studies at London University since 1944, Prin-

On March 31 Prime Minister Attlee was asked if he would state the political parties to which the press Commission members belonged. "No, Sir." A supplementary question: "While I do not for a moment suggest that any of these members will act other than impartially, does he not think it unwise to have appointed the chairman of a political party; and also is it not a fact that, while most of the members have some strong political association, none is in such a position in regard to the Conservative Party?" The Prime Minister replied simply that he knew the convictions of only some, not all, of the members. To another question whether he did not think it would have been a pleasing coincidence if there were a Conservative alderman and a Conservative barrister to balance the Socialist alderman and barrister, he said that the Government had taken a cross section of the community and did not necessarily want a spate of either aldermen or barristers.

That was the end of the matter of the Commission's membership, and even these mild queries were exceptional, as Parliament rarely says anything about composition once it has been announced.

The questions found no echo in the press. The *Times*

---

cipal of Morley College 1926-27, served on Royal Commission on Workmens Compensation 1938, and a well-known writer; Alderman Wright Robinson, associated with the Union of Shop, Distributive, and Allied Workers and former Lord Mayor of Manchester; Miss Eirwen Mary Owen, Deputy Regional Commissioner, Wales Civil Defense Region during the war; Sir Charles Geoffrey Vickers, Director-General, Economic Advisory Branch (Foreign Office and Ministry of Economic Warfare) 1944-45, legal adviser to the National Coal Board from 1946, member of London Passenger Transport Board 1941-46; Reginald Holmes Wilson, an accountant, Director of Finance at the Ministry of War Transport; and George Malcolm Young, a trustee of the National Portrait Gallery and member of the Standing Commission on Museums and Art Galleries and an authority on Victorian England.

(3/27/47) felt that there could be no complaint of any lack of variety in the experience and reputation of the members who had evidently been chosen to reflect different walks of life, different parts of the country, and different viewpoints. The independent and liberal *Economist* (3/29/47) went so far as to hope that "impartiality has not been carried to the point where no significant result can emerge." The moderate *Manchester Guardian* (3/27/47) thought the members a "pretty fair collection of eminent citizens none with any known bias against the present organization of the newspaper industry." The Labour *Daily Herald* (3/27/47) gave the names of the members but had no comment on their qualifications.

The terms of the Commission were to investigate the control and management of news media and to recommend any changes that would further free expression of opinion and accuracy in presentation of news.

The Commission began work in April 1947 and issued its practically unanimous *Report* in June 1949. In addition to the usual hearings and invitation to give testimony, the Commission appointed a special research staff to make content analyses of newspapers. It also employed a firm of accountants to collect financial and statistical data.

The Commission's verdict on the organization of the press was favorable. It found no monopoly, nor did it expect any reversal of the tendency away from concentration of ownership in the national press, which its research showed had begun in 1921. Newspaper chains were not undesirable in themselves—only if they unduly limited the number and variety of voices speaking to the public through the press. The Commission would not be averse to any increase in the smaller chains but would deplore any tendency of the larger chains to expand. The decrease in the number of newspapers was not yet so great as to prejudice the public interest, but the

Commission felt that any further decrease in national papers would be a matter for anxiety and that a decrease in provincial morning newspapers would be a serious loss.

But, while the Commission vindicated the organization of the press, it had severe criticism of its performance. The Commission held up two requirements: (1) although the selection of news may be affected by a paper's political or other opinions, the news that it does present should be reported truthfully and without excessive bias; (2) there should be such a number and variety of papers that all important viewpoints are effectively presented to the public in terms of the different standards of taste, political opinion, and education among the principal groups.

As to the second requirement the Commission reported that the press provided for a sufficient variety of political opinion but not of intellectual levels. There was a lack of newspapers more serious and better balanced than the popular papers but easier to read than the quality. "So long as this gap exists we cannot find that the Press adequately fulfills our second requirement."

The first requirement was satisfied by some of the quality newspapers, but the Commission condemned all the popular papers and even some of the quality for excessive partisanship or distortion for the sake of news value.

No one form of ownership, no external pressure (other than public demand) could be blamed. The public could therefore dismiss any misgivings of "hidden influences." Newspaper space is sold to people who want to address the largest possible public, however, and advertisers must bear some responsibility indirectly. For the reach for maximum advertising revenue stimulated the competition for higher circulation and the debasement of quality associated with it.

Apart, then, from the inherent hazards in collecting news at high speed, the Commission placed responsibility for shortcomings at the door of those who owned and operated newspapers. The standards of education were not high enough to enable journalists to deal adequately with the increasing complexity of events; the standards of publishing were not high enough to prevent distortion from excessive bias and from the scramble for ever higher circulation.

The Commission recognized that the press was part of the country's political machinery, which was essentially partisan. The need for public instruction on an entirely new scale had not yet, it charged, produced the corresponding demand or the corresponding supply. It felt the failure of the press to keep pace with the requirements of society was due largely to the plain fact that an industry that lives from the sale of its products has to give the public what it will buy. It cannot, therefore, raise its standards far above those of the public, and the more scrupulous are always in danger of being undercut by the lowered standards of a competitor. The problem of bridging the gap between the rising standards of mental nutrition required for healthy citizens and the fare provided by the press is, admittedly, not one solely for the daily newspaper. The radio, the periodical press, and the host of educational institutions that influence public taste and judgment are equally responsible.

All this the Commission accepted but still concluded that the press did not do all it might to encourage its public to accept or demand material of a higher quality. Some of its spokesmen were unduly "complacent and deficient in the practice of self-criticism." It had no one body concerned with maintaining either its freedom or its integrity. "Indeed, the Press has taken fewer steps to safeguard its standards of performance than perhaps any other institution of comparable importance."

Balancing its criticism, the Commission praised the press for considerable achievements—providing quickly and cheaply a mass of information and entertainment, acknowledging high standards of public service, and guarding jealously its independence.

The Commission regarded free enterprise, admittedly commercially profitable enterprise, as a prerequisite for a free press. It saw no solution to the problem in major changes in ownership or control of the industry; any form of state control would concentrate in the hands of the Government a power quite incompatible with freedom of the press. It placed primary responsibility on the press itself for maintaining free expression of opinion and the greatest possible accuracy in the presentation of news.

The major recommendation of the Commission was that the press should establish a General Council of at least 25 members representing proprietors, editors, and other journalists, with lay members amounting to about 20 per cent of the total. The chairman should be a lay member and should be paid. The lay members should be nominated jointly by the Lord Chief Justice and the Lord President of the Court of Session, in consultation with the chairman.

The General Council should safeguard the freedom of the press, encourage the sense of public responsibility and service, and generally further the efficiency and well-being of the profession of journalism. To these ends it should take such action as it saw fit—for example, action to improve the methods of recruitment, education, and training of journalists; to censure undesirable types of journalistic conduct and to build up a code of professional ethics; to consider a comprehensive pension scheme; to study any monopolistic tendencies; and to promote research generally.

The reaction of the British press to the report tended on the whole to emphasize its favorable aspects and to play down its criticisms. The London *Times* had this to say (6/30/49):

After labouring for two years and costing over 20,000 pounds, the Royal Commission . . . has produced a much-needed yardstick by which to measure both sweeping condemnation and complacent defence of British journalism. . . . Exaggeration and false diagnosis thrive on illusion, and no branch of national life has been more exposed than the Press to attack from sometimes well-meaning but almost always badly briefed reformers. Its undeniable shortcomings have tended to be lost in a dark cloud of sinister accusations. . . . The report . . . should save future discussion, including debate in Parliament, from being wasted on wild words.

Triviality and sensationalism rank first as charges against one section of the Press. Failure to supply the electorate with adequate materials for sound political judgment is a more controversial but tenable structure. . . .

This report deserves to be generally read for the wealth of useful information it contains, but its authors, like many sincere enquirers before them, have not succeeded in finding a sure way of improving the practice of Roosevelt's first freedom without robbing it of life.

The *Manchester Guardian* (6/30/49) was also unable to see what practical ends the proposed Press Council could serve, though the paper noted that a large part of the report was "extremely critical" of the press and that its

value lies almost wholly in the arresting way in which it sets out the strength and weakness of British journalism and the challenge it throws down to newspapers and to the public which sustains them. . . . The report disposes of the wilder charges. . . . Then, . . . having put the question of ownership in reasonable proportion, the Commission attacks the real source of public disquiet about the press—the change of standards which has accompanied the contest for mass circulations.

There follow the criticisms of the Commission. The editorial concludes: the "report is so patently right-minded and sincere, even if its remedies are not clear-cut."

The left-wing *Socialist Leader* (7/16/49) focused on the criticisms the Commission made of the press and welcomed the Council, which "should be urged by all who desire to see a cleaning-up of bad journalistic practices." The publication thought that if individual complaints would receive the attention of such a body it would act as a check on editorial distortions.

> This is one reason why a number of papers have already opposed the idea on the grounds that it is a limitation of their freedom. . . . The proposal is an inoffensive one and falls far short of the cleaning-up operations we would like to see but if it is given powers to "strike off the register" papers which practice unethical methods it will be of some value to society as a whole.

The *New Statesman and Nation* (7/2/49), which generally spoke for the Bevanite wing of Labour, felt that the Commission made "no recommendation of any substance at all," that it made its appointment "ridiculous," and that it produced a "pious little mouse" and a "respectful whitewashing of large-scale capitalist enterprise in the production of newspapers." It went on:

> When the Government appointed this Royal Commission it might have been thought that they were seriously concerned with the question whether the domination of the British press by a comparatively small group of big capitalist interests was compatible with the orderly progress towards Socialism of a politically adult democracy. If that issue was in their minds, they are relieved by the Commission's report from the embarrassing necessity of doing anything about it. In no single paragraph of this Report is there the faintest indication that the Commissioners consider the task of transmuting an acquisitive society to be in any way complicated by the present overwhelmingly capitalist structure of newspaper ownership. Why, indeed, should they be concerned with such a

problem, when it is clear that the conception of a Socialist Britain was from the outset completely excluded from
their political philosophy?

The Commission's report was debated in the House of
Commons on July 28, 1949. The Government there announced its acceptance, expressing the hope that the press
would set up a voluntary Council. If it did not, the Government and Parliament would have to consider the situation
that would then be created. This was the general sentiment.

Some critics charged that most newspaper publishers at
first thought the Press Council was unnecessary; then they
accepted the idea in principle; then they tried to restrict progress in its creation to a snail's pace; then they tried to secure
predominance in power for the owners.[4] At all events, even
with the implied threat of government intervention, negotiations among the various representative bodies were still proceeding more than three years later.

Finally, to forestall interminable drift, a Private Member's
Bill was introduced into Commons in November 1952. This
would have set up a statutory Press Council modeled on the
lines advised by the Commission. The Bill was withdrawn,
however, in May of 1953, when the Attorney General ap-
pealed to the House to give the voluntary Council, to be created in July, a chance to prove its worth.

The Press Council was duly created in that month as an
unofficial body. Contrary to the Commission's recommendation, there were no lay members. It was composed of fifteen
editorial representatives and ten managerial representatives.
Its expenses were paid by subscriptions from the constituent
organizations in varying ratios. Its functions were laid out
much as the Commission had proposed.

A second main recommendation of the Commission has

[4] See, for instance, Harvey Cole, *Socialism and the Press* (London: Fabian Publications, 1952).

also been implemented. A National Council for the Training of Journalists has been established. It provides no training itself but is engaged in setting national standards, working through the Ministry of Education with schools and colleges to provide the education needed by young journalists.

The functions of the Commission

Ever since the newspaper wars of the 1930s started the scramble for mass circulation, and even before, perceptive citizens had been worried about the social responsibilities of the press. But the formal charges leveled in 1946 by the largest professional group in journalism, with the subsequent Commons debate, brought this dissatisfaction to a head.

The situation, however, was very confused. There was no doubt of the importance of the public functions of a press— free expression of opinion and adequate and accurate presentation of news and public information. But there certainty and agreement ended. Newspaper proprietors, on the one hand, defended the press as having no other inadequacies than those inherent in the rapid dissemination of news. Critics at the other extreme charged that a privately owned and business controlled and profit motivated press could never be "free" and that anyway the proper function of a press should be to further the advent of a socialist state. Nowhere, in Parliament, in academic circles, in private research, were citizens able to find their way among all the arguments. Aside from an occasional specialized monograph there was only partisanship and confusion.

What really was the relation of advertising to newspapers? Were the chains really exercising monopolistic powers and distorting news? Would it help to limit the profits of newspapers, to prohibit certain kinds of ownership, to create a single professional association of journalists whose power to expel could enforce standards against owners?

What now was the society to do? The Government was unable to act directly, caught as it was in the cross-fire of charges from one side that it sought to muzzle the press because of its antinationalization attacks, and from the other that it feared to investigate thoroughly because that would have antagonized the press.

But, even without these particular suspicions of self-interest, no Government, at any time, would have been trusted with an inquiry into the press. For over 150 years what has been called the libertarian theory held that the press was a device for giving citizens the information they needed to check the Government and to make up their own minds on policies. If facts and opinion contrary to official policy were to emerge, the press had to be free of government control. Any direct investigation, therefore, was certain to be labeled a prelude to control, and the resultant distrust would have vitiated the findings.

Nothing, of course, prevented any private body from making its own investigation. But even assuming a university or a research agency would have been accepted as having the necessary balance of perspectives, no unofficial group could have commanded the authority needed to pry vital facts from newspaper owners. Nor would it have had the prestige likely to get action on any proposals.

Without an instrument like the Royal Commission, what else could the society have done but simply ignore the problem? And who could say in that event what damage the society would have sustained? How measure loss of confidence in leaders by the more responsible citizens? How measure the effect of confusion and dissension in the body politic? How measure the harm from the gap—undetermined in size—between effective and inadequate fulfillment of the functions of an important structure? If corrections were necessary, how measure the loss from delay in applying them?

It is obviously impossible to handle every problem at the same time, and normally a society can tolerate the resultant strains. But it needs no exact measurements to know that the sooner and more effectively any important problem is handled, the better.

The simpler part of the Commission's functions was to lay the press open, to find out how true the charges of monopoly and distortion were. And here, as did the police Commissions in their field, the press Commission supplied a far more accurate picture.[5]

Two illustrations of Royal Commission correction of segmental perspective are pertinent. The Commission gave individual journalists and officials of the National Union of Journalists every opportunity to substantiate their charges of distortion, suppression, advertising influence, the domination of profit considerations over public interest, and other evils, but

> neither . . . produced much positive evidence in support of their criticism, and some of what was produced

[5] As a result of a special study J. Edward Gerald has reported: "The Royal Commission . . . inquired searchingly into the stewardship of the press as the custodian of the mass mind. When its work was done, the web of dissatisfaction and conjecture about the performance of the press had advanced from the stage of gossip and social myth to the level of an objective evaluation; the public was reassured in many directions and forewarned in others; and the press —fearful and nervous as the investigation began—in the end dealt respectfully with the commission and the factual authority of its documents, even incorporating the general *Report* in the list of readings required of neophytes in a national training scheme which itself grew out of the commission's work." *The British Press under Government Economic Controls* (Minneapolis: University of Minnesota Press, 1956), p. 155.

did not stand up to examination. The Memorandum submitted to us by the Union was not a survey of the Press as a whole, but rather an attack on the right wing portion of it. . . . the fact that the *Daily Worker* and the *Daily Mirror* were the only national daily papers not criticized by name, while the *Daily Herald* was scarcely mentioned, is some indication of the selective nature of the document. The Memorandum gave us no coherent and comprehensive picture and no means of reaching general conclusions about the extent and character of the abuses which had been said to exist.[6]

To determine this extent and character the Commission appointed a team of researchers to analyze the treatment by the press of bread rationing, housing, one by-election, and certain aspects of the nationalization of coal. The results are recorded in the appendices of the report and formed most of the factual basis for the critical conclusions of the Commission.

There is another example of material which has one effect when presented by itself in a book but quite another effect when presented in the frame of a Royal Commission:

Mr. Wickham Steed in a postscript, dated October 14th, 1938, to his book *The Press* wrote: "Enquiry into this humiliating behavior on the part of our 'free Press' (its treatment of Hitler's speech of October 9th, 1938) elicited the information that certain large advertising agents had warned journals for which they provide much revenue that advertisements would be withheld from them should they 'play up' the international crisis and cause alarm which was 'bad for trade.' " We invited Mr. Steed to give evidence upon this statement. At his own request he was interviewed privately, but gave no precise information about newspapers and none of organized pressure on them by advertising interests.[7]

[6] Royal Commission on the Press, *Report* (London: H.M.S.O., June 1949), p. 107.

[7] Ibid., pp. 136-37.

Thus the Commission handled the first societal requirement of determining the facts of a criticized structure. It was
an acceptable surrogate for an untrusted Government. True, a
few newspaper defenders still remained satisfied with the industry's professional standards. Also, a few critics still believed the press was a monopoly, as did Michael Foot, a
Member of Parliament and left-wing journalist, who called
the Commission "complacent, timid and unimaginative."

But there is little evidence that these views were any longer
able to influence the public. For now citizens had a point of
reference. They could compare these claims and counter-
claims against the varieties of background of the Royal Commissioners and the way they arrived at their judgments. From
where else in the society—newspapers, union, Government,
opposition parties, private researchers—would come a better standard of reference, a closer approximation to the truth?
Whom else but the Royal Commission could citizens trust to
consider, fairly and competently, all sides of these complicated questions and then come to reliable conclusions?

In short, most leaders and citizens appeared satisfied that
the facts had been found and that attention could turn to the
problems of remedy. For it should be patent that the Commission had a far more extensive function than simply to find
the facts of press operation. Whether or not the Labour Government intended it, the Commission had essentially the delicate problem of developing guidelines on the future relations
between the press as individual, independent, profit-making,
and influence-seeking entrepreneurs on the one side and, on
the other, the total society with certain *public* needs. The
Commission sought a valid pattern of control.

It could not find it in the traditional *laissez-faire* system of
complete independence of governmental controls (except for
libel, obscenity, sedition, and contempt of court). This the
Commission rejected as even more unacceptable here than in

industry or business, where it had long already been modified. Nor could the Commission find it in the system advocated by socialists that the Government should impose legal regulations guaranteeing accurate presentation of news. The state was just one association in a democratic society, the Commission felt, and this would have given it such an overriding power as would destroy a free press.

The Commission therefore sought its control in a mid-area between total freedom and total control, between the influence of the unregulated market and the influence of the Government. In this uneasy balance of forces the professional spirit of journalism could develop standards all the more effective because self-imposed. And it was in the Press Council, as corporately embodying that professional spirit, that the Commission found its agency of control.

Though it fell short of the kind of structure envisaged by the Commission, the Press Council in its annual reports did show the beginnings of an improvement in the norms of press conduct. It investigated all serious complaints against newspapers. If they were found not justified, the Council gave an explanation. If they were justified, the Council tried to secure redress and was severe in criticism of the offending paper or journalist. With the publicity given the Council's statements in the press, there began to develop gradually the community opinion that is a necessary basis for the Council's effectiveness. It became evident that there was no intent to impose uniformity or to reduce the force of controversy but to condemn and publicize antisocial practices and offenses against the general sense of decency.

The Commission's remedial measures were received much as its factual findings. Newspapers feared a Press Council and, left to themselves, would probably never have created one. And, since the Press Council had no built-in function to further the socialist state, no element of governmental control, and no compulsory powers, other extremists dismissed it as hopelessly inadequate for making the press responsible.

But between these extremes, again, it is probably true to say that most citizens recognized the Press Council as an undogmatic attempt to balance forces, to leave the maximum play for free expression within self-imposed standards of accuracy and fair play.

There was no disposition in Britain to regard the problem of press performance as settled. Later private studies of the Council and parliamentary debates summed up to a feeling that the Council had done well with its limited funds and staff but that it had not yet secured a satisfactory reformation of the press.

The Royal Commission on the Press, 1961

In the meantime, events did not bear out the expectation of the Commission that the trend against concentration would continue. The death of two respected papers, the *News Chronicle* and the *Star,* and the merger of two giant newspaper and periodical chains, the *Daily Mirror* group and Odhams Press, brought to a climax a renewed concern with monopoly and production costs. Since the Commission in 1949 had warned against any increase in size of the larger chains, the Government was as worried as almost everyone else about this new concentration of power. But its policy on monopolies, here as in other fields, was uncertain, and it felt it had no right to interfere with the merger.

So, again, to bring the facts up to date and to chart its course, a Conservative Government in February 1961 called on the Royal Commission, as a Labour Government had called on it 14 years earlier.

The new Commission was a small impartial one, of five members.[8] Its focus this time was not on performance or ethics but on whether high costs and inefficient production, together with dependence on advertising, tended to reduce the number of publications and thus to narrow the opportunity for diverse opinion, an essential for a free society.

If the Press Council had been constituted as the 1949 Royal Commission had recommended, and if the Council had then fulfilled one of the functions which that Commission had laid out for it—to study the economic and social factors that affect monopoly—"much of our own inquiry might have been unnecessary," wrote the Commission in its unanimous *Report* of September 1962 (p. 101), "and public awareness of possible developments might indeed, of itself, have modified the course which in the end those developments actually took."

There was still a considerable range of choice in the press, the new Commission found, but it was less than in 1949 and it would be better for the country if there were more. Since 1949, 17 daily or Sunday papers had ceased publication, with only four new ones started. Amalgamations of surviving papers had markedly increased the concentration of ownership.

The Commission examined every conceivable method of helping new or smaller papers, such as uniform reduction of

[8] Chairman was Sir Hartley William Shawcross, retired barrister, former Attorney General, former president of the Board of Trade, former chairman of the Bar Council, and chairman of the British branch of the International Commission of Jurists; Sir Graham Cunningham was chairman and managing director of a safety glass company; Robert Browning was a Professor of Accounting in the University of Glasgow and partner in a firm; William Brian Reddaway was director of the Department of Applied Economics in the University of Cambridge, and a writer and editor; and William James Percival Webber was general secretary of the Transport Salaried Staffs Association, member of the National Coal Board, member of the General Council of the Trades Union Congress, and former member of the Labour Party National Executive.

costs, regulation of advertising, common printing facilities, and government subsidies of one form or another. None of these would be effective or were without serious disadvantages, the Commission found. It recommended instead that all projected amalgamations involving weekly circulations of three million copies or more should be submitted to a Press Amalgamations Court. This body should consent only if it were established, by statutory criteria, that the transaction was not contrary to the public interest. The Court should consist of judges of the High Court and the Court of Sessions and lay members appointed on advice of the Lord Chancellor after consultation with the Trades Union Congress and the Press Council.

Newspapers, furthermore, should not be permitted to control any television stations, the Commission decided; where they already did, the arrangements should be terminated as soon as possible.

Through personal investigations and from reports of an outside firm of management consultants it employed, the Commission concluded that newspaper production was grossly inefficient and over-costly. Nor was the development of new machinery and techniques exploited to best advantage. Management was to blame for this for not paying enough attention to good industrial relations and to the interests of the industry as a whole. But the unions were also at fault for feather-bedding and other restrictive practices and for excessive wage demands.

The Commission therefore advised reconstitution of negotiating machinery in each plant, and creation of a joint standing body of employers and unions charged with planning and development over the whole field of national newspaper production. This body should attend particularly to facilitating use of new machinery and methods and to long-term manpower and training requirements.

"There may be more than one view on the question whether the public interest is actually injured by the degree of concentration of ownership and control existing at any time," reported the Commission. "But no reliable view can be formed at all unless the facts are known. The first necessity, therefore, is to ensure that control can never be clandestine. . . ."

To this end the Press Council should be re-formed to comply with the 1949 Commission's directive for a lay chairman and substantial lay membership. If this was not done voluntarily by the press itself within a time limit the Government should set, the Government should provide for it by law. The Council should then be given the resources to enable it to investigate and report on changes in control of press undertakings. Newspapers should also show the name of the individual or company in ultimate control.

The Commission recognized public disquiet about the possible conflict of interest between editors and advertisers. It proposed, therefore, that the Press Council take on the added function of hearing and publicizing any complaints of undue influence by advertisers.

By 1964 action had been taken on the major recommendations of the Commission except for the creation of a Press Amalgamations Court. Almost immediately on issuance of the *Report,* owners and unions began negotiations to improve the technical efficiency of the industry. After several months' study the Press Council adopted a revised statement of objectives and announced that the number of its journalistic and managerial representatives would be reduced from 25 to 20 to make way for five lay members. This was effected by the end of 1963, and Lord Devlin, who had retired after a very distinguished career as a judge, then accepted the position of independent Chairman. In January of 1964 the reconstituted Council began to increase its staff to handle the additional functions suggested by the Commission.

As early as 1957, after only some four years' experience with the Press Council, Francis Williams (now Lord Francis-Williams), a former editor of the *Daily Herald* and a biographer of Ernest Bevin and the Labour Party, was able to make a tentative appraisal. Arguing that journalists needed standards of professional integrity not only to safeguard the public against malpractice but to provide the journalist himself with a counterbalance against the immense power of financial control in the newspaper industry, he goes on:

> It is possible that the Press Council will provide such a counter-power; indeed there are already some signs that it is beginning to do so. At the time of its foundation I took the view, as did several members of the Royal Commission out of whose recommendation it was born, that there would have been great advantage in establishing the Council as a statutory body with powers analogous to . . . those of the General Medical Council. Such a statutory body would from the beginning have entered the field able to provide a valuable counter-balance to the massive power of commercial interest, which ought not to be left to decide alone the standards by which popular journalism is to live. Yet it is possible that a voluntary Press Council may in the end succeed in doing this no less effectively. The moral pressures it can bring to bear, both on proprietors and journalists, are considerable. Its specific judgments may be overridden, but they can serve to create a general climate of public and professional opinion that cannot be ignored so easily and whose effects may be pervasive and far-reaching. To create such a climate is the most important of all the responsibilities that rest upon the Council. It is a responsibility to which it is applying itself with considerable courage and in which it needs all the public and professional support it can get.[9]

[9] Francis Williams, *Dangerous Estate: The Anatomy of Newspapers* (London: Longmans, Green; and New York: Macmillan, 1957), pp. 268-69.

By 1961 another respected British journalist, Arthur Christiansen, was able to write that the Council's influence on press standards had been "immense," and noted for example that the gossip columns had been largely cleaned up and that the number of cases of intrusion into individual privacy was noticeably less. And, now that the Council has been reformed as two Royal Commissions recommended, Lord Francis-Williams in March 1964 predicted that "at this stage of its existence . . . there is a real chance that it can become a serious and effective instrument of press guidance and establish a body of 'case law' to which newspapers can regularly refer. . . ." [10]

An American commentator in August 1964 noted that "The Press Council has, however, succeeded better than almost anyone predicted in improving press coverage of day-to-day events. Similar bodies have now been formed in Holland and West Germany." [11]

Thus the British attack on one of the most sensitive of modern problems. Both press Commissions ended confused public debate, the one on the performance, the other on the costs and production techniques of the press. Both then focused attention on the pace of improvement under the changes they recommended. They enabled the country to escape the paralysis resulting from the inability of the Government to act directly and from the inadequacy of other remedial agencies.

The first measures may be disappointing in not having achieved at one giant step a completely reformed press. But perhaps in a decade or so, if high standards have become a feature of the press as they have for example of the legal profession, the police, or the civil service, the distance trav-

[10] "Fleet Street" in the *New Statesman*, 3/27/64, p. 480.
[11] Helen Nelson, "Watchdog of the British Press," *Saturday Review*, 8/8/64, p. 43.

eled from the inception of the Press Council may be impressive. Without the good start prompted by the Royal Commissions there is little reason to suppose there would be any improvement at all. Who would even have initiated it?

Though the press is still in transition, there is, therefore, already ample demonstration of the role of the Royal Commission in guiding its development in the direction of a more responsible fulfillment of its 20th-century responsibilities.

4 Oxford, Cambridge, and the state

The role of Oxford and Cambridge in shaping British leaders, and through them much of the character of British institutions and life, hardly needs demonstration. Nor does the ranking long accorded them the world over. What is not so universally known is the contribution of the Royal Commission to that achievement.

We must suppose that all the brain-power assembled within these revered universities was still not enough to overcome certain human failings. For, just like civil service departments or newspapers, they have not always been conspicuous for self-criticism and self-improvement. Three times since 1850 dissatisfaction with the way they were meeting their national responsibilities has forced major operational audits by outsiders. It may not be surprising by now to learn that these were done by the Royal Commission.

There were two Commissions on Oxford and Cambridge in the 19th century, in 1850 and in 1872. Both are credited by scholars with the remedy of many defects and the introduction of more changes in a few years than had occurred in any previous century.

After the First World War, the fall in the value of money, the rush of new students, and the inadequacy of academic salaries and of most facilities all combined to present almost insuperable financial problems for both universities. In desperation they turned to the state. But after the most costly war to date, the finances of the state itself were severely strained. Even though, as alumni, most of the members of the Government would doubtless have been ready to help their Alma Maters, they knew the public would rebel against any spending except for the most pressing needs; and substantial public support for two ancient "class" institutions would not likely be regarded as having high priority.

The Labour Party expressed a widespread view. All persons capable of benefitting from an Oxford or Cambridge education should be able to have it. Living costs at both were too high and existing resources were not used with utmost economy, with the result that too many poor students were excluded. It was also improper to award scholarships for years to men who did not need them, when others were disbarred because of financial limitations.

There in substance was the societal problem. It was inconceivable that Oxford and Cambridge should be allowed to fail in the functions Britain required of them. But the difficulties were triple.

There was first the absence of sufficient public appreciation of the importance of the work of these two universities in the life of the country and, in a time of financial stringency, of their need of public funds. Without adequate public understanding, a policy of substantial help from taxes would be very risky, if not impossible, for any Government.

There was second the rigidity of administrative and educational policy which seemingly prevented both universities from adapting themselves to the changed conditions of the 20th century. They were unable to get the money they needed from increased fees or from private philanthropy. And they appeared unable, by themselves, to effect the reforms in structure and operation demanded by the Labour Party as spokesman for the majority of citizens deprived of an Oxford or Cambridge education.

The third obstacle in handling the problem was the handicap of the Government both in informing the public and in reforming the universities. The Government at the time was a coalition, with the Liberal Lloyd George as Prime Minister and the largest party in Parliament that of the Conservatives. These men were hardly in the best position to persuade citizens that they should pay substantially to underwrite the continuance of institutions long the almost exclusive prerogative of the upper classes. And just as no politically partisan Government would be trusted to modify the civil service or the press, so it would not be trusted, by itself, to make radical changes in the statutes of the two universities whose autonomy had long been so zealously guarded.

The Government therefore made small emergency grants, and informed each university that any further aid depended on a comprehensive Royal Commission inquiry into its resources and operations.

The large, expert Royal Commission on Oxford and Cambridge Universities was created in November 1919 and made its *Report* in March 1922. Chairman was the Rt. Hon. H. H. Asquith, Liberal Prime Minister, 1908-16.

The Commission traced the history of the two institutions

and their contributions to the nation. It laid open their current financial needs. It analyzed contemporary practices, vindicating some and criticizing others. It recommended a host of changes in administration, provision for research, facilities for poorer students, reduction of expenses of college life, scholarships, extramural work, and other areas. It also advised the Government to provide large annual grants to each university.

These recommendations were accepted by the Government and both universities, and by 1926 most of them had been carried out.

The first function of the Commission was educative, to demonstrate both the needs of Oxford and Cambridge and the justification for public grants in view of past and present services to the country. It appears to have fulfilled this function adequately. As the *Times* put it (3/25/22): "After this Report, there can be no excuse for ignorance or loose speculation about the affairs of the two ancient Universities; their needs ought now to become perfectly intelligible."

This is not to imply that almost every British citizen read the report and was personally persuaded of these needs. Although Royal Commission reports can top 100,000 in sales, they are not normally "best sellers." They effect their instruction primarily through the leadership: through teachers, writers, newspapers, political leaders; through top echelons in industry, labor, and other groups; through alert and knowledgeable citizens who set the tone and influence the attitudes in their private circles from home to office to pub to civic organization.

So, as an instance, in the June 22, 1923, debate on the Oxford and Cambridge Universities Bill, the Labour Party, which in 1919 had opposed public grants until the two structures had been reformed, now had no objections to the large sums recommended by the Commission.

An even more important function of the Commission was

to chart the course of reform that would ground justification for public grants even more securely on the adaptation of validated older educational practices to the service of all capable citizens and to 20th-century needs of the total society.

Here again, as an independent, relatively impartial and professionally competent body, the Commission had the confidence both of the universities and of their critics and could thereby act as agent in renovation. Its reforms were acceptable to the Labour Party, even though they did not go so far as to realize the Party's goal of transforming the ladders to Oxford and Cambridge into stairways.

Abraham Flexner thought that the greatest obstacle to the reformation of Oxford and Cambridge was probably the "impalpable, resistant tradition as difficult to penetrate as a London fog." In 1930 he wrote:

> Three successive Royal Commissions have during the last seventy-five years wrestled with Oxford and Cambridge problems; they have accomplished much in bringing the Universities into the main stream of modern life; but they have *in my opinion* [my emphasis] hardly touched the fundamental problems of University activity and organization—largely because, being composed mainly of Oxford and Cambridge men, their natural loyalties have interfered with incisive and objective analysis, . . .[1]

Extreme conservatives, on the other hand, felt the Royal Commission had gone entirely too far in recommending change.

It is impossible to know what might have happened had the Commission not been composed of so many members so sensitive to the complexities of these institutions. The changes they recommended were strongly welcomed by the liberal and

[1] Abraham Flexner, *Universities: American, English, German* (New York: Oxford University Press, 1930), p. 273.

progressive elements in the universities and at least acquiesced in by the conservative elements. Had the proposals been so radical as to incur the violent opposition of the conservatives, a bitter cleavage might have done irreparable harm to the universities. They might even have lost the character that still gives them their distinction.

Had the changes advised by the Commission not been effected, the universities would probably have been so much slower to adapt to modern needs that they would have been supported primarily, if not solely, by the minority upper classes. In the absence of broader approval, public funds would have been given them, if at all, only to a minimal degree; and either they would have retrograded to insignificant anomalies in a 20th-century democracy or they would have been transformed into the image of the newer universities.

It is hard to resist the conclusion that the Commission achieved a golden mean, not to be taken here as a bland compromise that left a nondescript shell, but as a balanced perspective that combined a historic sense with the sense of contemporary need, that preserved the best of the past as a secure foundation for the present—and the future.

In the history of Oxford and Cambridge, the three Royal Commissions are unquestionably landmarks. They would appear to have played as significant a role in the eminence of Oxford and Cambridge as other Commissions did in helping the British police and the British civil service (and, potentially, the British press) to their high rank.

The tremendous changes occasioned by the Second World War and the present scientific revolution might have been expected to require a reappraisal of educational processes—and one would expect that this would be done by Royal Commission. So it was, in all but name. For this time the Government decided that a Royal Commission would not be necessary and appointed instead a Committee on Higher Education, with

Lord Robbins as chairman. This was not to investigate Oxford and Cambridge alone, but to survey the nation's needs in the area of higher education generally.

This appointment of a Committee rather than a Royal Commission shows how closely related the two forms of inquiry are. Most generalizations about the Royal Commission as a societal agency apply also to these special Committees; they are, in effect, the second level in the ranking of advisory bodies. For they usually have the same high caliber membership, are unpaid, operate independently and in the same way, and meet the same standards as the Royal Commission—except that they lack the prestige of "Royal" origin. In this instance the Government felt no need for that special prestige. But the October 1963 report of the Robbins Committee on Higher Education is likely to have effects on Oxford and Cambridge as marked as those of its preceding Royal Commissions.

5 Stability and change: divorce

Although material interests were hardly absent from the Royal Commissions on divorce, the controversy here centered on ethical and religious principles, in the delicate area of conscience.

All the divorce Commissions had their origin in attacks on age-old norms. In few problems are the stakes of decision higher in personal happiness and social stability; in few is it harder, at best, to know what is right and what is wrong. But the search for wise public policy on marriage and divorce has seldom been comprehensive, dispassionate, philosophical. Private groups, reformers and defenders alike, have taken extremist positions. Governments have failed to provide leadership, mainly because they feared stirring up sentiments which would cut across party lines and endanger their tenure.

To resolve this impasse the Royal Commission has been called on three times in the last century, in 1850, 1909, and 1951.

A hundred years ago in England marriage was held to be indissoluble. Neither common nor ecclesiastical law recognized divorce. The only two ways of ending a marriage were through annulment or a Private Act of Parliament. For the legislature had recognized divorce; through procedure in the House of Lords it might grant it because of a wife's adultery, or because of a husband's when it was accompanied by aggravating circumstances. The difficulty of this remedy obviously put it quite beyond the reach of any but the wealthy and influential.

After half a century of middle-class attack on this aristocratic privilege, a Royal Commission was finally created in 1850. On its recommendation was based the first major reform in 150 years—the introduction of judicial divorce, itself the basis of present law and procedure. The Act of 1857 did not provide new grounds for divorce. It eliminated the exclusive procedure of the House of Lords and made its civil system of divorce more widely available through a newly created court.

For the next 50 years there continued two systems of legal remedy for marital failure. The centralized divorce court was used by the upper classes; those unable to afford a divorce could go to the magistrates courts and there get a judicial separation order. But the obvious economic inequities of this dual arrangement led to increasingly vocal resentment by the working classes, and this, with other dissatisfaction, was able by 1909 to force the appointment of another Royal Commission.

The Royal Commission on Divorce and Matrimonial Causes, 1909

The Commission was appointed by the Liberal Asquith Government in November 1909 with terms of reference to investigate the laws of divorce and separation "especially with regard to the position of the poorer classes," and to report whether any amendments should be made.

Fourteen Commissioners were appointed. Lord Gorell, former President of the Probate, Divorce, and Admiralty Division of the High Court and one of the most active proponents of reform, was made chairman. The Church was represented by the Archbishop of York. The legal element was strong (43%) with six members. Two distinguished women were appointed, Lady Frances Balfour and Mrs. H. J. Tennant, who had helped extend the work of the Women Inspectorate of Factories. One member was an experienced journalist, J. A. Spender. There were also Thomas Burt, a Member of Parliament representing the Northumberland miners for nearly 50 years; the Earl of Derby; and Sir George White, M.P.

The Commission found five different theological attitudes toward divorce. These ranged from the belief that all marriages are indissoluble to the belief that they can be dissolved not only on grounds of adultery or desertion but also on other serious grounds based on the necessities of human life. Each of these attitudes was sustained by persons equally eminent in scholarship, piety, and public spirit. Since there was no common understanding (even though the disagreement still turns largely on the actual words used in passages in Scripture) and since many non-Christians discounted the relevance of theological considerations, the Commission felt justified in basing its judgments solely on secular utilitarian grounds.

On the principle that "no law should be so harsh as to lead to its common disregard . . . or so lax as to lessen the regard for the sanctity of marriage," the majority of the Commission concluded that the state should permit divorce not only because of adultery but also because of (1) willful desertion, after three years; (2) cruelty; (3) incurable insanity, after five years' confinement; (4) habitual drunkenness found incurable, after three years from the first order of separation; and (5) imprisonment under commuted death sentence.

On grounds of religious principle and social stability, the Archbishop of York and two lawyers signed a minority report advising continuance of the current law, which allowed divorce only for adultery.

The Commission made a large number of unanimous recommendations, for example that men and women be placed on an equal footing with respect to the grounds for divorce, and that high court hearings for divorce should be decentralized so that persons of limited means could have access to this remedy. The minority members, fearing divorce might be encouraged if it became too accessible, thought that these local facilities should number less than the 89 recommended by the majority.

The *Report* of the Commission was published in November 1912. Nearly half a century later a commentator wrote that it is "a model of relevance, clarity and the thorough analysis of evidence. . . . Within three years this Commission produced four large volumes of evidence which are still essential reading, and a Report of remarkable clarity and intellectual distinction." [1]

In the next quarter century and more, many attempts were made to secure legislation implementing the Commission's

[1] O. R. McGregor, *Divorce in England* (London: William Heinemann, 1957), p. 26.

advice, but successive governments were always resistant because the issues were so controversial. The chronological sequence in which these attempts were successful illustrates the frequent time difference between Royal Commission recommendations and politically possible action—what we may call the time-lead of a Royal Commission in social direction.

During the First World War there was, of course, no hope for change. The post-war tide of feminism was responsible for the first breakthrough. Reform leaders directed public attention to women's disabilities, and one result was an Act in 1923 which would give a wife a divorce for her husband's adultery, even though there were no "aggravating circumstances." In 1926 the publication of certain details of divorce cases was stopped.

The most contentious proposals of the Gorell Commission had been the addition of five new grounds for divorce. In 1937 A. P. Herbert (later Sir Alan Herbert) was finally successful in securing passage of an Act which introduced the heart of the Commission's advice. This was the three new grounds: cruelty, three or more years of desertion, and incurable insanity after five years' confinement. Thus 25 years after the Commission recommended it, England received the first extension of the grounds for divorce since the Reformation.

The second main recommendation of the Commission took even longer to implement. It was not until 1956 that commissioners with all the authority of high court judges were sitting in London and 38 provincial towns to hear divorce petitions. A system of legal aid to poor persons was developed concurrently. The combination has given substantial reality to the principle that poverty should not bar any citizen from the divorce court.

It is plainly impossible to present the Gorell Royal Commission of 1909-12 as cause, and the major change in the substance of the Herbert Act of 1937 as effect. Indeed, the primary responsibility for this change in norms would seem to belong to the active proponents of the Act. Without their efforts the change might not have occurred for another quarter of a century. For none of the Governments in the preceding 25 years had acted. Yet it was really the Government that saved the reformers from still another failure. The members of the Government were privately divided in opinion, and the Government as such was neutral. But it did lend its own experts in the committee drafting stage. Then, when the time allotted to passage of Private Members' Bills had elapsed before the Bill had gone through its third reading, the Government supplied the necessary time from its own business. Without that, the Bill would have died.

There was also the influence of a quarter century of world-wide changes in habits and ways of thinking.

There exists no calculus of social causation that could assign quantitative weights to these and other relevant factors. The public record is usually, however, though unfortunately not always, sufficient for reasonable assessment of most Royal Commissions. And with the Herbert Act there is, by good fortune, a behind-the-scenes account of the action that secured passage of the Act. It leaves little doubt of the significant role played by the Royal Commission.

Herbert was justly credited with the leading role in guiding his Bill to the statute books. A year later he wrote a book, *The Ayes Have It,* one of whose purposes was to distribute, as he says, some of the excessive credit given him.

In his maiden speech in the House, he recounts, he had rashly announced that he would introduce a Bill on divorce. Even more rashly, he prophesied it would be passed during that Parliament. He was aware (though not so completely as at the end of his experience) of the difficulties ahead. For governments usually disliked Private Members' Bills, he felt, because they raised awkward questions better left alone, and they generally had the Report of a Royal Commission behind them.

At the opening of the session in December 1935, Prime Minister Baldwin (the Conservative Party was in power), announced that certain business of the House had to be postponed and that this would have the advantage of giving Members who contemplated bringing in Private Members' Bills "more time to think out suitable Bills." With his Bill already in his pocket, Herbert remarks, " 'Think out' indeed . . . when a Royal Commission had thought everything out nearly twenty-five years earlier!" [2]

In distributing credit for the Act Herbert writes: "There was, after all, a Royal Commission which made its Report in 1912; and it is right to remark how strongly that Report has stood the test of time. It provided the flesh, bones, and blood of the present Act. All that we have done is to give the picture a new frame, hang it in a better light, and sell it." [3]

It would have doomed his Bill, Herbert admits, to have put into it the smallest packet of divorce by consent.

> The Bill . . . was founded on the Royal Commission; and the Royal Commission stood firmly on the same basis as the existing law, that (apart from insanity) a marriage should be dissolved only because of a matrimonial offence, so found by a court of law. We were not proposing to build a new system, but to repair the old one and add a harmonious wing or two. We could not in one breath boast (as we were always doing) the tremendous backing of a Royal Commission, and in the next challenge its fundamental principles.[4]

[2] A. P. Herbert, *The Ayes Have It* (New York: Doubleday, Doran; and London: Methuen, 1938), p. 43.

[3] Ibid., p. 60.

[4] Ibid., p. 132.

When it was all over, Herbert observed that the whole experience showed that a democracy could deal decently, though candidly, with religious strife.

The Royal Commission on Marriage and Divorce, 1951

In 1951, nearly 40 years after the Gorell Commission had reported, another Royal Commission on the same problem was appointed under very similar circumstances, this time by a Labour Government.

Against a background of agitation by reform societies and their parliamentary supporters, Mrs. Eirene White, a Labour Member, had succeeded in getting a Private Member's Bill to a second reading. This Bill would have permitted divorce, upon petition of either party, where husband and wife had been separated for seven years with no prospect of reconciliation. Such a measure would have introduced into matrimonial law for the first time the principle of divorce by consent.

In the second reading debate, March 9, 1951, Mrs. White recalled that more than 200 Members of Parliament had recently asked for a Royal Commission on the subject but that Prime Minister Attlee had refused on grounds the time was not appropriate. The Attorney General, speaking after Mrs. White, stated:

It has long been a necessary tradition of our affairs that in matters such as are raised by this Bill the Government cannot seek to impose any collective view upon the House, nor can they usefully express a collective voice. As our debate today has very well shown, these are matters on which personal opinion . . . cuts across all po-

litical lines. . . . people in all parties hold views based
on their conscientious or religious beliefs which lead to a
variety of differing conclusions, all of them strongly and
sincerely held but nevertheless controversial for all that.

He went on to say that Mrs. White's Bill concerned only one
aspect of the marriage laws, and concluded that the Government thought it unwise to legislate on any one matter alone,
without full study. In short, "the best way of dealing with the
present proposals in the long run, the way which would arouse
least bitterness of religious or partisan conflict, would be to
recommend the appointment of a Royal Commission to study
the whole field of our marriage laws. . . ." He admitted that
this involved delay, "even if it is practical to suppose that the
present proposals have a great prospect of getting into law in
the immediate future."

Earl Winterton confirmed this observation: ". . . there is
not the faintest chance of this Bill going through. . . . The
only chance we shall ever get, whether a Tory or Socialist
Government is in power, of getting a real reform of the divorce laws is after a Royal Commission has reported. We
shall never get it otherwise."

Mrs. White's Bill was therefore allowed to lapse.

The Royal Commission was appointed by September 1951
(a month before the Attlee Government was voted out of
office), and reported in December 1955. Its terms of reference were similar to those of its predecessor—to report on
divorce and allied laws and to recommend any needed
changes "having in mind the need to promote and maintain
healthy and happy married life and to safeguard the interests
and well-being of children . . ." There were 19 original
members, 12 men and 7 women, with backgrounds in law,
administration, medicine, social work, education, and labor.
The chairman was Lord Morton of Henryton, a Lord of Ap-

peal, age 63, married, and since 1949 chairman of the Council of Legal Education.[5]

Although the Commission took evidence from spokesmen for Christian churches and for other religious bodies, like its predecessor in 1909 it decided it would examine its problem only from the point of view of the state, which had to legislate for all its citizens, whatever their religious beliefs. This position was accepted even by the Archbishop of Canterbury.

All the Commissioners agreed that the root of the problem of marriage breakdown was the tendency to take the responsibilities of marriage less seriously, to be less willing to try to overcome difficulties and to put up with the rubs of daily life, to regard divorce not as the last resort but as the obvious way out when things begin to go wrong. There was also agreement, however, that making divorce more difficult would not help.

[5] The other members were Lady (Viscountess) Portal, a widow, chairman of the Children's Committee for Hampshire; Lord Keith, Senator of College of Justice in Scotland and former chairman, Scottish Central Probation Council; Mr. Justice Pearce, judge of the Probate, Divorce, and Admiralty Division of the High Court; Lord Walker, K.C., former Sheriff and Dean of the Faculty of Advocates; Sir Frederick Burrows, chairman of the Agricultural Land Commission and former Governor of Bengal, and once a $10-a-week railway porter; Lady Bragg, former Mayor of Cambridge and married to a scientist; Mr. H. L. O. Flecker, Headmaster of Christ's Hospital; Mr. Thomas Young, solicitor, member of the Council of the Law Society of Scotland; Dr. May Baird, chairman of the North East Regional Board for Hospitals; Mr. Robert Beloe, Chief Education Officer, Surrey County Council; Mrs. Ethel M. Brace, former Mayor of East Ham; Mr. George C. P. Brown, Headmaster and principal teacher of English in a Glasgow secondary school; Mr. Frederick G. Lawrence, K.C. and Recorder of Tenterden; Mr. Darrell Mace, solicitor; Mr. Daniel Hopkin, Metropolitan Police Magistrate; Mrs. Mabel Ridealgh, Labour M.P. and former National President of Women's Cooperative Guild; Dr. Violet Roberton, the only unmarried woman, deputy chairman of the Corporation of City of Glasgow and member of Scottish Central Probation Council; and Mrs. Kate W. Jones-Roberts, member Advisory Council on Child Care, Joint Education Committee for Wales, Welsh Regional Hospital Board, and a County Councillor.

The Commission therefore strongly recommended a great extension of education and premarital instruction, and far more facilities for marriage guidance and conciliation. To help make parents face their responsibilities, the Commission also proposed that before making a final decree of divorce the court should satisfy itself about the arrangements for the children.

The existing divorce law was founded on the doctrine of the matrimonial offense. That is, certain acts, "matrimonial offenses" (for instance adultery, desertion, or cruelty), were regarded as being fundamentally incompatible with the agreements of marriage. The commission of any of these acts by one party to a marriage gave the aggrieved party an option to have the marriage ended by divorce.

The basic question posed to the Commission was whether this principle—that divorce is a remedy for a specific injury—should be abandoned, the existing grounds of divorce abolished, and a new principle recognized which would permit a divorce when the marriage had in fact irretrievably broken down. This new doctrine held that matrimonial offenses are not usually the cause of the failure of a marriage but its symptoms, and that to base the grounds for divorce on symptoms is bad social policy. It denies relief (divorce) when it should be available because the marriage has in fact completely broken down although there may not have been an offense, but it permits divorce (for instance for an isolated act of adultery which has been repented of) when there may be no reason why the marriage should not continue. Further, people deliberately commit offenses, or pretend to, in order to supply the grounds for divorce, and this induces contempt for the law. The suggested solution was to require the court to determine in each case whether the marriage has broken down beyond hope of reconciliation.

The Commission noted that the majority of witnesses who supported this doctrine of breakdown of marriage favored the addition to the present law of one or both of these new grounds: (1) divorce by mutual consent of husband and wife (all but one Commissioner rejected this); (2) divorce at option of either spouse after a period of separation (all but four Commissioners rejected this).

With one exception, the Commissioners all agreed that the present law based on the doctrine of the matrimonial offense should be retained. But nine of the remaining 18 Commissioners decided that the time had come to introduce the doctrine of the breakdown of marriage to a limited extent; that is, they wanted to make exceptions to the doctrine of the matrimonial offense. They recommended that where husband and wife had lived apart for seven years it should be possible for either spouse to obtain a divorce if the other spouse did not object.

In other words, these nine Commissioners allowed the fact of breakdown, without inquiry into guilt or innocence of either spouse, to be grounds for divorce in certain circumstances. Four of these nine thought this was second best to Mrs. White's Bill (which did not require agreement of the other spouse)—which the rest of the Commission rejected as enabling parties to profit from their own wrong-doing and forcing divorce on innocent parties.

Nine other Commissioners opposed the introduction of this new principle (or the exception to the old one) because they believed it entailed basically the recognition of divorce by consent. This they felt was fundamentally objectionable, threatening marriage as a life-long relationship by making divorce the "easy way out." The right of people to divorce themselves by mutual consent[6] would tend to foster an atti-

---

[6] In the House of Lords debate (10/24/56) Lord Merriman clarified the concept of divorce by consent. When there is a legitimate grievance, the fact that both parties are glad to be rid of each other does not turn what is a remedy for a proved wrong into "divorce by

tude to marriage that would be disastrous for the nation. People would enter marriage more lightly, with the reservation that if it were not a success they could always agree to put an end to it. When difficulties arose there would be much less incentive to overcome them. These Commissioners regarded marriage not merely as a civil contract between two persons but as a status arising out of that contract and of concern to the community as well as to the parties.

The Commission advised that divorce be granted for three new grounds: willful refusal to consummate the marriage; artificial insemination by a donor without the husband's consent; and detention as a mental defective of dangerous propensities. It rejected eight other proposed new grounds such as incompatibility, refusal to have a child, imprisonment, or conviction of murder.

To encourage reconciliation the Commission advised that estranged couples should be able to live together for a trial period without, if the trial failed, interrupting the three years' unbroken period which the current law required for desertion. In all, the Commission made 149 recommendations for England and 81 for Scotland.

The *Report* of the Commission was released in March 1956. In the House of Lords, October 24, 1956, the Eden Government announced plans to implement many of the recommendations. Grants were already under consideration to provide greater facilities for marriage guidance and conciliation. But no hope could be held out for major legislation. The even division in the Commission on the most controversial problem—whether to allow divorce after seven years' separation—reflected a similar division throughout the country, the Government spokesman felt, and therefore "few Governments would be ready to legislate . . . without first allowing

---

consent." "Divorce by consent" means divorce where the agreement of the parties is the only basis on which divorce is sought.

time for public opinion to crystallise." But he also felt a role here could be played, as in the past, by Private Members' Bills.[7]

Advocates of the principle of divorce by consent were, of course, highly displeased by the Commission's report. The *Socialist Leader* (4/7/56) thought that all this mountain of labor had produced "scarcely a mouse's squeak in the direction of substantial reform"; the *New Statesman and Nation* (3/31/56) called it a "fascinating reflection of official humbug." The chairman of the Marriage Law Reform Society said it should be treated as a document of "little social value." This appraisal, however, did not prevent the Society's using the prestige of the Royal Commission in preparing a Bill based on the recommendation that no divorce should be granted until satisfactory arrangements had been made for the children of the marriage.

This sort of response was doubtless to be expected. More responsible criticism centered on the Commission's procedure. Lord Chorley, Professor of Law in the University of London, charged in the October 1956 Lords' debate that the Commission had relied too much on conjecture and not enough on facts. How many uncontested divorces rested on collusion, he asked, as a sample? Witnesses before the Com-

---

[7] So it has proved. In fact it is now established procedure to effect reforms in this field through Private Members' Bills. Such a Bill, to implement the Commission's proposal for trial reconciliation, received Royal Assent August 1, 1963. Opposition forced dropping another part of the Bill which would have permitted divorce after seven years' separation under certain circumstances, as some of the Commissioners had advised. Judgment was apparently as divided then as it was seven years earlier in the Commission itself.

As early as December 6, 1957, at a second reading of another Private Member's Bill to implement other recommendations of the Commission, the sponsor reported that a great many of the 149 proposals for England and 81 for Scotland had already been put into operation by rules of court or by administrative measures.

mission had disagreed on this, and Lord Chorley felt that capable researchers could have found the truth. Then the country would know to what extent the law, which he regarded as a bad law, was evaded by this subterfuge.

O. R. McGregor, Lecturer in Sociology at the University of London, who had so warmly praised the Gorell Commission, made the same criticisms, charging that the Commission had failed to appreciate the importance of further research.[8]

McGregor's conclusions are based on his appraisal of the Commission's handling of the matrimonial offense versus breakdown of marriage controversy; his book admittedly makes no attempt to evaluate all the other recommendations. The leading articles of the *Times* and the *Manchester Guardian* may therefore supply something of a balance. On March 21, 1956, the *Times* wrote:

> It will be regrettable if the Royal Commission's dissensions about divorce by consent divert attention from their solid and united work on other important aspects of marital disharmony. All nineteen members agree on a list of very necessary improvements in the law and practice. . . . The first task of policy is indubitably to prevent marriages from breaking down. The commission offer wise observations on the importance of a really great extension of . . . services for . . . marriage guidance. . . .

[8] See his *Divorce in England*, p. 181. On p. 187 he suggests several research projects the Commission might have undertaken, e.g. a factual study of the consequences of their parents' divorce for a representative sample of children.

It is interesting that while he charges that "the absence [on the Commission's membership] of known opponents and advocates of change in divorce laws was striking," the *Economist* (3/24/56) comments that when the Commission was set up "it was widely reported that its members had been chosen in such a way that half were likely to approve of some major 'liberalization' of the divorce laws and half were bound to oppose it."

The liberal and independent *Manchester Guardian* on March 22, 1956, had no criticisms of poor membership, hopeless conservatism, or lack of research. It simply stated its opinion that the weight of evidence supported the nine Commissioners who recommended that divorce should be granted after seven years' separation if both spouses consented. It also emphasized the Commission's recommendations on other matters, especially marriage guidance and conciliation.

> It is hard to do justice to the rich variety of the Commission's proposals which range from broad principles to points of procedure. . . . The Commissioners deserve gratitude for the painstaking, humane, and reverent way in which they have tackled this vast and intricate network of human problems. . . . On civil marriage the Commission is entitled to be heard with an attention reflecting its own serious and high-minded approach.

Whether the Chorley and McGregor criticisms would have been made had the Commission recommended divorce by consent is beside the point. Whether the conclusions of the Commission would have been significantly altered by further empirical evidence it might have collected is probably impossible to know. But one criticism of the Commission seems unquestionably sound. Like Caesar's wife, a Royal Commission must be above suspicion—suspicion of professional incompetence. There will probably always be protests from those disappointed by the conclusions of a Commission. But it should never be possible to make even a plausible case that a Commission may be wrong because it did not properly investigate the facts.

The Commission might well have foreseen the objections that were voiced and made anticipatory rebuttal in its report, if it could. There seems little doubt that the Morton Commission suffered from the absence in its membership of persons able to approach its problem as research specialists.

It is probably also true that the division in the Commission on the question of divorce by consent reflected a basic uncertainty in knowledge and moral principles. But the Commission, with only one dissentient, recommended three new grounds for divorce, and this degree of consensus presents a clear guide for action.

An even more clear and certain guide lies in the Commission's emphasis on a very large expanson of facilities for education, premarital instruction, and marriage guidance and conciliation. There is already considerable evidence of a shift in public attention to this more positive and therapeutic course. If the recommendations are fully implemented the dimensions of the whole problem of divorce could be markedly reduced.[9]

[9] The division of judgment about divorce is shown in the 1957 results of the New York *Herald Tribune* World Poll conducted by International Research Associates. In response to the question "Do you believe that divorces should be made easier or more difficult?", 46% of those queried in Britain answered "more difficult"; 31% "easier"; and 23% had no opinion. In not a single European country polled were there more persons who favored easier divorce than favored more difficult divorce. The British divorce rate (per 1000 married couples) was reported in the poll as 2.8, with only the Netherlands lower at 2.6. See New York *Herald Tribune,* December 8, 1957, p. 30.

6 Objective justice: the coal industry

Two basic features set the frame of the Royal Commissions dealing with the coal industry. The importance of the industry to Great Britain has long been second only to that of agriculture. Next to land itself, coal has been the nation's greatest material asset and its chief export. As the only important source of power, it has been the foundation of the entire British industrial system. And, coexistent with this crucial significance to the country's economic well-being, the coal industry, especially since the First World War, has been marked by conflict between owners and workers more bitter and more destructive than in any other segment of the economy.

Since 1860 twelve Royal Commissions and innumerable

committees investigated one or another phase of the coal industry. By far the two most important inquiries were the well-known "Sankey" and "Samuel" Commissions in 1919 and 1925. Because the problems they handled were so controversial, these two Commissions provide the best context for viewing the relation of this mechanism to partisan governments and to a class or associational society. Their very dates, long before labor had achieved equality of power with industry, underscore the balance and independence of the Royal Commission.

The First World War profoundly disrupted the prevailing methods of operation in the industry and signaled a time of troubles which lasted through the Second World War. Owners and miners opposed each other not only on immediate issues of profits, wages, hours, and working conditions but with conflicting and inflexible philosophic, economic, and political faiths. But the ramifications of the "coal problem" extended far beyond their interests. Consumers demanded a steady supply of coal at lowest prices; dealers depended on it for their livelihood; the Government needed coal for exports; engineers were concerned with productivity. Coal had to be cheap enough for maximum sale at home and abroad; it had also to be priced enough to permit ever higher standards of living for a tenth of the population.

All these differing demands, each held passionately, reveal the limitations of thought inherent in all segmental approaches to societal problems. The partial solutions cannot simply be added up to make a total solution. It was basically, then, this strategic problem of how to evaluate and accommodate conflicting interests to attain equity and efficiency that was set to both Commissions.

It was set to them because the permanently responsible agencies were unable to handle it. Owners and miners pursued their private demands so fanatically the Government had to intervene in the interests of the total society. But the authority of the Government was so weakened by alleged partisanship that the warring factions refused to accept its directives.

At the end of the First World War the coal industry was prosperous, but the miners felt they were not receiving their fair share. Also, all during the war their Federation had been planning the changes in the industry they believed should be made. Two months after the armistice, therefore, the Federation presented its program to the Government, then still in control of the industry. It included a 30 per cent increase in wages, a six-hour work day, and nationalization of both mines and mineral.

The Coalition Government had the Liberal Lloyd George as Prime Minister and a large Conservative majority in Parliament. It refused everything but a 10 per cent wage increase and offered a Committee of Inquiry on the other proposals. This the miners refused and voted a national strike. The upshot was the agreement that the Government appoint a Royal Commission to survey the entire state of affairs in the coal industry. The Commission would present an interim report on wages and hours. If the miners accepted the findings, the Commission was to go on to consider the other demands. The miners in turn would postpone the strike until after the interim report.

Because the problems were so emotionally charged it was decided to make the Commission also statutory. Parliament passed a special Act creating a Coal Industry Commission and gave it all the powers of a high court: full authority to compel the appearance of witnesses and the production of documents, to take evidence under oath, and to punish for contempt. No evidence could then be denied the Commission, for instance on the touchy matter of profits. The Act called for reports "as soon as practicable" but did not set any time limit.

The (Sankey) Coal Industry Commission

The Commission was set up in February 1919 and was a "representative" one. Each belligerent nominated three members and to them the Government added six members independent of miners or owners—three to represent other industries (dependent on coal) on the employers' side and three to represent the workers' interests in other industries, or labor generally. For chairman the Government selected Sir John Sankey, a judge of the King's Bench Division of the High Court of Justice, a distinguished jurist of independent views who had previously had a large practice in the mining area of South Wales.[1]

The interim *Report of the First Stage of the Inquiry* was presented on March 20, 1919. The three miners' representatives, together with Webb, Money, and Tawney, recommended the full 30 per cent wage increase asked by the miners, and a reduction of the working day from eight to six hours. They stated that nationalization ought in principle to be accepted since individual ownership was wasteful, the method of retail distribution needlessly costly, and unification of mines in the hands of a "capitalist trust" intolerable.

The three representatives of the mine owners recommended a maximum wage increase of roughly 15 per cent

---

[1] As Commissioners the Mining Association (the national organization of mine owners) selected three of its leading members. The Miners' Federation selected its President, Robert Smillie (who was also head of the Triple Alliance), its Vice-President, and its Secretary. The Federation also designated the three "friends of labor" —Sidney Webb, Sir Leo Chiozza Money, and R. H. Tawney, all well-known Fabian leaders. The independent representatives of industrial employers were Arthur Balfour, managing director of a steel firm; Sir Arthur Duckham, a mining engineer who had served in official agencies during the war; and Sir Thomas Royden, deputy chairman of the Cunard Steamship Co.

and a reduction in hours from eight to seven for underground workers. They remarked that evidence was still insufficient for their judgment as to nationalization or unification.

Sir John Sankey and the three representatives of industrial employers recommended a 20 per cent wage increase, an immediate reduction of hours from eight to seven and a later reduction to six at the end of 1920 if conditions permitted. They had no final decision yet on reorganization but said that even on the evidence already given, "the present system of ownership and working in the coal industry stands condemned and some other system must be substituted for it. . . ."

The Government immediately accepted the chairman's recommendations. The miners were jubilant and voted thirteen to one to waive the strike. The Commission thereupon continued with its investigation and made its final *Report on the Second Stage of the Inquiry* in June 1919. It was split into four separate reports.

The chairman recommended that the Government nationalize both the mineral and the mines themselves, paying fair compensation. His scheme called for a Minister of Mines, responsible to Parliament, who would superintend fourteen district administrative councils, on each of which the miners would select four of the fourteen members. There was to be arbitration on local, district, and national levels and no strikes unless the dispute went to the highest level and there failed of settlement.

The three miners' representatives and the three independent friends of labor agreed with the chairman but objected to his arbitration provisions and wanted fuller representation for workers on the district councils. The three miners' representatives also opposed any compensation to mineral owners.

The third separate report was issued by the three owners' representatives and two of the independent representatives of

employers. It was based on the principle that private enterprise must be maintained, but it did recommend that the mineral be nationalized and that owners give workers more information on prices and profits of coal.

Sir Arthur Duckham, the remaining representative of employers, issued the last report. He accepted nationalization of
the mineral but rather than nationalize the mines he proposed
to amalgamate them within certain districts. Each district was
to be operated by a private corporation under majority share-
holder control but with a minority of members selected by
the miners. He also advocated a levy on coal to establish a
Welfare Fund to improve social conditions of the miners.

Lloyd George announced the decision of the Government
in the House of Commons on August 18, 1919. He agreed to
state purchase of the mineral and reported that a deduction
from the price would be made to create a Welfare Fund. He
rejected nationalization of the mines but favored amalgamation along the lines suggested by Sir Arthur Duckham. The
Government would oversee the amalgamations in the interest
of the whole country.

Faced with this decision the miners decided against carrying out their postponed strike. Instead they organized a two-
months "Mines for the Nation" publicity campaign. This,
however, failed to move the Government and had no appreci-
able effect on public opinion.

The Government in turn went ahead with part of its
scheme. Because the miners objected to compensation to
mineral owners and a powerful section of Commons was
against any nationalization, this feature was dropped. But the
Government passed the Mining Industry Act of 1920, which
set up a Mines Department to co-ordinate all governmental
mining activities. It also levied a penny a ton on all coal to
expedite housing schemes and pit-head baths. This was the
origin of the Miners' Welfare Fund, which over the years

made a great contribution to the living conditions of the miners.

A second part of the Act created machinery to deal with wages and profits, and a series of bodies representative of owners and workers to collaborate on operational problems.

The functions of the Sankey Commission

The Coal Industry Commission was created in what came very close to a revolutionary crisis. Here was the most powerful union in the country pressing wage and hour demands against the owners. This was critical enough, considering the disrupted times. But coupled to this familiar drive for economic advance was the formidable claim that the state should take over both the mineral and the mines. This was a direct political attack on private enterprise, on the system believed responsible for England's supremacy in industrial civilization. So to a traditionally accepted struggle between two segments in a private industry was joined a struggle between defenders of private enterprise and radical innovators. Finally, a national coal strike was threatened. This would not merely have deprived a small number of users of a product either unnecessary or duplicable; coal was central to the entire British economy, and the total costs of a stoppage would have been enormous.

The first function of the Commission was an invariable one: to present the facts of a controversial situation as a basis for policy.

The Government defended its refusal to grant the first wage and hour demands of the miners on the grounds that the facts simply were not available on which a responsible decision could be made. The miners argued that it was not facts that were lacking but Government willingness to grant just claims.

Whichever contention was right the function of the Commission was not affected. If the block to Government action was lack of reliable information, the Commission could supply that where Parliamentary debate could not. If the Government's argument simply masked the obduracy of conservative interests, the definitive information supplied by the Commission would remove the Government's excuse for inaction (or for its first offer of one third the workers' demands), and place the struggle where it properly belonged—in the realm of political "will." In the entire House debate on the Bill to create the Commission (2/24/19) no one even suggested that if a Royal Commission were appointed it could not be trusted to produce all the relevant facts.

The interim report, even though split, ended the debate on the facts of wages and hours. Attention could then turn to the more difficult problem of improvement in operation.

The Sankey Commission opened up the entire mining industry. It provided a forum that revealed the economic principles and administrative practices of mine owners, the place of mineral owners, the working and living conditions of the miners. Here was public instruction of the highest order. Before its report probably not a single person had the balanced picture of the industry that the Commission made available to the whole public.

In its disclosure of facts, in its demonstration that the methods of operation under private enterprise were intolerably inefficient and inequitable, in its examination of alternative schemes for reconstruction, and in its specific recommendations the Commission guided the way for successive improvement. It represented the first major cultivation of public thought on this problem. It gave authoritative support to those seeking remedial changes in the industry—changes that culminated some 20 years later in nationalization of the mineral and some seven years after that in nationalization of the mines themselves.[2]

The predominant weight of the Sankey Commission was in the direction of social change. But it also contributed to social stability. The Commission recommended unanimously to nationalize the mineral but, with the exception of the three miners' representatives, it also agreed that just compensation should be paid to the expropriated owners.

This characteristic Royal Commission balance was not an unprincipled watering-down of opposing claims. The national society was confronted by an industrial revolution superseding established ways based mainly on land. In the interest of stability it had to conserve what was valid in the established norms; in the interest of adjustment to change it had to decide which new ways would be most successful.

The mineral owners, as elder brothers, claimed they held their rights under full legal justification unchallenged for generations, and that it was only fair they be compensated for surrender of those rights, just as any other property would be paid for, were the state to require it. In upholding this well-established norm the Commission helped preserve property rights, the continuity of which was the basis of a good proportion of the economic security of every citizen—including the miners.

The miners, as younger brothers, challenged the norm that owners could continue indefinitely to exercise control over the use of their property. They contended that private

---

[2] "Perhaps the most powerful single stimulus ever given to the nationalization movement was the Sankey Coal Commission of 1919. No government commission had up to that date ever subjected an industry to so thorough an investigation nor uttered so plain a condemnation of accepted business procedure." Isador Lubin and Helen Everett in *The British Coal Dilemma* (New York: Macmillan, 1927), pp. 213-14 (a publication of the Brookings Institute of Economics).

control over mineral rights was both unjust in that it yielded high returns for no service, and inefficient in that it prevented sensible mining operations. And here the Commission decided that changes in industrial life required that the state should own and control the mineral itself. The Commission acted, in effect, much as a mediating parent.

This balance of the Commission, and its prestige, contributed of course to the influence of its judgments. This in turn, reinforced by the Samuel Commission six years later, may reasonably be taken to have facilitated voluntary acceptance of its directives when embodied in law. The 1938 legislation expropriating the mineral, though opposed by the owners, was accepted by them without revolt, without continued opposition supported by other property owners who felt threatened, without the use, as often in authoritarian decrees, of any external force beyond the orderly execution of the law.

The miners, similarly, accepted the reaffirmed norm of just compensation for expropriated property—something they would probably not have accepted from a Conservative Party alone. By so helping reconcile blocs to adverse rulings, the Commission aided both social order and orderly social change.

Quantitative measurement of the degree to which the Sanky Commission helped speed social change would be practically impossible. If, however, one posits the miners, as an underprivileged minority, the sole source of pressure for the changes, the mineral and mine owners would probably have been able to block legislation much longer than they actually did. The miners needed support from many other sources and among citizens generally. What, in fact, surely as much as anything else, did secure outside support for them were the Sankey and the Samuel Commissions. All the evidence testifies to the invaluable instruction of these Commissions in presenting the facts of the coal mining industry and those ways of handling its problems that promised most advantages. Owners and their supporters henceforth had to deal not with a splinter of "radicals" but with most of the body politic and most of the country's leaders, as they had been enlightened by the Royal Commission.

The Royal Commission, Parliament, and vested interests

It is possible at this point to consider the place of the Royal Commission in a class society. It may be felt that while theoretically a democracy attempts to balance conflicting interests on an equitable appraisal of social needs, actually class rights and a legally bolstered class system introduce a crippling bias. Labor may be relatively weak, general consumers inarticulate, different groups have varying access to data. As Tawney remarked, in England there was inequality on the scale of a national institution.

What happens, then, to objectivity in data-gathering and policy-making in a heavily class-stratified society? In this instance the miners may be presumed the weaker party, discriminated against and denied access to data—as indeed they were outside the frame of the Royal Commission.

The standards which safeguard the Royal Commission show up first in the absence of any bias in selecting the members of the Commission. Lloyd George, though himself a Liberal, was the leader of the Conservative Government. He was regarded by the miners as the guardian of all ruling-class interests. It was he, however, who appointed Sir John Sankey as chairman, a man in whom the miners had the fullest confidence. There was probably no other person in the country they would have preferred. Similarly, the rest of the membership suggested no packing to buttress capitalist interests. The six labor members were easily the equal of the industrial and employer representatives.

Regardless of respective strength in political or economic areas, there is no evidence that within the frame of the Royal Commission any group suffered any discrimination. Nor did class differences distort objectivity in fact-gathering. Class bias did clearly show itself in some of the Commission's recommendations—the miners voted against compensation to mineral owners, the mine owners against giving workers more than a nominal share in control. In other decisions, for instance to nationalize the mineral, presumed ruling-class bias was transcended.

There is another aspect to this question of objectivity. One may grant that the Royal Commission itself is as egalitarian and objective in data-gathering and policy-forming as human frailty permits. It might still be possible that the political system can and does use it as an appendage for partisan purposes, to the disservice of the society.

Aneurin Bevan's *Why Not Trust the Tories?* was a scathing denunciation of Tory methods in defense of their interests. In it the Royal Commission would appear to share criticism as a tool used by Conservative Governments to sidetrack reform. Bevan generalizes the Tory technique as "Death by Words"—that is, to ignore a demand for reform as long as possible, hoping it will die of political malnutrition. If the no-longer-to-be-avoided debate in Commons shows growing demand, the Government does not show open opposition, since this might lose support at elections. Instead it expresses interest but asserts the problem is complicated and requires examination by experts in a public inquiry. The reformers agree, for fear the reform will be rejected out of hand.

The Commission investigates. Then the Government delays issuance of the report for as long as possible, then delays debate on the report as long as possible. Then it promises a White Paper embodying its intentions, observing that the Government needs to take time to consider, just as the Commission did. The Government then delays issuance of the White Paper, made as vague as possible, because its consideration in Commons may be the start of a Bill which might then become law. It is to prevent this that the Tory technique is to add to the number of talking stages through which a suggested reform must pass. At each stage it suffers a further decline in vitality, so that by the time of the White Paper even its most ardent friends are likely to be sickened by it.

In describing the 1919 coal impasse, Bevan remarks first that the miners had a "healthy and natural distrust" of Commissions, regarding them as "face-saving and stalling devices." But they accepted the proposal for the Sankey Commission despite their suspicions. The interim report pleased them "beyond anything they had ever experienced" in their industrial history, and they felt that at last justice was to be done. The miners thereupon revoked their strike notices, and the Commission went on to its second stage.

> Then followed one of the most extraordinary series of public sittings ever held. . . . Day after day coal owners, royalty owners [and others] were cross-examined so thoroughly and efficiently that universal admiration was felt for the work of the Commission. . . . Day after day the newspapers carried banner headlines [N.B.] reporting the exposures of inefficient mining, exorbitant royalties and shocking housing conditions. . . . Never have the deficiencies of private enterprise . . . been so thoroughly exposed. . . . The Tory champions of property were alarmed. What had started as a conspiracy to blunt the edge of the miners' industrial militancy [i.e.

the appointment of the Sankey Commission] was turning into a weapon against the coal owners themselves.[3]

But the Government rejected what Bevan called "the Majority Sankey Report" to nationalize the coal mines and the minerals. Bevan sums up:

> . . . the mining crisis of 1919 and the Sankey Coal Commission . . . is in many ways a classic of its kind. It is by way of being a model of the working of the Tory mind in politics. It shows that the Tory is never concerned about implementing the democratic will, nor with industrial efficiency nor social justice. . . . The Sankey Commission had shown an indefensible state of affairs in the mining industry. . . . But the Tories chose private property and they defended it with every weapon in their armoury. . . . And they won.[4]

Regardless of the justice of this condemnation, surely Bevan's own words are the strongest confirmation of a fact: in the Sankey Commission, for whatever discreditable reasons it *may* have been set up, the miners found the fullest opportunity for voicing their claims, and in its proposals a notable advance toward equity.

By 1919 the Miners' Federation was a strong union. But its leaders had not had in the past the experience or education of their opponents, nor the same public attention. The Sankey Commission gave exploited workers not merely information they had previously been denied but their first significant public sounding board at a time when their spokesmen had the ability to take good advantage of it. In equalizing the chance to speak to the country, and in the influence of its recommendations, the Commission introduced

[3] Aneurin Bevan, *Why Not Trust the Tories?* (London: Victor Gollancz, 1944), pp. 18-19.
[4] Ibid., pp. 22-23.

a counterforce to the hitherto stronger power of the industrial and land-owning class. Here is a striking example of a latent function of a Royal Commission. One does not have to agree with all Bevan says to conclude that the Government never intended this result.

Did the Sankey Commission, nonetheless, delay reform? The question implies that, had there been no such mechanism, reform would have met one less obstacle. Surely this is not so. It is true that the Government, without a Royal Commission, could have nationalized the mineral and the mines in 1919. But, given the superior political power of the owners at that time, the hard facts were that no such action would have been taken. As Bevan suggested, the demanded reforms would have been rejected out of hand.

And if the purpose of the Government and its Tory supporters in creating the Sankey Commission was to delay reform, they badly miscalculated. For the Commission was actually a potent influence in undermining the power of the owners. So potent, in fact, that one commentator reports they regarded the Commission as a "catastrophe." [5] If an important bloc can so regard a Royal Commission, perhaps the structure to that extent may be dysfunctional for a society. But this is unavoidable in any accommodation of conflicting interests. Whenever blocs clash any equitable balance may be felt by one or the other, or even by both, as detrimental to its interests. But if they accept the decisions without external force the dysfunction is simply that imbalance which is an inevitable concomitant of adjustment to reality. Where its recommendations involve significant dislocation or other loss to any group, a Royal Commission

[5] Isador Lubin and Helen Everett, *The British Coal Dilemma,* p. 40, note that the Commission's report "was to have a far-reaching effect upon the movement for the nationalization of the mines. It added vital force to the miners' demands and aroused public interest in the issue; so much so, in fact, that the mine owners have come to look upon the report as a great catastrophe."

also advises fair compensation. If this is then provided, social change may be taken to have occurred with minimal ill effect.

Experience suggests, therefore, that it is not wise for reformers to regard the time a Commission takes to report as a delay in reform. If the Commission's findings go against a class policy of the Government either it must then yield—in which case the reformers have achieved their goal with only a relatively short delay—or the Government will use its superior power sometime *after* the Commission reports—in which case the Government is in exactly the position it was before. But now the reformers need no longer continue their agitation alone. They now have the support of authoritative facts, impartial recommendations, and the prestige of a Royal Commission.

Regardless of inability to measure the exact degree of strength this adds to their cause, it is indisputable that it adds *some* strength, and thus from a strategic point of view speeds, not delays, reform. Without this mechanism the body politic has no information or insight save the conflicting claims and counterclaims of the opposing blocs. It becomes a matter of "propaganda," and in this reformers have not usually credited ruling classes as being weaker. With no yardstick, no reliable facts on which to base judgment, citizens waver back and forth with the frequent result of the attitude expressed in "a plague on both your houses."

The Sankey Commission is an excellent illustration of a common experience: the functions of a Royal Commission are significantly independent of the partisan motivations of a Government. Once set in motion, a Commission has a life and power all its own. It cannot be controlled; its findings may seemingly be disregarded, but it initiates pressures which usually result in implementation in spite of segmental opposition.

The pressures it generates are no "unseen hand." They

comprise an increased awareness of a problem by citizens and a set of authoritative facts and judgments which give weight to those seeking a solution beyond the imposition of the stronger power of one or another bloc.

The Royal Commission is not in some idealistic sense aloof from party politics. Its structure and institutional context in Great Britain enable it to rise above class and party politics. It is the integrated relationship of the Royal Commission and political life—its appointment by the reigning ministry, its official status in constitutional law, the payment of its expenses out of the public treasury, the norms governing selection of members and terms of reference—that gives it its importance. These and many other political links do not pervert its Royal (i.e. impartial, fatherly) attributes or degrade it to the level of a tool of a biased Government. On the contrary, without these links it would indeed be aloof, uselessly ungeared to the societal need, simply a group of private individuals voicing private judgments.

On the other hand, it is the character of the Royal Commission itself—its relative independence of the appointing Government and of any private groups, the balancing perspectives of its members, cross-examination techniques, and other features—that raises it above its source, that yields facts and judgments going beyond the limitations of class and party and group prejudices.

The Royal Commission, in sum, is not some theoretically ideal mechanism which is corrupted by a class-biased society. Obviously most Commissioners, personally successful, accept the basic values prevalent in the society. But, provided only that its standards are observed, there is no more effective agency than the Royal Commission for overcoming the obstacles to reform imposed by limited perspective.

Why were not the Sankey Commission's recommendations more fully or more quickly implemented? Irrespective of responsibility for a representative Commission,[6] there was the fact of divided reports and their hindrance to implementation. There was, Lloyd George was able to argue in Parliament, no majority in favor of anything or why had no report signed by a majority been produced? G. D. H. Cole, however, has charged that these "secondary" differences were used by the Government as an excuse for inaction. Lack of unanimity could not have been the main reason for delay in implementation. For it will be recalled that the unanimous directive to nationalize the mineral was not followed either.

The real reason for the delay lies in the relation of a Royal Commission to Parliament and to special interest blocs.

The House of Commons had been elected barely a month before the Sankey Commission was appointed. Every Labour candidate had gone to the constituencies on a pledge to nationalize the mines and railways, yet the country had returned a large Conservative majority.

In Parliament are representatives of many different blocs and classes, all openly committed to press for programs furthering their special interests. Each of these representative groups has members whom impartial observers would rank as mature leaders, championing their group but also able in de-

---

[6] The opinion has been expressed that "The composition . . . would indeed suggest that its appointment was a political expedient, designed to quieten public feeling and—perhaps even more—to tie the hands of the coal workers who were threatening strike action."— J. Taylor in Vernon and Mansergh, *Advisory Bodies* (London: George Allen & Unwin, 1940), p. 379. Actually it was Sidney Webb who proposed the four sets of representatives and persuaded the Miners' Federation to press for such a composition. The intention of the Government had been to appoint eight representatives of labor interests and eight of the business community. Lloyd George had requested a dinner with Mr. Webb to consult with him on specific members. See *Beatrice Webb's Diaries, 1912-1924,* ed. by Margaret I. Cole (London: Longmans, Green, 1952), pp. 146-51, under date of February 22, 1919; and *Parliamentary Debates,* House of Commons, Vol. 112, February 26, 1919, Col. 1752.

gree to accommodate their interests to those of other blocs. Each group also includes extremist members, ignorant or dogmatic, who view their interests only in the most narrow, short-range perspective. In their policies, therefore, ranking leaders cannot get too far ahead of what the extremists will accept, lest the latter revolt and the group lose its cohesion.

Members of Parliament are also in close vertical interaction with their respective blocs outside Parliament. Among these outside members are, as always, extremists who press for their interests with a militancy untempered by the experience of lateral interaction with the leaders of opposing blocs. If Parliamentary leaders, in their attempts to adjust conflicting interests, go too far beyond what outside extremists will support, they risk replacement as leaders.

In contrast to Parliament, a Royal Commission lacks any vertical association with blocs or the general body politic. (Because of the representative character of the Sankey Commission the three union leaders and the three mine owners were exceptions to the usual situation.) Commissioners are not elected; they have no responsibility to any groups or to the Government; they disband on presentation of their report. They are usually individually, and always collectively, uncommitted and independent. Their recommendations therefore need not be tempered to the necessity of securing the immediate support of anyone; they can be designed to the requirements of the problem itself. An obvious qualification here lies in the ineradicable subjective perspective of any individual toward any social problem no matter how "impartial" the individual. But it is recognition of precisely this fact that accounts for the structure of the Royal Commission—its balance of perspectives, its procedural arrangements—and for its relationship to other societal agencies.

The Sankey Commission was not an impartial one; six of its members were as openly committed to opposing interests as was the House of Commons membership itself. Even so, the frame of a Royal Commission produced conclusions closer to realistic and equitable adjustment among contradictory demands than was possible in Parliament. It is true the split reports tended to obscure what consensus there was. But the independent observer has no great difficulty in identifying that consensus or in recognizing its superiority to the policy actually adopted.

It was into such a Parliament with ultimate responsibility for action, the final adjustment among competing wills and conflicting interests, that the recommendations of the Sankey Commission intruded. What happened was the usual struggle between the recommendations of a Royal Commission, as approximating valid social direction,[7] and the demands of segmental interests. Since the recommendations represented a balanced perspective, which opposing blocs had not yet reached, the problem, as always in a democracy, was to set a course of action as close to valid social direction as would be accepted by opposing blocs with a minimum of external force.[8]

If ranking leaders inside or outside Parliament were willing to accept the directives of a Royal Commission but extremists were not, immediate implementation might trigger very disruptive action. The group might be split. The leaders might be

[7] By "valid" (valid social direction, change, policy, action, or national interest) I mean simply what would appear to be to the best interests of the largest number of persons so far as that may be known or approximated at the time. This may or may not coincide with policy or action that would be to the best interests of given blocs in the country as those groups would see them. This key question is considered in Chapter 8, in the section entitled "Social Fact."

[8] No data were collected on this time-lead of Royal Commission recommendations over policy. It is a familiar observation in the literature, however, that it often takes from 5 to 20 years to effect implementation. This question is further considered in Chapter 9.

replaced by a more extremist faction. Or perhaps compliance could only be secured by force. The more force that is required the less secure the social order or the social change; to that degree a society has taken a turn toward disorganization.

How far policy is able to incorporate the more balanced directives of the Royal Commission depends, then, on the quality of the leadership and the strength of opposing attitudes. This is always a delicate problem of tactics, and extreme caution is required in any attempt, certainly by outsiders, to evaluate this process and its final outcome.

In this instance, when the Government outlined a fuller implementation of the Sankey Commission recommendations—calling for nationalization of the mineral, greater share in operation by the workers, and other features—the miners rejected it mainly because it did not go as far as nationalization of the mines themselves. In turn, the owners were able to prevent any further changes in traditional operation than were finally adopted.

The degree of implementation that was effected at the time was thus the result of a complex struggle between opposing political wills. It constituted a step in the direction of valid change, and may be presumed to be the maximum distance that actual policy was then able to go along the direction mapped by the Commission.

It must also be recognized that the effects of the Sankey Commission were not limited to its prevention of a crippling strike or to the legislation of the time. The Commission's importance can only be appreciated in the light of its long-range effects. Its dissection of the problems of the industry, its analysis of alternative methods of reconstruction, most of its specific recommendations—all threw significant weight against obsolete practices. At the same time it reaffirmed certain established norms such as just compensation for confiscated property. It thus helped preserve social order, and it guided social direction to that kind of change that is securely rooted in voluntary acceptance.

The (Samuel) Royal Commission on the Coal Industry

The story of the Sankey Commission would be incomplete without some account of the Samuel Commission six years later, and of how the coal problem was finally settled.

In 1924 began a depression in the coal industry that by mid-1925 found over 300,000 miners unemployed and over 60 per cent of coal being sold below cost. In this emergency the Conservative Baldwin Government took the unprecedented step of granting a nine-month subsidy to the industry. This made up the difference between current wage rates and the lower terms the owners had intended to impose. In those nine months a Royal Commission was to try to find a permanent resolution of the problem.

This time the Government appointed a technically impartial Commission of four members, none connected with the mining industry. The chairman was Sir Herbert Samuel, former Home Secretary in the Asquith Government and former High Commissioner in Palestine. Sir William Beveridge was an economist who had had numerous government positions and since 1919 had been Director of the London School of Economics. The other two members were Sir Herbert Lawrence, a distinguished retired soldier, an industrial financier, and managing director of a banking firm; and Mr. Kenneth Lee, a leading cotton manufacturer and a member of several important public boards.

The Commission was appointed September 3, 1925, and made its unanimous *Report* March 11, 1926. It castigated the owners for holding that little could be done in reorganization and that only lowered wages and lengthened hours could improve the position. It stated that before any sacrifices should be asked of the miners all practical means of improving efficiency should be adopted as quickly as possible.

The Commission concluded that prosperity would come through greater application of science to mining and the use of coal, through larger units of production and distribution, and through fuller partnership between owners and miners; and its recommendations spelled out the means to these ends. The Government should stop the subsidy at the end of the nine months and never repeat it. The Government should also nationalize the mineral, with just compensation to the owners, and should give financial support to research.

The Commission rejected the new form of nationalization of the mines which the workers and labor generally presented. It found this quite unworkable and offering no advantages that could not be more readily secured by the method the Commission proposed. This was to form larger units of production, which were imperative, not by compulsory amalgamation but by flexible schemes initiated by the owners. The Government should itself promote desirable amalgamations, for example as owner of the mineral when granting new leases or renewing old ones, and legislation should be passed permitting the use of compulsion when opposition was unreasonable.

The Commission's report came out six weeks before the subsidy was to end. The Government quickly announced it would accept it in its entirety provided—this was to prove the fatal error—the owners and miners also accepted it. For this practically invited the blocs to pull the report to pieces and reject what they disliked.

The owners protested that the recommendations would restrict the individual freedom of action which "sound economic conditions" required. The miners stood immovable on the recommendation that before wages were lowered all practicable improvements in efficiency should be made. Since the owners presented no remedial measures, the miners would accept no sacrifices. And since the two parties could not agree, the government would not itself initiate the Commission's program.

The deadlock over these issues dragged on from one futile conference to another. It defied innumerable mediation efforts. It was unbroken even by the General Strike of nine days, the first, and last, attempt by British organized labor to tie up essential services. The deadlock continued on for some seven months during the longest and most disastrous stoppage in the history of coal mining. It was finally ended only when the miners could no longer hold out and had to accept the terms of the owners. The conflict marked 1926 as perhaps the most crucial year in British industrial history. Its cost was well over a billion dollars, and the owners secured a victory that bankrupted and virtually disrupted the Miners' Federation.

During the next 12 years successive governments made attempts to implement the Samuel Commission report, but they were all either half-hearted or aborted. By 1938 12 of the 17 main recommendations had been adopted, but the available powers were exercised so poorly that amalgamation of mines was hopelessly behind what the Commission had reported necessary. In the Coal Act of 1938 a Conservative Government finally nationalized the mineral. It also strengthened the power of the Government to force amalgamations, but the extent of the power was still too limited.

During the Second World War the industry came again under Government administration. Shortly before peace the Conservative Party issued an alternative to the Labour drive for nationalization. This criticized the slowness of amalgamation in the thirties and advocated both strengthening the compulsory power of the Government and reducing the industry from some 150 concerns to about 50. But the Labour Party won the election and by July 1946 had passed a bill nationalizing the industry.

The Coal Nationalization Act set up a National Coal Board to operate the mines. Its members were to be appointed by a Minister of Fuel and Power, who had authority to issue general directives to the Board and who was the link between the Board, as a public corporation, and Parliament. The Corporation was exempt from the usual civil service requirements on personnel, and its finances were separated from the usual Treasury control.

In the extensive powers given the Minister over the Board, the Labour Party reversed the previous trend toward, and its own previous preference for, greater autonomy for government corporations. The workers were given no *de jure* representation on the Board, but two well-qualified Labourites on the first Board indicated *de facto* representation. The scheme also reversed the earlier guild socialism of worker control.

Studies of the result of nationalization indicate that the miners feel it has definitely improved their condition but that it has not come up to all their expectations. Judged from the optimistic forecasts of the Labour Party, nationalization has not been a notable success in improving human relations within the industry. But judged from the predictions of a disastrous drop in production and loss of freedom made by the Conservatives, the effects of nationalization have been very favorable.

The Samuel Commission continued the fact-finding and educational functions of its predecessor. But, since the ownership of the mines was definitively settled by nationalization, it would seem that though the recommendations of the majority of the Sankey Commission were thus ultimately implemented, the recommendations of the Samuel Commission on this point were directly contravened, a rarity in Royal Commission experience. Some feel that its rejection of the form of nationalization demanded by labor at the time, far from being a positive influence in social change, actually delayed reform. As Harold Wilson wrote in 1945, the report of the Samuel Commission was "the most comprehensive factual study of the industry ever made, but its conclusions are timid and disappointing, and have been quoted ever since by the opponents of nationalization, in spite of a substantial change in circumstances in the 19 years since the Commission reported." [9]

In the first place, the Samuel Commission helped permanently to dispose of a defective type of nationalization, that calling either for dominant worker control or for mixed worker and governmental control. And to clear away mistaken ideas is an important function of this structure.

Secondly, when it came, nationalization was not adopted because the Samuel Commission's advice had been followed and had failed to secure the desired improvement. For the advice on amalgamations had never been effectively implemented. Had it been, it is quite possible the industry might have been led to a level of efficient and equitable operation such that nationalization would not have been necessary as a final remedy.

Labor groups attributed the reason for the Commission's preference for a reorganized private ownership over nationalization to its conservative prejudices. The more responsible leftist critics acknowledged that the members were able, not the "hard-faced" type, and that they would try to be fair and might even find some plan that would be a vast improvement over the current system. But the critics felt that none could really understand poverty or the comradeship of wage earners and that they would be psychologically unable to yield the case for nationalization.

No Government would have any difficulty in defending the

[9] *New Deal For Coal* (London: Contact, 1945), p. v.

selection of either Sir Herbert Samuel or Sir William Beveridge. But in combining the backgrounds of all four Commissioners there seems little doubt that it would have been harder for them psychologically to assent to the new idea of nationalized industry than to the established idea of private enterprise. That the Government's choice of members was within (though perhaps just within) the norm that proscribes "packing" is evidenced by the fact that the miners made no complaint and did co-operate fully with them. But had the Government selected, instead of the soldier-banker or the textile manufacturer, at least one member who had the complete confidence of the miners, the Commission would certainly have been more fairly balanced.

It is pertinent to realize, also, that since the 1945 Labour Government's large-scale nationalization program, public debate in Britain has become much more sophisticated, more empirical, and less dogmatic. It is no longer the relatively simple problem of whether the means of production should be publicly or privately owned. It is appreciated that both forms of ownership face precisely the same sorts of problems —administrative initiative, public responsibility, morale, sense of participation by all workers, and many others—and that there are many different approaches to these problems involving various degrees of government participation.

With this insight, it is safe to say that if the question of control of the coal, or any other, industry were to come up for decision at this time it would certainly not be regarded as *ipso facto* "timid and disappointing" if an impartial body were to advise in favor of private ownership with proper governmental powers in areas where they were needed.

The main reason that the Samuel Commission recommendations were not any more quickly or completely implemented than those of its predecessor lies in the uncompromising opposition of both owners and miners. Lord Birkenhead,

Secretary of State for India in the Baldwin Government, has been quoted as commenting in 1925: "It would be possible to say without exaggeration of the miners' leaders that they are the stupidest men in England if we had not frequent occasion to meet the owners." [10]

A secondary reason lay in the tactic of the Government in accepting the Commission's recommendations conditional on acceptance also by owners and miners. Had the Government, instead, acted at once to implement, both blocs might perforce have yielded.

What was lacking, in retrospect, was Will—on the part of either bloc to subordinate its partisan perspective to the decision of the Commission and on the part of the Government to make effective use of that mediating decision.

In speaking of schemes for reorganization of the American coal industry, Walton H. Hamilton and Helen R. Wright note all the problems involved: how to work out the scheme, how to persuade others of its validity, how to get action. In a footnote they comment:

> In utopian books on social organization it is written down that there are simple and easy ways by which needful changes in institutional arrangements may be accomplished. But as matters go in society as it is currently organized there is no orderly way by which an industry may doff the old scheme of control and don the new. There is neither a body before which, nor a procedure whereby, questions which have to do with the organization of an industry can be raised, alternative schemes considered upon their merits, and a decision rendered upon the basis of respective promises of performance. If there were some tribunal, made up of able, far-sighted and disinterested persons, before whom the cases for various schemes of arrangements might be presented; or

[10] Quoted in D. C. Somervell, *British Politics Since 1900* (London: Andrew Dakers, 1950), pp. 174-75.

if in the affairs of industry the decorous processes of justice could be invoked and the question argued before a judge, or a jury of twelve good men and true, the better order might become the prevailing one. But, as our ways of disposing, or of not disposing, of such questions go, a change in the organization of an industry is a protracted and complicated performance . . . like nothing so much as a long drawn out and involved trial by ordeal.[11]

The renovation of the British coal industry from 1920 to 1945 shows that in Great Britain there is a body which furnishes decisions of precisely the kind which these authors rightly view as essential to smooth social change. Indeed, had the proximate validity of these decisions been sufficiently recognized, especially by the Government, and at once implemented, the better order might well have become the prevailing one with something very close to utopian ease. Though, in the event, the British reorganization was a protracted ordeal, the Royal Commission, intruding into the violent class struggle of opposing blocs, in which Governments themselves were partisans, still delivered competent, fatherly, mediating decisions—the weight of which operated to produce the better order of social justice and needed institutional change more quickly (25 years) than would have occurred without such a mechanism.

[11] *A Way of Order for Bituminous Coal* (New York: Macmillan, 1928), pp. 290-91n. (a publication of the Brookings Institute of Economics).

7 Crisis in the health service

The forty-odd years since the Sankey Commission have not notably reduced the lengths to which private blocs will go to gain their ends. Nor have they seen the competence and impartiality of Governments so increased that they always forestall crises by equitable adjustment between conflicting interests. A crisis in 1957 in the British Health Service showed that the functions of the Royal Commission in impasse are as timely as ever.

When the medical and dental professions entered the National Health Service set up by the Labour Government of 1945, they understood they would be protected from a depreciation in the value of money. With the post-war inflation continuing, the doctors and dentists felt their pay was not giving them the living standards they had enjoyed before the war.

For some time, therefore, they had been agitating for an increase of 24 per cent above levels received in 1956. By 1957 negotiations had reached a standstill. The Government felt a 24 per cent increase was unjustified, and the professions refused any lesser amount. The doctors thereupon started developing plans to stage a "phased withdrawal" from the Health Service. This would have been a strike against the state, with the threat that unless the Government yielded they would return to the pre-war private practice of medicine. This, of course, would have wrecked the entire national health program, by now endorsed by the Conservative as well as by the Labour Party, and regarded by almost all citizens as one of the most essential public services.

In this crisis, on February 20, 1957, Prime Minister Macmillan announced in Commons that a Royal Commission would be appointed.

The immediate reaction of the doctors was negative. They wanted the dispute submitted to an arbitrator at once, arguing that neither party would be bound to accept the Commission's verdict. The Government contended that the Commission was needed as the only way a permanent system could be devised. As an interim adjustment, however, the Government on March 29 approved a 10 per cent increase for junior hospital doctors and a 5 per cent increase for all other doctors and dentists.

The Commission was technically an impartial one of nine members. It included persons with Conservative and Labour backgrounds, from the financial and business worlds, and from academic, legal, and other professional circles.[1] The terms of reference called for the Commission to determine

[1] The chairman was Sir Harry Pilkington, chairman of Pilkington Bros. glass manufacturers, and a director of the Bank of England;

proper levels of compensation in the Health Service "in the light of . . . remuneration received by members of other professions, by other members of the medical and dental professions, and by people engaged in connected occupations," and to consider what arrangements if any should be made to keep remuneration under review.

The medical profession bitterly protested the terms. It charged they unfairly restricted the Commission by asking it to advise on their pay in the single light of what other professions and connected occupations were currently earning and not permitting it to take into consideration also what the position of the profession had been prior to the National Health Service. After discussion this amendment was accepted.

The Government seems on this occasion to have come very close to violating one of the norms governing the creation of a Royal Commission—its terms of reference must not restrict a fair inquiry. One may assume the Government did not deliberately try to slant the terms. At the least, however, the original wording shows the Government failed to consult properly with interested parties to make sure the terms would be acceptable.

Even the expanded terms did not at once mollify the doctors, but finally, on June 12, 1957, they decided to co-operate with the Commission. Later they also voted to table plans for withdrawal, though a committee was authorized to consider

---

Mrs. Kathleen Baxter, secretary to Cambridge University Women's Appointments Board; Mr. A. D. Bonham-Carter, director and formerly personnel manager of Unilevers; Mr. J. H. Gunlake, vice chairman of the Institute of Actuaries; Professor John Jewkes, Professor of Economic Organization, Oxford University; Mr. I. D. McIntosh, Headmaster, George Watson's College, Edinburgh, and a member of the Committee on Recruitment of Dentists; Sir David Hughes Parry, Professor of English Law, London University; Sir Hugh Watson, Deputy Keeper of Her Majesty's Signet; and Mr. Samuel Watson, Durham Miners' Association.

the possibilities of medical care on some basis other than the National Health Service or the former private practice.

The situation, therefore, was that professional trade unions were seeking to advance their special interests to an extent apparently contrary to the broader interests of the country. They refused to accept an adverse decision of the Government as presumed representative of the total citizenry. On the other hand, the Government was directly involved through one of its own departments—the National Health Service—and was accused of "lack of statesmanship," "dishonouring pledges," "autocracy," and "refusal to arbitrate." It could not, therefore, convincingly assert the impartiality and competence needed for any attempt to find the facts or to draw up principles of equitable pay.

With no other way of resolving the crisis the Government would have to yield to the blocs on the best terms it could get; or, if it were successful in using its power to force doctors and dentists to continue in the Health Service, it would have to operate that Service with highly antagonistic practitioners; or it would have to accept the return to the former system of private medicine. Any of these results might have been very damaging to the society.

One last possibility remained, an arbitrator. If he were simply to strike a balance between the maximum the Government would grant and the minimum the professions would accept, he might break the deadlock. But he might also fall considerably short of doing justice to others—taxpayers, patients, comparable professions. If he tried to base his award on a set of principles balancing all other interests he would be attempting exactly what the Royal Commission was set up to do. But what person, alone and in private, could hope to achieve the variety of perspective, the prestige, the educational effect, the general acceptability of a Royal Commission?

Once again, it was this mechanism that offered a way out of the dilemma. Everyone, Government, blocs, citizens, could trust it to investigate and award with a view to the best interests of the total society.

And the mechanism fulfilled expectations. The *Report* of the Royal Commission on Doctors' and Dentists' Remuneration was issued in February 1960. It concluded that the salaries of these professions could not be settled by any formula based on living costs, but only by "the faculty of good judgment" exercised in the future by an independent review body on a combination of relevant factors. This review body, much like the advisory committee on the higher civil service, should be set up with an eminent chairman and its members must have the confidence of the Government and the professions. The Government should accept their advice save for some very rare and compelling reason. The Board of Inland Revenue should provide the statistics that the review body would need, and it should collect these in strictest confidence.

For some of the statistics on which it based its own immediate salary recommendations, the Commission sent out over 42,000 questionnaires seeking confidential data from members of 11 professions on earnings in 1955-56. Without enumerating the exact weights attached to all the factors of its calculations, the Commission recommended that general practitioners should receive increases of 22.8 per cent. Similar increases were granted specialists and other categories, and an immediate payment of twenty million pounds was granted as a token for years of waiting. Detailed proposals were made about the pool method of determining pay, and, to give a special stimulus, "merit awards" were recommended for distinguished work.

With the two interim increases already granted, these recommendations substantially met the 24 per cent claims made in 1956. Professor Jewkes, in a Memorandum of Dissent, wanted a 30 per cent increase and felt no back payments should be made.

The Commission found there was a shortage of dentists and that they worked longer hours than the National Health Service had intended. Modern methods also enabled them to work faster and thus handle more patients. They therefore earned more than had been planned, and more even than the general medical practitioners, contrary to experience elsewhere in the world. The Commission decided they should receive no increase in salaries until a permanent "Dental Rates Study Group" was set up and fixed rates that would ensure the intended level of dental earnings. As expected, the British Dental Association protested that they alone should receive no "retrospective payments" or immediate salary improvements. But beyond this public declaration there was no attempt to counter the findings.

The Government accepted the Commission's report in its entirety and invited the professions to implement it through joint working parties.

At a special meeting in May 1960 the British Medical Association voted to accept the Government's offer. At this meeting the report was hailed as a "really great victory." As a spokesman put it, "the Government had accepted their defeat with dignity and generosity." He added that

> this is a fair report in which there is ample evidence of the Royal Commission's desire to assure us in the future of a standard of living which will not be depressed by arbitrary Government action. In its turn the Government as agreed to accept all of the recommendations . . . although it cannot have found many of them to its very great liking.[2]

It is not overstatement to conclude that the Royal Commission saved a health system approved by all political par-

[2] The London *Times,* May 20, 1960, p. 6.

ties, by the public, and by the medical profession itself. The decisions of the Commission validated the claims of the doctors and restored equity. The Government's acceptance meant it was yielding not to a strike threat but to the moral authority of a group of trustworthy citizens. This in turn removed from the doctors a problem that usually accompanies a victory won by force: that rather than co-operate the loser will continue wherever possible to oppose. Where the dentists would probably have resisted the Government's refusal to increase salaries, they simply expressed disappointment at the Commission's judgment of their case, and may be presumed reconciled as much as possible to waiting for the later judgment of the Study Group.

The gain to British citizens in this mutually satisfactory resolution of the whole problem needs no comment.

8 The functions of the Royal Commission

A study of every Royal Commission would, of course, be the only way to total up the contributions of this structure to Great Britain. Glancing through the list of Commissions just since 1900 (Appendix 2) gives some idea of the range of problems handled but little appreciation of their importance. Who would gather from the title The Royal Commission on Doctors' and Dentists' Remuneration, for instance, that the whole Health Service of the country was at stake?

But examination of more Commissions would reveal no importantly different functions from those already disclosed; it would only show additional problem areas where those

CHART 1

Functions of the Royal Commission

Purposes of government appointment	To help overcome problems or obstacles or deficiencies		Consequences intended or latent
	of citizens or blocs	of government	
When Government unable, or unwilling, to assume sole or immediate responsibility for a decision:	1. Are outside decisional process	1. Does not include all able citizens	1. Secures facts, makes value judgments, provides policy directives
1. To resolve policy uncertainty or disagreement	2. Are indifferent or uninformed or confused or with narrow perspectives	2. Is too busy	2. Approximates equity in balancing conflicting interests
2. To gain support for a policy	3. Refuse accommodation of conflicting interests, or seek to impose a minority view	3. Has limiting organizational perspectives	3. Provides operational audit and correction of structures
3. To overcome distrust	4. Perform functions inadequately	4. Is partisan	4. Co-opts additional intelligence
4. To avoid premature commitment; to satisfy agitating group		5. Self-interest (fear of political damage or loss of office inhibits	5. Educates, widens two-way social communication
		a) Self-criticism and self-correction of structures	6. Extends democratic controls and self-governance
		b) Leadership initiative	7. Aids social control and voluntary acceptance of decisions
			8. Increases respect for leadership(?)
			9. Increases morale and self-respect(?)
			10. Guides social direction

functions were applied.[1] We should have sufficient basis, then, for systematizing these functions and the problem-situations that occasion them, and for trying to assess the significance of this structure, what it can do for the society that uses it properly.

Purposes of government appointment

A Government assumes the leadership in decision-making. If it needs more information it has an elaborate civil service to get it. Why then call on a Royal Commission? From the surface political view there appear four functions the mechanism can fulfill.

The Government may be uncertain or in disagreement about what to do—say about the press or population growth. Here the Commission is to get the relevant facts, assess the strength of conflicting interests, and recommend the best or the most acceptable policy.

The Government, on the other hand, may have decided what it wants to do but finds it inadvisable to proceed because the public is poorly informed or because private blocs are inflexibly set on some contrary course. Even though it cannot control its findings, the Government hopes then that a Com-

[1] It would be especially valuable evidence of usefulness, however, to consider such Commissions, for example, as the 1944 one on Population, the 1949 Commission on Capital Punishment, and the monumental 1927 (Simon) Commission on India, which show perhaps better than any others the research capacities of the structure; the three pioneering Commissions, 1904, 1924, and 1954 in the field of mental illness, or, in the field of city planning, the 1937 Commission on the Distribution of Industrial Population and the 1957 Commission on Local Government in London; or the 1919 and 1951 income tax Commissions, which played so valuable a role in the development of an equitable tax system in Britain.

mission will educate the public, dissipate opposition, and thus secure maximum support for the Government's policy.

In a variation of this, the Government may be neutral or want to do nothing, perhaps because it fears splitting party loyalties on some explosive issue like divorce. Yet it may also fear to be accused of neglecting the problem. A Commission then enables the Government to avoid political commitment and at the same time should satisfy any agitating group that its views will receive fair and authoritative treatment.

Lastly, citizens may feel that because of a disqualifying partisan or class interest the Government in office is not to be trusted, say to take remedial action in some criticized executive department or to mediate fairly between opposing groups. Here the Commission is to act, in the place of the Government, as the acceptable representative of all societal interests.

As the case studies showed, the circumstances leading to the creation of a Commission are usually complex, and it is rare that a Government appoints a Commission for only one reason.

Governments have been accused of misusing the Royal Commission to deceive the public. If a Government is opposed to certain action (coal industry or divorce reform, for instance) but fears voter displeasure if it shows that opposition openly, it may appoint a Royal Commission, so runs the charge, ostensibly for the purpose of getting more information but actually to prevent or at least delay the action itself or disclosure of the Government's opposition. The public is deluded into thinking necessary work is being done, and the Government gains time without risking any political penalty.

It is difficult to know when, if ever, such charges are true. Certainly this use must be rare, or the Royal Commission would have long ago come into disrepute.[2]

2 Where such a charge is not part of bloc controversy it is some-

We take judicial notice of the partisan character of modern democracies. If a Government, whatever its bias, is genuinely perplexed and seeks a nonpartisan solution to some problem, the Royal Commission will supply it. But if the Government sets up a Commission only as a pretext for not taking action the functions of the mechanism are not thereby nullified. Facts, judgments, and recommendations, rather than being immediately incorporated into governmental policy, usually then become important weapons in the continued assault against the obstructing blocs; they really speed reform, as witness the coal Commissions. It may therefore be futility more than virtue that restrains such misuse. On the other hand, if a Royal Commission supports the Government, it then has impartial justification for its position and can use the Commission's endorsement as a shield against segmental opposition.

In the scanty literature on the Royal Commission, discussion stops with these immediate political purposes, except for elaboration or an occasional incidental allusion to some other possible societal effect. It is probably owing in large measure to this myopia that we have no adequate analysis of this structure. It is true that most of the functions of the Royal Commission are implicit in these intentions, but they are also effectively obscured. For the seeming simplicity of such purposes as to "get the facts" or to "secure public support" tends

---

times found repeated second hand in the literature. But invariably then the charge is couched in cautious language, as in this typical sample: "It *may* [my emphasis] be true that Royal Commissions are often resorted to by a Government under pressure of public opinion with the hope of shirking responsibility or of postponing action." And even here the writers continue: "But it is evident that this can never be the chief use, for the appointment of a Commission would soon be recognized as an evasion rather than an attempt at solution."—H. M. Clokie and J. W. Robinson, *Royal Commissions of Inquiry* (Stanford: Stanford University Press, 1937), p. 217.

to let the mind glide past without consciousness of their complexity. As a problem-solving mechanism the Royal Commission is not likely to be understood or used with full effectiveness without clear awareness of all its possible consequences for the larger society, some of which are latent or unintended and go far beyond manifest political purposes.

For clearer vision one must look at the Royal Commission not from the point of view of the Government, which is hardly all-encompassing, but from the point of view of the national society as the totality of all citizens and groupings. We may then see this mechanism, through its various functions, as a means for overcoming certain obstacles to the handling of societal problems and, in so doing, simultaneously a means for strengthening democratic processes.

Social fact

It is the function of every Royal Commission, publicly stated in its Royal Warrant, to secure the operative facts of the problem assigned it and then to recommend the best solution in the form of specific policy directives. Finding facts and making policy judgments both involve the basic problem: What may be called "social fact"? We encounter here the first obstacle in valid decision-making: the difficulties of determining objective reality in social relationships.

When anyone looks at an object in space his decision about its characteristics and relation to other objects is affected not only by his personal make-up but by the position from which he views it. If he comes to his decision from his own observation alone, from one position, he has no way of knowing whether he is objectively correct, however sincerely he may believe it. If his conception of the object is to match the object's reality, he must first recognize these inherent sources of error. He must then devise ways to juxtapose the observations of others, from various points of view. So may he secure a composite picture closer to the truth.

This relative nature of visually perceived objects is evident enough. But the same difficulties exist in the field of social knowledge, where they are not so readily admitted. Here, too, reality in the form of social facts and relationships is distorted by personal conditioning and by the position occupied by one's group or class.

The personal roots of intellectual bias have long been recognized. The more recent insights into the sociology of knowledge emphasize knowledge as a function of social and class structure. Ruling classes, for instance, tend to be blind to facts that would undermine their sense of domination; oppressed minorities concentrate exclusively on elements that will transform their condition. So it is with all the groups in a society. The objective facts of a social situation are determined and interpreted from the special-interest viewpoint of the group, be it political party, trade association, union, church, or profession.

The admission of the inherently relational structure of human knowledge, Karl Mannheim has remarked,

> does not imply renunciation of the postulate of objectivity and the possibility of arriving at decisions in factual disputes; nor does it involve an acceptance of illusionism according to which everything is an appearance and nothing can be decided. It does imply rather that this objectivity and this competence to arrive at decisions can be attained only through indirect means.
>
> .   .   .   .
>
> It is not a source of error that in the visual picture of an object in space we can, in the nature of the case, get only a perspectivistic view. The problem is not how we might arrive at a non-perspectivistic picture but how, by

juxtaposing the various points of view, each perspective may be recognized as such and thereby a new level of objectivity attained.[3]

The sociology of knowledge as a field of study has many unresolved problems. What does "knowledge" include— folkway maxims, empirical science? What is the relationship of knowledge and social structure—mechanical cause-effect, invariable, or "correspondence," influence? What are the criteria of validity of knowledge? "Nor does Mannheim satisfactorily indicate how the 'translation of one perspective into the terms of another' is, on his view, to be attained. Once given the existential determination of thought, who is there to judge among the babel of conflicting voices?" [4]

Such questions are of the greatest importance in the never-ending attempt to refine human thinking. They are in a sense, however, on the frontiers of this crucial study, and a society is often faced with the immediate necessity of securing as close an approximation as possible to objectively valid knowledge. It cannot delay decisions until all these questions are definitively answered.

Who indeed, then, *is* to judge among the babel of conflicting voices, to decide what the facts really are, what the policy should be? Whence are to come the directional guidelines for a society—guidelines that are not simply the unwilled result of competing forces but that represent a rational, valid, social direction of ultimate benefit to the total society—so far as it can be known at any one time? To make such judgments, to supply such guidelines—these are the keystone functions of the Royal Commission as the advisory Supreme Court, the ultimate advisory Yes or No.

[3] Karl Mannheim, *Ideology and Utopia* (New York: Harcourt Brace, 1949), pp. 269-70, 266.

[4] Robert K. Merton, "Karl Mannheim and the Sociology of Knowledge," *Journal of Liberal Religion*, 1941, Vol. II, No. 3, p. 147.

The method of the Royal Commission for determining "social facts" and making evaluations and prescriptions is precisely that of juxtaposing various points of view of a problem to achieve not an impossible "nonperspectivistic" picture but a new level of objectivity. All the individuals and groups concerned with a problem bring to it a view which derives from their respective positions within the society, and from their dominant interests. Each view is therefore partial and distorted.

Recognition of this truth is implicit in the structure and operation of the Royal Commission. It represents a collective, balanced, not an individual or segmental, approach to social problems. It is based on the assumption that even the best-trained mind is autobiographically biased, that the individual group, no matter how large or dominant, is also situationally restricted in its view of reality. Its arrangements of members, of unquestioned integrity and competence, with least self-interest in the problem, yet bringing to its consideration the viewpoints of important interests; its mediating chairman; its impartial expert assistants; its evidence from every source of relevant information and bias; its due process and cross-examination techniques—all combine to reach a closer approximation to social truth by balancing partial and conflicting perspectives.[5]

[5] I am not positing any single, completely knowable entity like "social truth" or "national interest." I refer simply to the problem of trying to determine as accurately as possible what the operative facts of a social situation are when the facts are either not yet known or are disputed; and to the problem of trying to determine, as closely as it can be determined at the given time, what action would most benefit the largest number of citizens when that action is either not known or is disputed. It might be an instructive exercise for the political imagination to try to devise a process more likely than the Royal Commission's to yield a "more valid" decision about a societal problem, or one better calculated to gain voluntary acceptance of its results.

Conflicting interests

The first obstacle in problem-solving is determining what is true, what is right. The second obstacle is resolving conflict to effect what is right.

Any society of any complexity includes blocs whose interests are considered by members, mistakenly or not, to be opposed to the interests of other groups or of the generality of citizens. The concern of workers for maximum wages is opposed to the concern of owners for maximum profits and to the concern of consumers for lowest prices. Industrial workers, middle classes, farmers, unemployed, stockholders, and countless other groupings, however much all may benefit from certain national policies and the development of "common interests," still compete for shares in the total national wealth, for power-position, for freedom of action.

How, then, does a society evaluate opposing interests? How does it avoid physical conflict or crude compromise? More positively, how does it achieve equity and freedom, particularly in those crises when the opposing blocs cannot agree?

This problem of satisfying legitimate group interests and integrating them into the requirements of the total society has been approached from many angles. F. R. Bienenfeld has generalized it into the problem of approximating "objective justice" by balancing simultaneous and yet contradictory demands. He starts with the nursery. As children we all want equality of treatment with our brothers and sisters (communist principle). But we also demand reward for our own endeavors (socialist principle). We want the right to keep our possessions and prerogatives (conservative principle) on the basis not necessarily of need or effort but simply of their having been acquired earlier, as by an elder brother. Everyone wants the right of unrestricted freedom to do whatever he chooses (liberal principle). And we want to exclude from these rights all outsiders (nationalist principle).

These claims to satisfaction Bienenfeld sees as a universal constant. In the nursery, parents adjudicate between elder and younger brothers. In governed communities the State, as embodied in King, Parliament, or Judge, tries to reconcile the conflicting interests, with minimum of force, by allowing as much scope to each as is compatible with like consideration for the others.

Democracy is thus based on tolerance and compromise, on the realization that any one demand, carried to extreme, will obliterate the others. Impartiality is the very soul of objective justice; and fanaticism, which insists on the fulfillment of one demand alone as a panacea for all evils, is the greatest obstacle to social co-operation and order.[6]

Gerard DeGré comes to the same conclusion in his study of stratification. He shows diagrammatically that optimum freedom and well-being do not lie at the polar extremes either of atomized individualism, such as frontier anarchy, or of totalitarianism, where the leviathan state has destroyed all independent groups. They lie rather at some midway point at the top of a bell-shaped curve, where the various constituent associations, such as industrial organizations, labor unions, press, church, and state, have achieved a rough balance of power.[7]

In this kind of society, paternalistic or authoritarian settlement of conflicting demands has little place. As most repre-

---

[6] See F. R. Bienenfeld, *Rediscovery of Justice* (New York: Oxford University Press, 1947).

[7] See Gerard DeGré, "Freedom and Social Structure," *American Sociological Review,* October 1946; and Robert M. MacIver, *The Web of Government* (New York: Macmillan, 1947).

sentative of the totality of national interests, the central Government may, of course, intervene when bloc conflict is not otherwise resolved. But if the Government, as participant in the conflict or as a partisan political organization, is unable to emulate the impartial parent mediating disputes between brothers in the nursery, what is left for the society to do in a crisis?

Here the function of the Royal Commission. By virtue of its composition and procedures this structure can be accepted by all private and government groups as having the competence and impartiality to determine a more valid accommodation of all interests and thus to approximate "objective justice." Most Royal Commissions show this function, but it is seen most clearly, of course, in the coal and in the doctors and dentists Commissions.

Performance of structures

The deficiencies of both private and public organizations in holding to satisfactory levels of performance, or in adjusting to change, raise a third set of obstacles to the handling of societal problems.

Poor performance of industries or newspapers or any other private structure may be due naturally to factors outside their control. If not, the reason for failure usually reduces to the narrow perspective of special interest. This sometimes results in resistance to change, in insistence on immediate gain, in blindness to other considerations.

As the presumed guardian of all societal interests, the Government, again, may seek to intervene; and often it can effect improvement by itself. But though their range of concern is much broader, Governments have limitations of their own, both in bringing private structures to account and in self-correction. For at any given time the Government may itself be partisan, not so much in that it owes its control only to a majority or plurality of the country's voters but because more exclusive blocs exert decisive pressure on it. This may disqualify the Government for any acceptable attempt to evaluate a particular private structure or give it new directives. With its superior power a Government may be able to override such rejection. But the imposition of decisions by force is in a democracy normally a last resort, to avoid a greater evil.

In self-correction every Government suffers from another disability. This is a more narrow self-interest, a fear of criticism, of political damage, ultimately of loss of tenure. A Government is responsible both for over-all policy and for the day-to-day acts of its agents, the civil service. If administrative policy is in error or is widely condemned, or if some serious defect is charged to exist in the execution of policy, the Government is in a dilemma. To admit error or inefficiency is always politically damaging. To stand firm on simple denial may strengthen criticism. And self-investigation is almost certainly foredoomed to failure. For who would trust the investigator when he is also the accused—and the judge?

The usual course of a Government here is dictated by well-developed conditioning—the hands-up defensive posture, the fast footwork to evade the next attack. First consideration may be given not to the public interest in improved operation of some government department but to minimizing the political damage to the office holders.

The point is not simply that *any* Government flinches from self-criticism and self-correction because it fears political damage. The point is also that even if the Government were willing to investigate thoroughly it would be hampered by the suspicion of self-interest. How could it persuade citizens that its understandable urge for political self-preservation would not affect its impartiality?

The Royal Commission, again by virtue of the competence and independence of its members and the fairness of their methods, is acceptable to both private and governmental structures for this function of operational audit and correction.

Co-optation of intelligence

Governments have other limitations in handling societal problems. No methods of selection have yet been devised to ensure that members of the legislature, the executive, or the civil service will be those most capable of solving the country's problems. Electoral appeal, for instance, is a primary qualification for political leaders and much of this is irrelevant. In any event, the continuing structures of the government obviously could not at any given time include all able citizens in the society. Persons very knowledgeable in the innumerable fields in which decisions must be taken, exist by the thousands in the professions, the universities, industry, and elsewhere.

But even if the most able persons did fill the highest elective and appointive positions they would still be handicapped in handling important problems—first by lack of sufficient time and second by a restricting organizational outlook.

There is much critical analysis in the literature of the composition of political institutions and of their relationship and methods of operation. There is agreement that there is simply not enough time for Members of Parliament to serve their constituencies and still give adequate attention to the substantive aspects of complicated problems. More work in the standing committees of Parliament would force neglect of attendance in the full House. These committees, moreover, end with the legislative session.

Ministers are plagued by inexpert but nonetheless exacting Members of Parliament, by the daily succession of visitors, by the inconsecutive immediacies of administration. They are of necessity tired men, improvisers, and opportunists; their frame of work hardly encourages sustained thinking. The occupational hazard of re-election, too, fosters a distinguishing political perspective on problems that is something less than all-inclusive.

Civil servants suffer from most of the same disabilities and lack even the saving grace of a respite on a change of Government. They are subject without intermission to the constant impact of minor administrative difficulties and are traditionally prone to view questions in the light of administrative requirements: ease of handling, uniformity of application, consistency. They consequently tend to develop certain intellectual and emotional attitudes which citizens both respect and distrust.

The effect of these deficiencies is two-fold. A problem may be poorly handled not because intellectual resources are lacking but because they are not properly marshaled to bear on it. Alternatively, citizens may fear the problem is being mishandled. The resulting distrust inevitably tends to lower public morale, decrease respect for leaders, and weaken voluntary acceptance of governmental decisions.

These deficiencies are, of course, a constant in Government, but while they may be among the underlying reasons for appointment of Royal Commissions they are not often the immediate or sole reason. The Government was basically unable to handle the question of divorce, for instance, because even among all its branches, its members lacked enough time, knowledge, and broadness of perspective. But the immediate governmental deficiency leading to use of Royal Commissions was the lack of leadership initiative, a fear of assuming sole responsibility for changes that might arouse antagonism cutting across party lines.

The Royal Commission, then, is an institutionalized method, available at Government will, for helping overcome these political limitations. The Government co-opts from outside itself persons of established capacity, from different areas of national life, so that their balancing perspectives avoid the restrictions of party-organizational outlook. It then gives them adequate time and resources for study. This distribution of the work load of leadership, this increase in the number of able persons contributing to decision-making, should *a priori* secure better solutions to problems. And the record is proof that it does.

Education and feedback

When significant numbers of citizens are indifferent about a problem, ignorant of its requirements, or confused about alternative approaches, they may be a passive but nevertheless serious obstacle to its solution. In general, the lower the level of citizen identification with decision-making the less able the society to find the best policies or to get them accepted. At the other extreme, when citizens, as organized in blocs, seek excessive special advantage they are an active obstacle to right policy.

The evident solvent here is education. And of course this is a constant effort, from civic projects in local schools to top-level political press conferences. But direct attempts at education by the Government are often handicapped. A Government could presumably rely on party members to accept its statement of facts and its judgment on any question. But members of other parties or uncommitted citizens might on occasion resist this acceptance. They might suspect the statements to be colored by the partisan or personal interests of the Government, much as they are in a political campaign.

If the Government believes this handicap is immaterial it may disregard it. But if the object is the most effective education, the teaching is better done by others able to speak with authority and impartiality or, at the least, with biases reasonably balanced. So, for example, the Royal Commission educated citizens on the need of public funds for Oxford and Cambridge and on the problems of the mining industry.

Just as important as an informed public is a Government informed on the needs and desires and ideas of citizens. There is a reciprocal relationship here. The more fully the Government understands the attitudes of citizens, the more able it is to shape suitable policy. The more fully citizens understand the nature of problems and the difficulties in handling them, the more ready they will be to accept better policies—better because incorporating less compromise with ignorance or intransigence.

The Royal Commission is equally effective in this function of widening upward communication. The list of organizations and individuals who contribute factual information or express official or personal judgments (a list invariably included in the appendices of the Commission's report), bears witness to the large number of responsible sources of information made available to the Commission.[8] Most Commissions, in addi-

[8] "A great deal of the criticism of royal commissions is that they take a long time to get anywhere. They do. A great deal of that is owing to the time that it takes many organizations before they are ready to give evidence. Bodies such as the . . . lawyers, doctors, and local authorities cannot produce their evidence quickly; they must consult their members and give a considered view. A large national organization will probably appoint a special committee to draft its memorandum of evidence. Then that memorandum will have to go before its council; then be sent to all its provincial branches. . . . Then all the comments from all the branches will be examined in London; the special committee will submit a fresh draft, and with any luck the Council will now be able to pass the memorandum. All that may very well take twelve months; it would be wrong to hurry it because when, in the fullness of time, a Bill is before parliament, it

tion, receive innumerable communications from the public.

The Royal Commission serves as a national sounding board for alternative solutions to problems. Here is a social proving ground where different ideas can contend for mastery, where established norms can receive reinforcement or rejection, where new directives commend themselves for acceptance. In this open forum, so much more informative than a debate, the Government can learn what may have support and what may not and thus perhaps overcome a political timidity. Opposing groups can learn the reactions of others to their demands and perhaps modify accordingly. The general public can learn something of the complexities of the problem and thus perhaps be more prepared to help shape, or accept, a better solution.

Self-governance

So far, the obstacles to handling problems really reduce to one—limited perspective—as found in a variety of forms (ignorance, indifference, misconception, vested interest, partisanship, fanaticism) on the part of Government, blocs, the public, or individual citizens. In contrast stands the relational structure of the Royal Commission in its central principle—the combination of brains, impartiality, and balancing perspectives whereby it is able to overcome the obstacles.

The Royal Commission has additional functions in strengthening democratic processes.

The deficiency of Government in that it does not include

---

may be very material to know whether certain of its clauses are in agreement with the recommendations of such-and-such bodies." R. M. Jackson, "Royal Commissions and Committees of Enquiry," *The Listener* (London: B.B.C., April 12, 1956), p. 389.

all able persons, affects the quality of the decisions on national problems. The exclusion of the mass of citizens from anything like the full political engagement of their forebears in ancient Athens or in the old New England townships, however similarly unavoidable in larger and more complex societies, affects the ability of citizens to control their own destinies.

One of the major insights of democracy is the realization of the psychological inadequacies of imposing policy solely from above, even right policy. The importance of optimum participation of citizens in governance is by no means limited to its utility as means—to prevent tyranny, to jog complacency, to secure more valid solutions to problems. Self-governance, self-determination, and self-development are fundamental values in themselves. It is therefore a constant problem how to increase efficient participation of citizens in decision-making without succumbing to the dominance of the least-informed.

The Royal Commission, though appointed for more immediate purposes, as latent function makes one of the most effective contributions to the solution of this problem: the initial enlistment of Commissioners from many walks of life, usually not already holding government office; their secondary enlistment, as witnesses or researchers, of many more citizens from an even greater variety of social, economic, and occupational spheres; and the provision of a deliberative forum, open to the public, itself instigating other citizens in the press, the universities, the professions, and in other areas, to add their contributions.[9]

[9] "The point which must, however, strike any reader of the reports on the more controversial subjects is the immense number of organized bodies which come forward as interested parties to plead their cases. . . . it . . . gives some ground for hope that, besides securing expert advice they [the Commissioners] have done something to strengthen the democratic control of government." A. J. Brown, in *Advisory Bodies,* ed. by R. V. Vernon and N. Mansergh

This Royal Commission function of extending democratic controls and self-governance is not to be discounted because the actual participants in the work of any one Commission are only a small proportion of the total citizenry. For most participants are, of course, associated with innumerable additional citizens, if not as representatives of organizations then in some way so that others can influence them or at least make known their views. So the Royal Commission reaches down into the body politic much further than to just the number of witnesses or researchers listed in its reports. Also, every Royal Commission extends a general invitation to all members of the public, and any citizen who feels he can make a contribution can respond. Again, a public opinion poll or census may be used by the Royal Commission whenever it would be appropriate.

The Royal Commission extension of self-governance is not a naïve, normative idealization of the "common man" in whom power should rest and to whose level standards must be adjusted; it is not based on the theory that effective self-governance is synonymous with equal participation of every citizen in every public decision—as if citizenship by itself conferred equality of knowledge and experience. On the contrary, the structural frame of the Royal Commission surrounds even actual participants with safeguards, for its own purposes, much as the frame of a court of law with its presiding judge, its prosecuting and defense attorneys, its cross-examination, its expert assistants, and its precedents and traditions, safeguards the twelve ordinary citizen-jurors from many of their own limitations. Both frames shape the social contributions that their human components could not otherwise hope to make.

(London: George Allen and Unwin, 1940), pp. 124-25. This is typical of the passing allusion to other possible societal effects of the Royal Commission which is found in the literature.

Social control

In so far as it promulgates facts and policy directives, a good proportion of which are sooner or later implemented, nearly every Royal Commission promotes social control, the voluntary acceptance of decisions.

It is not enough that a society sets up processes for finding the right answers to questions of social fact and policy. It must also get the right answers accepted. If an investigation is made of criticism of the police or the press the conclusions must not be seriously questioned; any charge of "whitewash" would vitiate the whole inquiry. If a judgment is made on what norms should be maintained or what established ways should be changed, say in divorce, the decision must not be suspect as unreliable. If some accommodation is reached between opposing interests, a bloc must not refuse to abide by an adverse ruling.

This presents the problem of control (or "sanctions," as the term is sometimes used), the process by which decisions of the society are accepted by or enforced on citizens. Control may be either "external," as represented by such specialist organizations as police and courts, or "social"—informal, internal, voluntary, self-enforcing control.

A population whose overwhelming majority accepts the norm against theft and would fear "disgrace" more than imprisonment, requires the external force of police and prisons to a minimum degree. Although the Law stands as ultimate deterrent against violation, the norm is actually upheld by these social controls or sanctions. Here, as Sir Alfred Zimmern has remarked about the English people, "to break the law is more than a crime. It is a breach of etiquette, an offence against custom and social convention, a thing that is 'not done.' " [10] The contrast can be seen in street betting in England or in Prohibition in the United States, when a high proportion of citizens is not so restrained and all the external controls of the law are hardly sufficient to gain compliance.

The less external force a society is required to use in maintaining norms, in getting new directives accepted voluntarily, and in effecting the acceptance of blocs to adverse decisions, the more secure is the social order, the more orderly is the social change, the less conflict there is between opposing blocs, and the fewer the number of estranged citizens.

For a Government to pursue a policy in the absence of sufficiently widespread agreement is to risk a response ranging from covert anger to outright revolt. This in turn might require the imposition of additional force, leading in a vicious circle to further disorganization and conflict. If the inadequate acceptance is due to the indifference or confusion of citizens about the problem, the Royal Commission can fulfill its recognized educative function. If it is due to distrust of the Government, the Royal Commission can overcome that obstacle also. For the body politic will accept a decision by the Royal Commission, because of its competent enlistment of many citizens, that it might strenuously resist if presented by the Government.

When the national interest requires rejection or serious modification of the claims of one or another group, how does the society bring the group most smoothly through its inevitable dissatisfaction? If the claim is disposed of simply on the basis of the superior power of the Government there will be resentment, a lessening of respect for the society's leaders and processes of decision, even perhaps a sense of alienation or enmity. Here again are steps in the social direction of disintegration, weakening morale and the bonds of community.

[10] *From the British Empire to the British Commonwealth* (London: Longmans, Green, 1941), p. 11.

No matter with what judicial temper the Government may try to soften its ruling it may be under a handicap. Whether the group sincerely believes the Government overrules its view because the Government favors opposing interests or whether the group uses that charge simply as a tactical weapon to strengthen its position, the Government's effectiveness is reduced. If this is the inevitable result of the suspicion of partisanship or self-interest, the Royal Commission remedy suggests itself. A group will be far more likely to accept an adverse decision when it comes from persons demonstrably competent and disinterested.

So, also, structures that may need modification in operation, as did Oxford and Cambridge, will voluntarily accept investigation and correction from the Royal Commission that they would accept from a political Government only under duress if, indeed, they would accept it at all.

Respect for leadership

Respect for leaders is an obvious requirement for all successful organizations, from local clubs to the largest societies. It may be taken that, other factors being equal, the more citizens respect and trust their leaders, the more stable the social order is and the more easily new directives can gain voluntary acceptance.

There is no doubt the Royal Commission, by co-opting able citizens, helps secure better solutions to problems. It certainly seems reasonable to assume that this should not only gain respect for the mechanism itself but should transfer at least some of that respect and confidence to the political leadership that uses it.

The extent to which a given Commission may have this

result probably depends on its success. If it has performed well and if its conclusions are implemented, both Commission and Government may be presumed legitimate sources of pride—provided citizens reflect on the matter at all. If the Commission does a poor job it suffers disrepute, some of which might attach to the Government for its selection of Commissioners. Hence every Government and every Commission has a heavy responsibility. Every poor performance will lower much the respect of citizens; every fine performance should raise it.

Morale

In view of the unquestioned influence of Royal Commissions they do extend self-governance. Another reasonable assumption is that this should increase the morale and self-respect of citizens and strengthen the bonds of community—values, again, in their own right, not only important factors in the survival of a society.

This possible latent function would depend on whether those who participated directly or vicariously in a Commission's work articulated their roles, became conscious of helping to set their own norms and solve their own problems, and hence became conscious of their own dignity. Very little evidence of this awareness is available in the literature and no effort has yet been made to probe for these possible psychological effects. Consciousness of the immediate burden of work and time and expense that participation lays on citizens could easily pre-empt appreciation of the personal and communal values implicit in the participation.

However, just as men speak prose, knowing or unknowing, so also, knowing or not, citizens do have in the Royal Commission a mechanism that enables them to help guide their own development. Anything that would stimulate fuller realization of all the concomitant values of self-respect and sense of community should be highly beneficial for the society and its members personally.

Social direction

The functions of the Royal Commission in fact-finding and in policy directives might be summed up in the over-all function of helping to supply a guide to the social direction, the long-range strategy, of a society.

It has been charged that democracies never know where they are going. Three factors complicate their present situation. They are essentially fatherless, having outgrown dependence on Divine or Royal Authority. There is the welter of claims and ideologies that are brought into open conflict when ultimate responsibility for state policy is shifted from ruler to ruled. And the times are characterized by unprecedented technological and social change.

In a very real sense the Royal Commission is a Supreme Court of final jurisdiction—advisory, not compulsory. It can be called on for decisions on problem cases when they have reached a point of conflicting judgments and when an authoritative conclusion of facts and policy should be made—a conclusion that the continuing private or governmental structures are handicapped in making by themselves because of some deficiency. The qualities of its members and of its methods (provided their standards have been met) make the decisions of the Royal Commission probably as free of partial perspective, of self-interest, and of bloc control as errant human beings can presently make them. They should, therefore, and they do, furnish trustworthy guidelines to a social direction of ultimate benefit to the whole society.

Can the Royal Commission be dysfunctional? Can it have consequences that are in some way harmful—disruptive, delaying needed action, guiding in the wrong direction? Apart from possible deliberate misuse, it should go without saying that a given Commission may be composed of less than first-rate minds and that even first-rate minds may be wrong in their findings of fact and in their evaluations and may make recommendations not in the best interests of the society.

But the possibility of error is ineradicable from human affairs. The society's main protection against possible Royal Commission error is the cardinal fact that the structure is advisory only, with no power to impose any errors. Its decisions, unlike those of a legally compulsory Supreme Court, unlike those authored by a vested-interest group pushing for their adoption, are accepted by the Government, by the body politic, by affected groups, only by free choice, only through the moral or intellectual or practical persuasiveness of the decisions themselves. That they continue to be so accepted, at once or eventually (or that later events validate them), in the overwhelming majority of cases suggests a reduction in possible error perhaps close to its maximum.

9 Principles and problems of effective use of the Royal Commission

How are we to account for the Royal Commission? Services so distinguished, over so long a time, without interruption, under all kinds of Governments, under vastly different social and economic conditions—this does not suggest historical accident. Is it a measure of some unique political genius of the English?

Societal structures or processes cannot often be blueprinted as is a bridge. Yet they need not be utterly closed to descriptive analysis.

To fulfill its functions the Royal Commission requires certain qualities in its members, certain methods of operation, and an environment of norms and structures that will support it.

I. MEMBERSHIP

Ideally, Commissioners should have proved themselves competent; they should have shown the knowledge, experience, and sagacity to master the intellectual problems of their subject and to deliver a judgment on which a whole society can rely. They must be persons of unimpeachable integrity. For representative Commissions, they should not be so intransigently committed to one course that they are incapable of comprehending opposing points of view or arriving at some accommodative conclusion. For impartial or expert Commissions, they must have no conflict of interest which would prevent a judgment on the merits of a case itself. They should be capable of weighing conflicting interests to get a fair decision. This cannot be taken to preclude a personal perspective on social problems. Since this is psychologically impossible, a Commission should have members who complement each other in their emotional understanding of the basic issues. They must also be willing to sacrifice time and money as a service—not use membership on a Commission to enhance their public image in return for a minimum of personal effort.

Does this bring a smile, as at some utopian vision? Or do persons bearing a reasonable resemblance to this ideal actually get appointed in England most of the time, allowing, of course, that among themselves Commissioners will vary in these qualities along the usual normal curve?

The existence of enough persons both qualified and willing to serve presupposes an educational system to develop these qualities and a social and cultural milieu to sustain them. Here several acknowledged features of British life are especially relevant: the public service orientation in higher education; the sense of public duty and the influence of the older aristocratic *noblesse oblige;* the high ranking given public life generally; the honor in being selected a Royal Commissioner. With this nourishing milieu there appears little doubt either that enough qualified persons exist or that they are willing to serve.[1] With the exception, for obvious reasons, of the Sovereign and the Prime Minister, there is no office in the country too high for its holder to serve on a Royal Commission. A Prince of Wales, an Archbishop of Canterbury, a Lord Chancellor, an Archbishop of York, a Lord Chief Justice, a former Prime Minister—all have been Royal Commissioners.

There is not a single serious study, not of a particular Commission but of the Royal Commission itself as a societal mechanism, that charges its membership is characterized by mediocrity, incompetence, or bias. Yet one is sometimes struck by a sort of hit-and-run comment in the literature that leaves exactly this impression. A few samples of this may help prevent misjudgment of the Royal Commission.

One type needs only mention. This is the kind of epithet used by extremists angry at certain conclusions, as when the latest divorce Commissioners were accused of "official humbug" and of "bringing forth a still-born mouse." Such comments are so obviously irresponsible one hopes (against

[1] "It is remarkable that . . . there are still enough experts and public spirited laymen in England willing to serve. . . . To serve upon a Royal Commission is not only regarded as a public duty and responsibility, but is also sought by many people as an opportunity of making a contribution to the welfare and progress of their nation, though it means the surrender of leisure, and, indeed, considerable time which might otherwise be devoted to professional advancement." Herman Finer, *University of Chicago Law Review,* Spring 1951, pp. 556-57.

"Any number of persons with whom I talked were quite frank in saying that, even though they were very busy, they would welcome the sacrifice in time and money to serve on a Royal Commission." Jack A. Rhodes, *Southwestern Social Science Quarterly,* June 1952, p. 31.

reason, probably) that only the most ignorant or fanatic would be misled by them.

Less self-revealing is a more frequent type of response to a report by a commentator whose own opinion was not confirmed by the Commissioners. A whole volume of these derogatory comments could be compiled. A report may be said to make "disappointingly cautious reading," or the Commissioners may be accused of an "unacceptable naïveté." Or the writer may hold up one witness as evidence of the "complacency" or inefficiency of a Commission, as the *New Statesman* in its June 8, 1962, piece on the recent police Commission remarked: "One solid sergeant of my acquaintance is wondering whether the social survey [which reported good relations between public and police] found its informants in the same planetary system as the people he meets daily."

No one, of course, denies the right to express individual opinions; and it is probably too much to expect that public commentary should always do justice to the complexity of its subject. What is inexcusable is ignorance or bland disregard of the caliber of the Commissioners and of the balanced nature and comprehensive scope of their procedures, coupled with the simple-minded implication that the writer (usually anonymous at that) is Olympian in his knowledge and detachment and has conducted such a rigorous investigation of the problem that the Royal Commission is amateurish by comparison.

One can, again, only hope that not too many readers will be swept along by the superficial plausibility and pseudo-sophistication that usually mark such professional writing but will pause just long enough to compare what they may know about the single writer or publication with what they may know about the Royal Commission and its procedures.

Sir Alan Herbert has written an amusing little poem about

an old man who is watching couples in a park and who explains that he is the sole remaining member of the Royal Commission on Kissing, "appointed by Gladstone in '74." The old man describes the history of the Commission, its study of existing legislation and of the limits of its terms of reference, how it collected evidence but "carefully dismissed the opinion of anyone who actually kissed," the interruptions of world wars and the loss of its Minutes, and how each step in its procedure "took a long, long time." The old man concludes by saying he intends to see the task through, "Though I know, as an old politician,/Not much will be done if I do." [2]

The satire is so broad that few are likely to take it seriously. Yet few also may resist the suspicion that this picture of doddering old men engaged in interminable, pedantic, and futile research may come too close to the truth to dismiss entirely. If a knowledgeable humorist chooses so to caricature the Royal Commission does it not probably reflect, at least in part, his own opinion of it? Here the misdirection can only be corrected by knowledge of Sir Alan Herbert's more responsible judgment of the Royal Commission. He reports this in his book recounting his successful efforts to implement the 1909 divorce Commission's recommendations.[3]

William A. Robson's comment may be recalled:

[2] First printed in *Punch,* Vol. 186, 6/27/34, p. 708; reprinted in *Mild and Bitter* (New York: Doubleday, Doran, 1936); and in H. M. Clokie and J. W. Robinson, *Royal Commissions of Inquiry* (Stanford: Stanford University Press, 1937), pp. 236-38.

[3] See A. P. Herbert, *The Ayes Have It* (New York: Doubleday, Doran, 1938). Sir Alan has long been concerned with improving the use of advisory bodies. He charges that Governments too often appoint outside investigating committees and even Royal Commissions when they should rather do their own homework better or when they should rather take needed action. He suggests that Governments secure Parliamentary approval before appointing such bodies, and that their

We can compare these qualities [of Sir William Beveridge] with the type of Departmental Committee and Royal Commission which is nowadays [this in 1943] so frequently entrusted with the task of enquiring into difficult or controversial matters. The chairman is apt to be an aged High Court judge, ignorant of the subject, or a superannuated politician—often an ex-Minister who has been elevated to the peerage. Such a chairman tends to regard a mere investigation as a matter of minor importance compared with an important law suit or a debate in the House.[4]

This suggests the same sense of responsibility felt by those who call United States Supreme Court Justices "old fogies." It is unfortunate that statements of this order cannot simply be ignored as relatively harmless bacilli in the body politic. But it is a serious disservice to blur understanding of a societal agency. There is no explanation of the suspicious internal inconsistency: how odd that Governments should so frequently entrust difficult or controversial matters to Commission chairmen who regard them as of minor importance! There is no substantiation whatever of this alleged frequent feebleness, ignorance, or indifference, and it would be rather difficult to sustain the charge under cross-examination. For the fact is that Royal Commission chairmen are usually among the genuinely distinguished figures in British life.[5]

It might also be recalled in passing that Sir William Beveridge's talents (justly praised by Professor Robson) had al-

members be paid. Though it may confuse or mislead almost as much as it informs, see his essay "Anything But Action?", *Radical Reaction,* ed. by Ralph Harris, 2nd ed. (London: Institute of Economic Affairs, 1961), pp. 249-302.

[4] William A. Robson, in *Political Quarterly,* April-June 1943, p. 150.

[5] Data on the backgrounds of Royal Commissioners are given in a separate section of this chapter. See especially the information on Commission chairmen.

ready long before been used by the Royal Commission. He had, for instance, been a member of the well-known 1925 coal Commission, whose chairman was Sir Herbert Samuel, hardly a superannuated politician.

Are persons willing to sacrifice to serve on a Royal Commission? Let two witnesses testify. Sir John Simon and Clement (later Earl) Attlee were respectively chairman and member of the 1929 Commission on India. Earl Attlee wrote that the preparation of the report absorbed all his time and that during that period his activities in the House of Common were confined to voting in the Division lobbies.[6] Sir John (again far from an ignorant judge or a superannuated politician) wrote that his service "meant the complete abandonment of my practice at the Bar and the devotion of all my energies to an immense and laborious inquiry, which ended three years later. . . ." [7]

Here is no personal exploitation of the office of Royal Commissioner, leaving the burden of actual work to an anonymous staff.

Factors in appointment

Granted qualified persons exist and are willing to serve. Do they get appointed? Wilhelm Dibelius has remarked that the Royal Commission is an English device "for bringing the best brains in the country to bear on great legislative tasks. . . ." Is it, rather, politically acceptable brains that are brought to bear?

[6] Clement Attlee, *As It Happened* (London: William Heinemann, 1954).

[7] Viscount Simon, *Retrospect* (London: Hutchinson, 1952), p. 144.

The first choices for members may, of course, for some reason not be available. They may have other duties at the time, from which they cannot be released; they may have some vested interest that would conflict with the Commission's work. Hence "best brains" means the best brains available at the time. Also, it may be decided that a Commission should be representative in type, which means the best brains available who would also be acceptable as representatives of the interests involved.

The chief factor militating against selection of the most qualified persons is partisanship. If a Government knew in advance that a Commission would recommend unacceptable policy it would probably never appoint one. It follows that a Government is always concerned to appoint Commissioners who will give it what it wants, be that valid directives or relief from political pressure. Since the Government is not only the agency for total national interests but also has a private interest in holding office and a partisan interest in the fortunes of the political party, the social class, or the economic groups it favors, there may often be a motive for packing a Commission or slanting its terms of reference to further these more exclusive interests. This potential bias is counterbalanced so effectively, however, that it can rarely find overt expression.

If Commissioners were incompetent it is evident they would be unable to master the problems set them and there could be no hope of valid directives. If they were dishonest or partisan there could be no hope that the public or opposing blocs would accept their findings. Since an appointing Government is looking for one or the other or both of these results, its own self-interest is the first pressure making for appointment of qualified Commissioners—though not always for the most distinguished persons.

Another element of self-interest lies in the fact that failure to appoint properly qualified Commissioners would be to lose face, and might incur for the Government a more specific political penalty. For the criticism it would draw could well lead to an entry on the debit side of the Government's balance sheet at the next election.

The prestige of the Crown is an added pressure making for selection of qualified members. When the Monarchy was tied in the minds of citizens with the interests solely of a ruling class or a royal family, "Royal" Commissions were often resented, as their early history shows. But ever since, centuries ago, they have been created through Parliament, and the King was felt to represent parental concern for the interests of all segments of the population (always within the limits of the "cultural mentality"), the association of Royal Commissions with the Crown has helped to raise them above more narrow partisan considerations.

This means not merely a formal linkage to the political functions of the Monarchy; it means that the norms associated with the Crown apply also to the Royal Commission. Just as it would violate these norms if the Monarch were to show partiality against one segment of citizens, so it would be a violation if a Government were knowingly to appoint on a Royal Commission a majority of members who favored one side of a case; or for the Government to slant a Commission's terms of reference against any one group.

There is also that sense of fair play (again within the limits of the cultural mentality) which British schools are so famous for instilling. This attitude is hardly limited to sport. If a Government purports to set up a Royal Commission to make an independent investigation of a problem and to supply impartial recommendations, it would violate every canon of fair play to rig the inquiry from the start.

Then there is the sense of balance. No one perspective is completely trusted, be it that of experts, of the academic mind, of business or labor. Where this sense of balance is not effectively implemented one might well fear that unpaid Commissions would be weighted in favor of those who could afford to donate the time, either by being independently wealthy or, more likely, by being business-compensated. Able persons without such support—the working-class representative or the independent—might be conspicuous by their absence. But on any controversial problem a British Government would be guilty of a serious breach of established procedure were it to select such a biased Commission.[8]

The self-interest even of a partisan Government, plus these effective norms, combine, then, to put a decisive pressure on a Government to select Commissioners and to frame their terms of reference so that competent and honest investigations can be made.

Parliament rarely intervenes in the selection of Commissioners. It may suggest representation of different parts of the country, or of specific perspectives, or that women as well as men be appointed, but it almost never suggests names. "It is understood that since all parties desire that a Royal Commission shall render an impartial report, Parliament itself ought

[8] "The membership is generally made up on some scheme of representing major bodies of opinion and interests, but a great deal depends upon the subject matter of the inquiry. For some purposes it may be desirable that members should be drawn from different parts of the country. The only principle that is always [N.B.] adopted is that no particular interest will be dominant; thus if there is a Member of Parliament for one political party, there will almost certainly be a Member from the other side. If there is someone who is recognisably from the employer's side in industry, we should expect to find someone from trade unions." R. M. Jackson, *The Listener* (London: B.B.C., April 12, 1956), p. 388.

On October 31, 1953, the London *Times* in an editorial cautioned against weighting from a perhaps unexpected quarter. Universities, it remarked, are the most fruitful source of supply but "although commissions would scarcely be complete without including university members, there can also be a danger in having them too heavily weighted."

See also Chart 2 (this chapter) and Appendix 3, Table 5 for information on the occupational distribution of Commissioners.

to remain impartial in its choice, leaving to the Government the responsibility of objectivity and competence. It is rare that any of the parties to such an undertaking are disappointed in their hopes." [9]

The standards for Commissioners cannot be taken to mean that most Commissioners, whether appointed by Labour or Conservative Governments, do not have the basic conservatism of personal success. They do not view their assigned problems from outside the system of values (ideals of conduct, standards of education, party system of government, for instance) given consensus in the society. A Royal Commission composed of those acceptable only to advocates of the most far-reaching changes would be so unbalanced as to be obviously unable to fulfill most of a Commission's functions.

The structure has, however, fruitfully used the brains of many persons whose thinking was hardly congenial to those in power. The labor union leaders on the Sankey coal Commission were regarded as revolutionary radicals. And many of the Fabian and socialist leaders have been appointed Commissioners, for instance Sidney and Beatrice Webb, Richard Tawney, Graham Wallas, Philip Snowden.

It may be thought that if partisan bias is unable to pack a Commission it can still determine its composition type. A representative, rather than an impartial or expert, Commission could be chosen with the hope that it would stalemate and give the Government an excuse for inaction.[10]

[9] Herman Finer, *University of Chicago Law Review*, Spring 1951, p. 555. In the same issue, p. 476, comparing American and British legislative-executive relations with reference to the doubt that Congress would similarly trust the President or the Attorney General to name members of an investigative body, Professor Lindsay Rogers makes the point that the Congress is too suspicious: "A President would realize the risk of losing public esteem through appointments which Congress (and the country) could not applaud."

[10] About half of all representative Commissions have divided reports, and the chances of a divided report from a representative

The problem of proper composition type is usually a complex one and, it is difficult if not impossible in any given instance to decide whether the Government's choice was partisan. The Sankey Commission was representative at the insistence of the miners. And the next Commission, the Samuel one, was made impartial by Government choice. Even if a Government did hope for a divided report, it could never blatantly select a representative Commission if the circumstances clearly called for some other type.

So far we have considered membership as affected by partisanship. Even when this is not involved, appointing ministers vary in their wisdom and may err in their assessment of a situation. Their appointments, while not directly violating the norms, may therefore still be unsatisfactory because the intellectual quality of the appointees is not high enough or because they are not wisely distributed among the differing perspectives on a problem. The Morton Commission on divorce and the Tomlin Commission on the Civil Service suggest these deficiencies. Probably nothing could prevent such occasional lapses from standards. But it must be realized that mediocrity could destroy the Royal Commission just as effectively as partisan perversion.

Proper balance in composition poses difficult questions. Should experts be placed directly on a Commission or can their knowledge better be gained as witnesses? What is the place of the layman? Under what circumstances may interested parties usefully serve as Commissioners? Should chairmen be lawyers? [11]

Commission are more than twice as great as from an impartial Commission and more than three times as great as from an expert Commission. Only one out of every six Commissions since 1900 has been representative. On divided reports see also the section of this chapter entitled "Unanimity in Reports."

[11] K. C. Wheare, *Government by Committee* (Oxford: Claren-

Generalizations are risky; each Commission must be custom-fitted to its problems. But in principle the members on a Commission should adequately represent the conservative, liberal, socialist, and other universal attitudes analyzed by Bienenfeld. Secondly, experts must be balanced by laymen, specialists by the broadly educated; the aristocratic by the self-made man; the official by the independent student; the "practical" mind by the "philosophic."

Every Commission that meets the norms reinforces them and makes subsequent violation the more difficult. Alternatively, any time the norms are violated they are weakened, with repetition the more likely—unless the violation incurs such disapproval that the very instance of it serves to make the norms more conscious and effective. Consider a case in point.

Sir Lionel Leonard Cohen had been the original chairman of the Royal Commission on Taxation of Profits and Income, appointed in January 1951 by Sir Stafford Cripps of the then Labour Government. He resigned his appointment when he was made Lord of Appeal in Ordinary, and the succeeding Churchill Government appointed in his place Lord Waverley, who had had a distinguished career: Chairman of the Board of Inland Revenue, Permanent Under-Secretary at the Home Office, Governor of Bengal, member of the war-time National Government, for three years Chancellor of the Exchequer, and a Member of Parliament with a university seat. He had been made a peer after he lost his seat. Since the war he had been chairman of the Port of London Authority. As the

---

don Press, 1955), esp. pp. 78-88, has a valuable discussion of these questions. It is significant to note the level on which the discussion proceeds, for it is typical. There is the implicit assumption that the persons selected will have integrity and competence, and it is solely to prejudice, to perspective, and to background experience that he directs attention.

Times put it (3/1/52), "The bitterness of the Opposition's reaction to the new appointment took the Government . . . by surprise. It had been thought that Lord Waverley . . . had some obvious qualifications for this chairmanship."

Here was clearly the first violation of established practice —failure to consult with Opposition leaders or to have had prior knowledge that the appointment would be satisfactory.

When the announcement of Lord Waverley's appointment was made on February 26 in Commons there was a "storm of angry disapproval." Hugh Gaitskell led the attack, asking Prime Minister Churchill whether he realized the importance of having as chairman of this Commission "a man of acknowledged impartiality, of no political bias, and accustomed to the exercise of judicial functions," and whether Churchill realized that "Lord Waverley has shown by his political speeches and his bearing in the 1945-50 House of Commons, that he holds strong political opinions, corresponding broadly to the right wing of the Conservative Party, and is therefore quite unsuited to fill this post?" Mr. Gaitskell also suggested that the fact that Churchill had made this appointment "only shows that the Government are determined to influence the conclusions of this Commission for their own party advantage."

For debate the next week the Labour Party presented a Motion "That in view of the strong political views expressed by Lord Waverley on financial, fiscal and social questions, this House regrets that the Prime Minister should have recommended his appointment as Chairman . . . , thus departing from the normal practice [N.B.] by which such posts are occupied by persons of acknowledged political impartiality."

The Liberals felt that, whatever Lord Waverley's merits, the fact that his appointment was so unacceptable to the Opposition as to bring about a debate would likely prejudice fair judgment of the Commission's work. And, although at first he was not inclined to resign "having regard to the dignity and constitutional status of a Royal Commission," Lord Waverley later came to the same conclusion and resigned before the debate could take place.

The original terms of reference of the Royal Commission on Doctors' and Dentists' Remuneration will be recalled as another example of violation of the norms. This time the attack came not from a political Opposition but from the bloc most closely concerned, the doctors charging that the terms of reference were slanted to prevent a fair hearing. In this instance also the Government yielded.

The process of selecting Commissioners and framing their terms of reference is implicit in the foregoing norms. The Government must be sure that the decisions will reasonably satisfy the leaders of all interested parties. This does not necessarily mean formal consultation and specific approval of every Commissioner. For, because of the association which goes on constantly through political clubs, society, and school connections, the Prime Minister and his colleagues are already likely to know whom these leaders would approve. Occasionally a failure actually to consult will result in a grievous error, such as Lord Waverley's appointment. But such occasions are infrequent.

Where the best brains were not selected, the blame is properly directed against the Government, not the Royal Commission. Since its history demonstrates high usefulness, most members must have been well qualified. But obviously the more distinguished the members the better they can fulfill their functions. Anything, therefore, that makes more evident the importance of the mechanism and of the norms that sustain selection of the most highly qualified members can only add to the pressures already operating against the partisan selection of the "politically most acceptable" brains and thus help to improve still further the high level of performance.

Background of Royal Commissioners

Examination of their backgrounds and then of the political character of their reports should yield pertinent evidence on the qualifications of Royal Commissioners and on possible bias in their recommendations.

Royal Commissioners receive no salary; they devote personal attention to their duties; they have established reputations. But beyond these facts there is only the general acknowledgment of their superior quality. No information is available on their actual social, educational, and occupational backgrounds.

In an attempt to throw some light on these characteristics, biographical material was assembled on the members of a random sample of Royal Commissions. The selection of every sixth Commission appointed from 1900 to 1965 yields a total of 23 Commissions: ten impartial, nine expert, and four representative. They cover seven of the nine fields of problems with which all the Commissions dealt (there were none in the fields of military and colonial problems). Their members total 288, with an average membership of 12.5. There were only 277 different Commissioners, as 11 served on two different Commissions.

Chart 2 shows the general picture of the social, educational, and occupational backgrounds of the 277 sample Royal Commissioners. For complete information, see Appendix 3.

On the basis of this sample, we can say that in background Royal Commissioners are predominantly middle and professional class. They are persons of outstanding achievement. They are, as to age, at the peak of their powers.

Commissioners are not numerically representative of the

CHART 2

Sample Royal Commissioners

Mean Age: 56

Sex: 21 of the 277 (7.5%) were women

Social Origin: 10% aristocratic

Father's Occupation: 28% total professional; 13% clergymen; 9% from business; 4% from labor; probably 45% from lower-middle- and working-class occupations

Secondary Education: 40% from public schools in the Headmasters' Conference; 23% from 8 ranking public schools

Collegiate Education: 42% from Oxford and Cambridge; probably 14%-25% no collegiate education

Occupation: 22% in government; 20% in universities; 15% in business; 14% in law; 6% in labor and unions; 4% in church; 4% in social work

Achievement to date: 92% in *Who's Who;* 53% given Peerage, Baronetage, or Knighthood; 46% in *Dictionary of National Biography*

population with respect to class, education, or occupation. For only a small proportion of all citizens have aristocratic or professional background, public school or "Oxbridge" education, or are themselves in government, university, or professional work. Nor, of course, do most citizens achieve titles or inclusion in the *Dictionary of National Biography* or even in *Who's Who.*

The spread of occupational background, with 102 Commissioners from art, social work, and a variety of professions, and another 102 from governmental, judicial, and military service, certainly suggests no weighting on Commissions of the business- or labor- or profit-oriented person. Nor does there appear any significant weighting from any particular bloc in the body politic. The largest specialized group is that of the law, some 14% of the total. The reasons are mainly that so many public problems have legal aspects, and that legal and particularly judicial training is often advantageous for chairmen. Of the 24 chairmen of these 23 Commissions, four were lawyers early in their career; two were barristers, though one of these later became a Professor of Law; and five were judges.

Businessmen were more than balanced by university men. Labor and union leaders, while more numerous than any single group of businessmen, bankers, industrialists, or accountants, were overbalanced nearly two and a half to one by the total of businessmen. Even though Britain is increasingly middle class in outlook, there would appear room for a definite increase on Commissions in the number of members from labor and trade union and socialist areas, i.e. an increase in more "radical" thought.

Royal Commissions are, however, less exclusive and better balanced than cabinet ministers, Members of Parliament, or the upper echelons of the civil service. Fewer members are aristocratic in origin, and a smaller proportion attend public schools or Oxford or Cambridge. Compared with cabinet ministers, who have a higher proportion of parents who were businessmen or rentiers, those selected for Commissions have a higher proportion of parents who were clergymen or in some profession or sphere of government service. Royal Commissioners, although not numerically representative of the occupational divisions of the population, still come from a larger number of occupations than do cabinet ministers or Members of Parliament. They are not unbalanced by so disproportionate a number of rentiers and landowners as are the ministers, or by so disproportionate a number of lawyers and company directors as is the House of Commons. Table 6 in Appendix 3 gives the details of these comparisons.

The caliber of the Commissioners is evidenced only indirectly by percentages titled or included in *Who's Who* or the *Dictionary of National Biography*. But the pattern of eminence becomes obvious from the biographical sketches, as one after another of the Commissioners is seen to be present or past chairman or president of his professional association or otherwise designated leader in his field. Here are clearly some of the best brains in the country. Four men in this random sample were holders of the highest-ranking Order of Merit.

The chairmen are outstanding here. All 24 are in *Who's Who* and 16 of the 20 who died before 1951 are in the *Dictionary of National Biography* (the present edition does not include anyone who died after 1950). All but two were raised to the Peerage (13), or the Baronetage (1), or were Knighted (6), or inherited a title but were themselves advanced in the Peerage (2).

Political character of reports

It is hazardous in the extreme to infer a fixed direction of policy from a given social background, as witness a Clement Attlee, a Hugh Gaitskell, a Bertrand Russell, or a Beatrice Webb. It is on the *content* of their policies that judgment should be primarily based, not on the social or political or economic origin of the policy-makers.

In addition to the evidence of the case-study Commissions and of the biographical data, rather clear-cut evidence of the balanced and impartial character of the Royal Commission is also available from Commission reports whose policy recommendations were not unanimous.

There are clearly differences in the degree to which the various problems handled by Commissions are themselves subject to class cleavages. At one extreme are such problems as London Traffic or Registration of Title in Scotland, which are more likely to engender technical differences of opinion than violent class controversy. At the other extreme might be the problem of Trade Disputes and Combinations, on which a Commission was set up in 1903, after the famous Taff Vale case, to decide the extent of liability of trade unions for tort. Here the trade union world was so enraged it refused to testify before the Commission, a distinctly rare phenomenon. Perhaps between these extremes might be such problems as poor laws, how to reduce pauperism or destitution, with its obvious class approaches; the problem of the coal industry, involving the opposing interests of mine and royalty owners and miners; or the problem of divorce, on which judgments cut erratically across all class lines.

In all, about one quarter of the advisory Commissions reporting since 1900 presented a majority and one or more minority reports. Appendix 4 lists these Commissions and gives some capsule impressions on how the reports were split. In 17 of these 31 divided reports the political complexion is clear enough to permit discussion. Chart 3 shows the number of minority reports produced by each of these 17 Commissions, what Government appointed the Commission, and, very crudely indeed, the political character of the reports— whether more conservative or more radical than the majority reports.

In getting at possible class bias in recommendations, it should be helpful to consider this distribution against a hypothesis. If it is taken that Royal Commissions are subservient to the class-political apparatus, it would seem reasonable to expect that their reports would show that (1) the more deeply class interests were involved the more likely the whole Commission, certainly at least its majority, to report along

CHART 3

*Certain divided Royal Commissions
by political character of minority reports*

Minority reports MORE RADICAL than majority report			Minority reports MORE CONSERVATIVE than majority report		
# Min. rpts.	Title	Gov't. app't. by	# Min. rpts.	Title	Gov't. app't. by
GOVERNMENTAL					
2	Local Gov't. of Greater London, 1921	Coalition	1	Superannuation in Civil Service, 1902	Conserv.
1	Justices of Peace, 1946	Labour	1	Civil Service, 1912	Liberal
1	Honours, 1922	Coalition			
ECONOMIC					
1	Poor Laws, 1905	Conserv.	2	Trade Disputes, 1903	Conserv.
2	Coal Industry, 1919	Coalition	2	Coal Industry, 1919	Coalition
1	Food Prices, 1924	Conserv.	1	Food Prices, 1924	Conserv.
1	Unemployment Insurance, 1930	Labour			
1	Taxation Profits, 1951	Labour			
SOCIAL					
2	Divorce, 1951	Labour	1	Divorce, 1909	Liberal
1	Licensing, England, 1929	Labour	2	Licensing, England, 1929	Labour
CITY PLANNING					
1	Distribution of Industrial Population, 1937	Conserv.	3	Canals & Inland Navigation, 1906	Liberal
HEALTH					
1	National Health Insurance, 1924	Labour			
15			13		

the lines the appointing Government's class interests would be felt to lie—Commissions appointed by Conservative or Liberal Governments having at least their majority on the more "conservative" side, those appointed by Labour Governments having at least their majority on what might even more loosely be called the more "radical" side; (2) since Conservative, Liberal, and Coalition Governments appointed 11 of these 17 Commissions, the majorities would be on the conservative side by nearly two to one; (3) the net effect of Royal Commissions would be to conserve the *status quo* or to modify only in name and detail.

It is difficult, however, to find any patterns from the foregoing table which confirm such a hypothesis. No such pattern shows up, for instance, in Commissions most deeply concerned with class interests. The Commissions on Trade Disputes and Combinations, on Poor Laws and Relief of Distress, and on the Coal Industry are interesting illustrations.

In the Trade Disputes Commission, if anywhere, one would expect a good majority to be on the more conservative side in attempting to limit the effectiveness of trade unions and strikes, especially since this was over fifty years ago. In point of fact the majority of three, which included Sidney Webb, was on the more radical side. They recommended, as a sample, that central union authorities should be protected, in suits, against unauthorized acts of branch agents; that union benefit funds should be made immune to seizure for tort if they were not used for militant purposes; that trade unions, picketing, and strikes, including sympathetic but not breach of contract ones, should be made legal; that an individual should not be liable for any act, not in itself an actionable tort, only because it interfered with another's trade, business, or employment.

It was the minority, two, who signed more conservative reports, disagreeing with these recommendations. Yet it was a

Conservative Government that had appointed the Commission. The Commission reported after the general election of January 1906 returned a Liberal Government, which later introduced a Bill based on the majority report.

In the famous Poor Law Commission, also appointed by a Conservative Government, it was this time the majority that reported on the more conservative side. Their conservatism, however, by no means meant opposition to reform. On the contrary, they advised drastic changes, agreeing with the minority of four in proposing the abolition of workhouses and of the Poor Law Guardians and the transfer of most of the latters' functions to County Councils; in condemning the idea of a deterrent poor law and in advising extension of old-age pensions and medical services. As one commentator put it, all the Commissioners agreed on demolition but differed on construction, mainly about the able-bodied. Here the minority discarded completely the long-established principle that "character" had something to do with poverty and advanced the idea that only the national Government could effectively handle the varied programs needed to reduce unemployment and prevent destitution.

If the class-political end intended by the Government in appointing the Commission was a return to the principles of 1834, as Beatrice Webb charged, the Government did not attempt to achieve it by packing the Commission. The appointments show the strength of the norms. Some of the ablest opponents of the 1834 principles (including Beatrice Webb herself) were among the 19 members. These opponents also included (about 16% of the total) two socialists and one trade union official—and this in the year 1905.

Nor was the effect of the Commission what the Government may have wished. For not only did all the Commissioners advise a further break-away from those 1834 principles, the minority denounced them altogether. The recommendations of both minority and majority were too far-reaching for subsequent Liberal or Conservative Governments for 20 years. But the final effect, at the end of that time, was the implementation of the minority report and thus the break-up of the very system the appointing Government allegedly wanted to restore and strengthen.

The Sankey Coal Industry Commission was appointed by a Coalition Government. The Prime Minister was a Liberal and the largest party in the House was that of the Conservatives. Four final reports were issued. The chairman's report and that of the three miners' representatives and the three "friends of labor" may be considered the two more radical reports; those of the one "friend of industry" and the other two friends plus the three owners' representatives were the more conservative reports, though both these latter recommended nationalization of the mineral.

Here again the presumed class interests of the appointing Government find no discernible reflection in the Commission itself. Its membership certainly did not embody a class bias—the six labor members outmatched in competence the six owner members, and no other chairman would have been more pleasing to labor than Sir John Sankey. Nor did the Commission report favorably to the alleged political ends desired by the Government. All 13 Commissioners recommended nationalization of the mineral, seven recommended nationalization of the mines, only five did not recommend drastic changes in operation of the industry. Nor were the effects of the Commission, again, what the Government presumably would have desired. The mine and mineral owners regarded the Commission as a catastrophe, and it was, in fact, the greatest single influence in the nationalization movement. Nearly twenty years later the mineral was nationalized; seven years after that the mines themselves.

These three Commissions, because appointed by Governments essentially conservative, because involving class differences so deeply, and particularly because so long before labor achieved any equality in strength to business and industrial groups, are fair evidence that the net effect of Royal Commissions is not to conserve the *status quo*.

In Commissions appointed by Labour Governments there is similarly no pattern indicating biased memberships subservient to political ends, this time of the Labour (or socialist) Party. In only one Commission out of six, that on Licensing in England, was the majority more to the left side. In all the others, including such important Commissions as those on Unemployment Insurance, Taxation of Profits and Income, Divorce (1951), and National Health Insurance, it was, contrary to what might have been expected, the majorities that were the more conservative—though again this does not mean they recommended no reforms. In one case, indeed, in an interim report, five of the seven Commissioners appointed to advise on unemployment insurance recommended increases in payments and decreases in benefits, a policy utterly unacceptable to the Labour cabinet and one of the factors precipitating the crisis of 1931 and the replacement of the Labour by the National Government.

The totals of these divided reports also fail to show any class patterns. Instead of all four majorities of the four Commissions appointed by Conservative Governments reporting on the more conservative side, only two so reported.[12] Instead of all six majorities of the six Commissions appointed by Labour Governments reporting on the more leftist side, only one so reported. Instead of all ten majorities of the ten Commissions appointed by Conservative, Liberal, and Coalition Governments reporting on the conservative side, only four so

[12] Not including the Commission on Food Prices, whose majority was between the two minorities, one more conservative and one more radical.

reported. Instead of conservative majorities outnumbering radical majorities by nearly two to one, they outnumber them only nine to seven.

The content of Royal Commission recommendations thus lends little support to any theory that its members are reliable supporters of the class-political ends of the Government that appoints them. Nor does it substantiate Wilhelm Dibelius' comment that the statesman who selects Commissioners "can almost always determine the course that it [the Commission] is going to take, since he will have a pretty good knowledge beforehand of the minds of the experts whom he puts on it. . . ." [13]

II. METHODS OF OPERATION

The methods of operation of a Royal Commission must be adequate to its functions. According to the nature of its problem a Commission must be able to use any of the techniques of social science—questionnaires, personal interviews, collection of historical materials, research teams to make any kind of statistical, field, or other study. Members must themselves be free to make any inquiry they choose. A Commission must have expert direction of its procedures, as supplied normally by a senior civil servant. It should not go outside its terms of reference to give gratuitous advice. It must give attention to every relevant, responsible source of information and should be able to take testimony in secret if important information would not come out in open hearings.

There must be scrupulous due process in handling witnesses, and cross-examination techniques to check their evidence. The conclusions of the Commission must represent a collective decision. Although a unanimous report is most

[13] *England* (New York: Harper Bros., 1930), p. 254.

effective, individual Commissioners must nonetheless have the right of reporting any dissenting judgment; otherwise the report might represent either the conclusions of a dominant member or the kind of watered-down compromise that would bring the mechanism into disrepute. The Commission must be entirely independent in its work and have normally no time limit. The Government must not be able to withhold its report from the public.

Research

It may be thought that the procedure of the Royal Commission is essentially a "horizontal" one, bringing together for consideration just a variety of different points of view. This may make for some correction of perspective in approaching a problem, but does it rely too much on statements of opinion from purported well-informed persons and not enough on careful assembling of factual data? Is the result merely a compromise formula susceptible to practical action by Parliament or private groups? Does the Royal Commission then simply help to resolve a conflict-situation enough so that the institutional system, particularly the Government, can continue with somewhat less pressure? Is it, even, a pre-modern research device, inferior, as a guide in social direction, to research not tied so directly, if at all, to the hope of immediate pragmatic action?

It is the nature of the problem set the Commission that determines as a matter of course the methods it uses. The important principle is that Royal Commissions are independent. Once created, their procedures are entirely their own choice. They can call whomever they wish as witnesses; they can examine whatever data they want. They can employ as research staff whomever they choose. They can set the staff any type of research. They can take as long as they need, reasonably. If any Commission does a poor professional piece of work, therefore, it is the fault of those particular Commissioners, not of any inherent defect in the mechanism.

Because the open hearings at which oral testimony is taken attract wide attention, it is perhaps natural that this part of a Commission's work might give rise to the impression that a Royal Commission relies chiefly on the opinions of its witnesses—though few would deny that these witnesses are uniformly the best informed.

The kinds of problems that are given Royal Commissions are so varied, however, that it would be hazardous to generalize on the proper weight to be given to judgments of witnesses. What should be emphasized is that there is nothing in the mechanism itself to prevent any necessary factual study, granted that unlimited funds and time are no more available to the Commissioners than to any other human beings. It is also true that the attitudes of interested parties may be just as relevant to a solution of a problem as are "objective" facts.

There are definite limitations to the value of secret testimony. Usually the more public the work of a Commission the better for most of its other functions, education for one. During the hearings of the press Commission, Prime Minister Attlee was asked in Parliament whether evidence heard by the Commission in private the preceding week would be published. He replied that this was entirely up to the Commission, which was not a court of law and set its own procedures. Supplementary questions by Sir Anthony Eden and others indicated criticism of secret hearings on grounds that unless the findings of the Commission were based on evidence also available to the public, the public would have less confidence in those findings.

The norms that govern Commissioners in taking evidence

are very important. There is no known record of a Commissioner violating the trust of a witness that what was said in private sessions would not be disclosed outside. And browbeating a witness or violating any other rule of fair play is another thing that is simply "not done."

When well-informed persons cannot supply necessary information but it can be secured by factual investigation, the Royal Commission can proceed to get it. But though Royal Commissions are not accountable to any other structure in the Government this does not preclude attention to the fiscal requirements of the Treasury. Each Commission has in effect a blank check, but it also has a sense of responsibility. It therefore presents its financial needs to the Treasury and must be prepared to justify them. There are no known instances of a Commission being unable to do its work properly because of financial limitations imposed from outside.

If a Commission proposes some very special project the matter would come up for decision by the highest political level. This happened with the Royal Commission on Population set up in 1944 to investigate population trends and to decide what might be done in the national interest to influence them. The Commission decided it needed to take a special family census and made a successful request of the Government to do this.

The unusual organization of the population Commission shows the adaptability of the mechanism to any research requirement. Three expert committees were set up as formal subsidiaries of the Commission to advise it on the statistical, the economic, and the biological-medical aspects of the problem, and three expert members of the Commission proper were respectively made chairman of these committees.

Another illustration of superior fact-finding is the 1949 Commission on Capital Punishment, which collected statistics from and visited many foreign countries. The results of the work of both these Commissions are among the most authoritative factual studies ever made on these subjects.

Royal Commissions usually use the civil service for their fact-finding, and the suggestion has been made that they might well use outside experts more frequently. The Guillebaud Committee of Enquiry into the cost of the National Health Service, set up by the Ministry of Health in 1953, hired private scholars to do the research. These specialists found that the conventional government accounts were inappropriate and misleading, and pioneered a whole new approach to the measurement of cost trends in a complex public program. This

> made dramatically evident the wisdom of encouraging departmental committees and Royal Commissions to employ independent technical staff . . . instead of depending for statistical and professional services solely upon the civil service. Part of the functions of such bodies should be to bring a fresh view to a problem. They are impeded from doing so effectively if they cannot have the full-time help of technicians who have not been nurtured in the existing methods of handling the data.[14]

Relation to social science

The central question about the methods of the Royal Commission is whether research that is not geared to immediate action might not be a better guide. The Commission bases its decisions on the knowledge that is attainable at the time; might not research into facts not yet accumulated lead to a different and better solution?

[14] Herman M. Somers and Anne R. Somers, "The Health Service: Diagnosis and Prognosis," *Political Quarterly,* Oct.-Dec. 1956, p. 417.

When a Commission feels a valid decision cannot be made on the basis of facts already known, it can undertake any research necessary, and in the same way social science would. But clearly a Commission cannot go on seeking that objective knowledge which, if found, might provide the certainly valid solution to a problem, if that research would take so long as to put the Commission's report into an indefinite future. The Royal Commission is not social science developing a discipline whose first concern is the accumulation of knowledge regardless of the immediate practical use of the knowledge. So if the research for new knowledge would take the Commission far past the time when the Government needs a policy, the Commission will act on available knowledge and the judgment of the well-informed. What better choices are there?

Certainly not a decision by the Government unaided by the Royal Commission. And social science would not accept the responsibility of making the value judgments required. But even if it did, since it cannot at this time always predict the valid decision on the basis of established hypotheses, it could only proceed as does a Royal Commission: collect and interpret existing knowledge and evaluate the judgments of well-informed persons. It would beg the question for social science to accept the problem on the basis that when and if, proceeding on a pure science course, it developed the necessary knowledge it would supply it to the Government. For then the Government would simply have to make its decision alone.

But suppose social scientists could be persuaded to step out of their professional roles temporarily. Might they not provide better policy directives than the Royal Commission? They would not be appointed by a political Government, and they would not have to "water down" their advice to meet the claims of partisan power blocs.

In the first place, any presumed greater freedom from political influence would be more than offset by the absence of other perspectives than those of the scholar-scientist-researcher.

But any supposition that the Royal Commission, by nature or in usual practice, discards first-best solutions or dilutes them by compromise to placate power blocs, would be hard to confirm. Time and again Royal Commissions rule against the largest and strongest groups in the society: against the Government, for instance, in the matter of doctors and the health service; against farming interests in the matter of a cattle embargo; against the church in the matter of divorce; against the most powerful industry, and the most powerful union, in the coal controversy—to mention only a few Commissions. Here were flat and uncompromising findings, nothing weak or equivocal.

To cite the almost even division in the Morton Commission on the problem of divorce by consent as a "compromise" based on fear of a forthright verdict against outmoded beliefs of church and upper classes; to see the decision of both coal Commissions to expropriate the mineral but to compensate adequately for it, as another compromise (something for the workers and something for the owners); or to charge that the press Commission's recommendation for a voluntary Press Council represented a compromised retreat from what the Commission knew to be better (i.e. a state-imposed Council) because the Commission feared the press or some of its own dominating members—these would be quite gratuitous opinions which would find no responsible support.

There is, of course, give and take in the deliberations of a Commission. But to equate this with unprincipled compromise is to apply an epithet which obscures insight into one of the cardinal features of the Royal Commission: the balancing of perspectives to get a collective judgment. Charges of this order are usually inspired by disagreement with a Commission's recommendations.

It is in the Government and Parliament that any crude power compromises are made. The Royal Commission can transcend current "political realities." Further evidence of this lies in the frequent time-lead of Commission recommendations over their implementation in policy. The very fact that this well-known time-lead is often many years demonstrates that the findings arrived at by the Royal Commission are ahead of the political compromises of the Government and the power blocs.

No study has yet been made of the time gap between issuance of the recommendations of every Commission and their implementation. Much depends, of course, on the subject matter and the degree of controversy. Many recommendations are given relatively immediate administrative or legislative effect. In many of the more controversial problems it is a familiar observation that it takes "many" years for implementation. One estimate was given by Harold J. Laski: "On the average . . . it takes nineteen years for the recommendations of a unanimous report . . . to assume statutory form; and if the Commission is divided in its opinion, it takes . . . on the average about thirty years. . . ." [15] This is probably an exaggeration. Another estimate was given by Lord Silkin during the Lords' debate on the Morton divorce Commission. He remarked that it takes about ten years to implement a Commission's report.

It is hard to reconcile this time-lead with any view of the Royal Commission as a typical committee, operating on compromise and therefore rarely if ever able to be as fundamental in diagnosis or as far-seeing in prescription as a creative individual. Creative individuals (and radical groups) have their essential role in any society, and in Royal Commissions. But as sole originators of policy advice they would suffer the discount placed by most citizens on all single perspective.

[15] *Parliamentary Government in England* (New York: Viking Press, 1938), p. 93.

The very complaints about how long it takes to implement Royal Commission recommendations show how often and how far they are ahead of what is currently acceptable. And it is just because they are balanced, collective products that they can exert the greater influence as a guide in social direction.

Against this background, how differently one reads another example of indirect hit-and-run criticism: "It is often said, rather by way of a grim joke, that the result of having a royal commission is that nothing is done about the matter for ten or twenty years." [16] A reader unaware of the function of directional guidance would naturally get the impression that the Royal Commission *delays* action for ten to twenty years.

What this time-lead actually shows is the difference between the knowledge of what should be done to increase efficiency or equity, a knowledge supplied by the Royal Commission to the society, and putting the knowledge into effect; between the intent that right be done, as held up by the Royal Commission, and the timing of its actual doing, by Government or blocs, given the hard realities of groups with differing interests and varying degrees of insight—and power.

Unanimity in reports

Unanimity in a Commission's report undoubtedly gives it additional weight. The *Report* of the 1910 Departmental Committee on the Procedure of Royal Commissions urged chair-

---

[16] R. M. Jackson in *The Listener* (London: B.B.C., April 12, 1956), p. 389. The unwitting disservice of this statement is not notably remedied by the author's following comment that "Things are not really as bad as that in all instances." Nevertheless, this article is the best introduction to the Royal Commission.

men to do everything reasonable to minimize the differences among their colleagues on the grounds that a unanimous finding would be fruitful while a mere record of divided opinion would be "absolutely useless."

Yet there are other considerations. If Commissioners cannot arrive at consensus save by some artifically forced, lowest-common-denominator kind of agreement, it may be more serviceable to ultimate truth to bring into the open the differences in judgment and thus stimulate further thought. Commissioners should therefore have the right to make a dissenting report; and it has happened that minority rather than majority reports have come to be implemented. At the same time, as R. V. Vernon has observed, "Minor differences are no good excuse for minority reports and hardly even for 'reservations.' There should be some give and take even in the tendering of advice." [17]

In view of the wide range and controversial nature of the problems that Royal Commissions consider, and in view of the diversity in their membership, it may be rather surprising that 45 per cent of all Commissions making final advisory reports since 1900 were completely unanimous in their analysis and recommendations. Seventy-five per cent were unanimous in that all the members signed the report, though some had Reservations or Dissents of major or minor importance, which they felt impelled to note publicly. Only 25 per cent of the Commissions disagreed to the point where one or more members felt it necessary to sign a separate report.

About half (48%) of the representative Commissions had divided reports; and, as might have been expected, the chances for divided reports are greatest for this composition type—more than twice as great as for an impartial Commission (23%) and more than three times as great as for an expert Commission (15%).

[17] Vernon and Mansergh, *Advisory Bodies* (London: George Allen and Unwin, 1940), p. 442.

This problem of compromise and unanimity and dissent raises the more general question of the nature of Royal Commission findings. These findings incorporate description, evaluation, and prescription. Just as scientific attempts to describe the physical universe may be incomplete or untrue, so, obviously, may be the pertinent descriptions of a Royal Commission. Though in the social world there are not often such objective criteria of truth as exist in the physical world, it is also possible for evaluations and prescriptions of a Royal Commission to be partially or completely untrue in the sense that if acted upon they would have effects demonstrably different from those predicted. For all the delineated features of the Royal Commission calculated to reduce the chances of such error, it is still that possibility that lies behind the essential right of minority Commissioners to record publicly their differences from the majority. Thus may they "stand as an invitation to future change."

Charles Evans Hughes' comment about a minority judge has direct relevance:

A dissent in a court of last resort [read Royal Commission] is an appeal to the brooding spirit of the law [read statesmen, scholars, body politic], to the intelligence of a future day when a later decision may possibly correct the error into which the dissenting judge [Commissioner] believes the court [majority Commissioners] to have been betrayed." [18]

III. SOCIAL MATRIX

It is the paradoxical nature of the Royal Commission that to be an influential guide in social direction valid for the entire country, it must be linked to the partisan political system and yet able to transcend it.

[18] *Wisdom Magazine,* Beverly Hills, Nov. 1956, p. 33.

In modern associational societies the national Government is guardian of the totality of interests. But it views those interests from the perspective of a political party. Any structure, therefore, that is linked to the Government is subject to neglect or misuse to further the Government's more exclusive partisan interests. This possibility, together with that of mediocrity in membership, is the major threat to the usefulness of the Royal Commission.

The strength that the Royal Commission derives from its political linkage should, however, be equally appreciated. Precisely because it is a formal structure in constitutional law it exercises a strong influence, to its own ends, on Governments, blocs, and the body politic. Once a Government has accepted the responsibility for creating a Commission, it is under a stronger pressure to follow the Commission's leads than if the Commission were outside the governmental process. The Commission is similarly more influential with blocs and citizens if only because it has official status, and shares the dignity and supra-party character of the Crown and the public responsibility of elected Members of Parliament.

If a structure comparable to the Royal Commission could be established that was not linked to the political system, could it be maintained that it might then *not* be subject to bias, imbalance, limited perspective, to any number of distorting forces? Would a group of Oxford or completely unaffiliated scholars be more capable of unbiased research and policy directives? A group of specialists sponsored by business or trade unions or socialists or consumers?

Any private, as opposed to official, governmental, research would have to find financial support; someone would have final authority on when the structure would be set up, on what problems, with what membership. Those supplying the funds and those making these decisions would have their individual perspectives of social problems, their own positions in the society, their own personal and class interests. Enter therefore exactly the same kinds of problems that are encountered with the Royal Commission: the search for independence, integrity, and competence of members, balance of perspectives, and proper procedural and research techniques.

On the other hand, of course, were the Royal Commission not as independent of the political system as it is, it would be of no greater importance as a guide than a Parliamentary Select Committee or a Tribunal of Inquiry, with their limitations of membership and of time-span. Or it might be like a research group or task force set up by a party to guide its own policy-making. Only as it can transcend limitations imposed by interests less inclusive than those of the total population can the Royal Commission fulfill most of its functions.

Distorting influences

A Government could pervert the Royal Commission in four ways: to the hypothetical, impartial observer it could appoint a Commission when it should not; it could fail to appoint one when it should; it could weight the Commission's membership or slant its terms of reference; or it could fail to implement its recommendations.

Improper appointment of a Royal Commission, as a tactic to avoid both action and open opposition to it, is a doubtful abuse for two reasons. One can rarely be sure that this was the real purpose of any Commission's appointment. For a Government always asserts a legitimate purpose, and this must have sufficient plausibility else the appointment of the Commission would be seen as subterfuge, making it then ineffective for the Government's scheme. Secondly, even if the public could be so deceived, the Government would gain a respite from decision only for the time it would take the Commission to report. After that the Government would be worse off than before. Probably the clearest example of this alleged misuse is the Sankey coal Commission, and the experience there is not very encouraging to would-be manipulators.

The norms that protect the mechanism from attempts to slant its terms of reference or to weight its membership in favor of one or another set of interests have already been discussed. There are then the two possible sins of omission: failure to appoint a Commission and failure to implement its recommendations.

A Government will not normally set up a Commission if it feels it can handle the situation by itself, or if the problem involves a sensitive area of national security or international relations. This usually requires a secrecy in investigation for which some other type of advisory committee may be just as suitable. For a Royal Commission, the more open its work can be, the larger the number of functions it can serve.

Nor would a Government set up a Commission on a problem of too wide or indefinite a scope. It is universally agreed that the terms of reference should not be so broad as to invite an essay of generalities, so rarely helpful in framing legislative or administrative policy. The problem given it should be specific enough that practical results may follow. "A roving Commission is a roving nuisance," as R. V. Vernon has remarked.

Problems, therefore, that alert citizens may feel to be very important are not necessarily within the proper scope of a Royal Commission if they involve questions that the contemporary state of knowledge is unable to answer with any reasonable degree of sureness or if the answers would embody advice that has little chance of being followed. What busy and responsible citizens would, more than once, lend their services where results would be so nebulous?

Consider several problems on which a Government has elected not to create a Royal Commission.

On April 29, 1954, Prime Minister Churchill was asked in Commons if he would set up a Royal Commission to inquire into communist activities in Great Britain. He answered in the negative, noting that with England's free institutions and long experience there were few countries where communism had more difficulty in making headway, and that the security aspects could be handled adequately by established laws.

What to pay Members of Parliament had long been a troublesome question. On July 15, 1954, a Member asked if a Royal Commission could not be appointed to consider the amount and form of remuneration that would be best for the whole country. The Prime Minister answered simply that the Government did not feel any further inquiry was advisable at the time.

The reported romance between Princess Margaret and Peter Townsend stirred some quarters to see a widening gap between the law of the land and the teachings of the Church of England against remarriage of a divorced person. A Labour Member of Parliament on November 15, 1955, asked if the Government would not appoint a Royal Commission on the relationship between Church and State. Prime Minister Eden answered that in the last few years both the Church Assembly and the Free Church Federal Council had appointed bodies to investigate the relationship and that both reports had indicated that the separation of Church and State at this time would be to the detriment of both. He therefore declined to consider a Royal Commission inquiry.

In an editorial on March 2, 1957, the London *Times* noted the constant clamor for more money raised by cultural organizations—Arts Council, Royal Societies, British Museum, Sadlers Wells, and others. The paper had no criticism whatever of their vociferous claims, acknowledging that if they did not demand loudly they would get even less. Nor did the

Times blame the Government for not meeting the demands; admittedly the Government walked an economic tightrope. But the writer felt the whole business was degrading and proposed a Royal Commission "to make recommendations on the whole field of Government patronage of the arts. . . . The more comprehensive its enquiry could be the better. . . ." The *Times* urged "an examination of the whole cultural life of the United Kingdom in relation to its needs from public funds. . . . For out of the undertaking could emerge a set of modern principles that could guide the State in its role of patron, replacing the hand-to-mouth illogicalities of today." The Macmillan Government did not see fit to adopt this suggestion. Commons debated the subject again on February 26, 1960.

In the House of Commons on July 11, 1957 mounting concern for the dangers of inflation led to a request for a Select Committee or a Royal Commission to inquire into the problem. The Government replied that the Radcliffe Committee were already considering monetary policy. Other Labour speakers continued to press, but the Government was firm that such an inquiry would not be appropriate in relation to matters which cut across every possible line of Government policy.

There is a rather wide range of problems. An outsider without intimate knowledge might agree that on the surface the question of communist activity was too broad to be suitable for Royal Commission inquiry. On the other hand, the question of pay for Members of Parliament might seem very appropriate; as also perhaps the question of government patronage of the arts, if the terms of reference were made specific enough. But who could say with confidence that a Commission should or should not have been appointed on any of them?

Sometimes a Government might consider it advisable to

use a substitute, perhaps a departmental or special committee, if only because too frequent use of the Royal Commission might weaken its prestige. Or since a Government is usually plagued by wanting more legislation passed than Parliament can handle, it may feel that it does not have the time for the additional action that would probably be demanded by the recommendations of a Commission.

But undoubtedly there are problem-situations when a Government has not appointed a Royal Commission and could justly be criticized for neglecting its national duty because of political timidity, lack of vision, or subservience to partisan interests. Granted the advantage of having Commissions linked to the political system, there is probably no way of preventing this, though perhaps more understanding of the superiority of the mechanism might carry more severe political penalties for the Government that neglected it. As it now stands, those convinced a Commission should be set up on some problem must accept the responsibility for continuing to pressure the Government until it does appoint one.

The last point at which partisanship might impair the Royal Commission is by preventing implementation of its recommendations. Successful use of Royal Commissions obviously demands that a sufficient number of their recommendations be followed, sooner or later. Without this the mechanism would be reduced to the level of a debating society or a research bureau, and ranking leaders, seeing no proportionate results from their work, would no longer continue to serve on the Commissions. A corollary of this is that a sufficiently high percentage of the implemented recommendations must be found valid in the light of experience.

A Government may disregard a Commission's advice not because of bias but because of honest difference of judgment on how to handle the given problem. Here Sir Arthur Salter has justly commented that except for unforeseen later events, a Government should be reproached if, having appointed Commissioners of its own choosing and having itself defined their problem, it then concludes that it or someone else is better qualified to decide the same question.

Where the reason for nonimplementation lies deeper than this, it is usually because the more balanced directives of the Royal Commission are ahead of what partisan interests will accept.

The basic relationship of the Royal Commission to Parliament and special-interest blocs has already been discussed in Chapter 6. Implementation usually involves imbalance, shifting individuals and groups from one intellectual and emotional set to another. Most of those who come to an important problem bring definite conceptions they believe correct or definite interests they feel must be served. So any decision that incorporates other viewpoints or accommodates other interests may be displeasing. Indeed, it may be felt so threatening that the Government or blocs (either on their own or through pressure on the Government) may refuse acceptance for many years.

It is in this light that most segmental criticism of a Royal Commission's findings must be evaluated, whether the source of the criticism is labor, industry, a government department, a newspaper, or any individual. For anyone to accept such criticism, or his own judgment, as superior to the conclusions of the collective Royal Commission is to accept a frightening responsibility.

If then, a partisan political structure is given the final authority, it is always possible that the policy directives of a Royal Commission will be disregarded. But this is a calculated risk; to avoid it would be even more disadvantageous. When special interests in one form or another override a Royal Commission its work still remains as an important weapon in continuing the pressure to induce a change of policy, as seen, for instance, in the coal or divorce Commissions. The directives of the Royal Commission become part of the cultural climate and help ripen the time for their implementation.

Supporting influences

A condition for successful use of the Royal Commission is that it be effectively linked to the political system. It is an equally necessary condition that it be able to transcend the limitations of that linkage. It can do this for several reasons, most already cited in the sections on membership and operation. There are additional reasons that merit attention.

Probably the most important of these is the prestige of the structure. Also because of its prestige a Royal Commission is able to draw on the most authoritative and knowledgeable persons in government departments, in business and labor groups, in universities and other private organizations—an obvious requirement for its success. These people feel that their collaboration is worth the effort, that the work of the Commission will be taken seriously. Because a Royal Commission has prestige its findings of fact and its conclusions are normally accepted by the body politic, another obvious requirement if it is to fulfill many of its functions.

The Royal Commission gets its prestige from many sources: its co-ordinate ranking in constitutional law; its concern with important problems; the personal reputation of its members; association with the most deeply rooted traditions and the highest ranking public symbols; its record of past success; the fact that important people collaborate with it; the fact that its findings are accepted as authoritative. Here is a clear example of the reciprocal relation of the Royal Commission and its environment. Prestige is necessary for its effective operation, yet is itself basically the result of that effective operation.

Association with the Monarchy also helps lift the Royal Commission above its partisan political origin. It is true that the reigning ministry exercises most of the powers of the Crown. But implicit in the very word "Royal" are historical, psychological, and practical connotations that go far beyond party considerations. There is no need here for an elaborate psychological analysis of the emotions felt for the Monarchy or of the transference of those emotions to whatever comes to be linked with it. The point is that these emotions have developed and are transferred to a significant extent to the Royal Commission. And what is transferred is very important to its functions. The Monarchy represents supra-party, supra-partisanship, even supra-class. It represents concern for the total—the equivalent of the concern of the father for the whole family, but on the national level. It represents the best, the highest-ranking, whether that be personal (as in standards of conduct) or impersonal (as patron of science, scholarship, and the arts). It unifies.

When, therefore, the Crown appoints a Royal Commission, even though through a political figure, the "Royal" element curbs partisan influences by imposing the norms implicit in the Monarchy. Any attempt to make a partisan instrument of the "Royal" Commission would be quite offensive. The citizens appointed to a Commission are conscious of the dignity and standards of excellence associated with their title, and are impelled to procedures that meet expectancy—that is, are inferior to none. When witnesses are called they are co-opted into the same frame of expectancy and are likewise impelled to their best efforts. For this reason a Commission rarely needs subpoena powers. When facts and policies are presented they receive greater attention because of the deference attached to the Monarchy.

It should be evident, however, that this Royal association, while adding to the prestige of the structure, is not important to its successful operation in anything like the same degree as are the integrity and balance and competence of Commissioners or the efficiency of their procedures.

Widespread publicity for the work of Commissions is important for many of their functions. To improve dissemination of reports the Government might advertise them more. It, or the Commission itself, might supply popular versions aimed at different levels of readers. Summaries of reports could save busy journalists some mechanical work and thereby perhaps induce fuller consideration in the press.

But apart from publication of reports themselves, it is the press that is of greatest help here. Upon it lies a heavy responsibility. It should realize the importance of publicizing the work of Commissions. It should be alert to any violations of the norms of membership, terms of reference, or procedures. It should exert its pressure when a Government fails to appoint a Royal Commission when it properly should, or fails to implement its findings. Yet it must be sensitive to the place of segmental criticism. It should, in short, fulfill its role in the inter-structural system of the Royal Commission.

It should be clear from all this that the Royal Commission could hardly operate successfully, were not the other structures to which it is linked sufficiently kindred in character, and were there not a host of effective norms and values congenial to its spirit.

It should also be clear that the proper use of the Royal Commission calls for knowledge and skill: knowledge of the nature of this societal instrument and of its political and social and cultural matrix, in whatever country that might be; and skill in seizing those opportunities when it might fruitfully be used.[19]

[19] To such questions as at what phases of problems Commissions are "usually" appointed; on what kinds of problems they are "most

often" successful; under what circumstances their recommendations are "most likely" to be implemented, there are few, if any, useful generalizations. The conditions of each Commission are so varied; each has so many individual, even unique, aspects; and whether a Commission is appointed or its advice implemented depends on so many factors—the relative strength of opposing groups, the historical development of particular ideas or attitudes, the personalities of leaders, the existing economic or political situation, accidental features such as some unexpected scandal—that all that is useful, perhaps all that is possible, is the sort of general discussion of underlying principles and major problems that I attempted here.

10 Conclusion

At some point in the handling of societal problems some persons or some process must be trusted to certify facts and to make judgments on which action will be taken, or there will be tyranny, anarchy, or schism.

Review now the character of the Royal Commission. It incorporates in social structure the insight that no one person, no group from any single class or social or economic stratum, is capable of total perspective, has the qualities of temperament, the knowledge, and ability, to comprehend the totality of a societal problem. It has a balanced, not an individual or segmental, approach to problems; it juxtaposes relevant points of view to attain not an impossible "nonperspectivistic" picture but a new level of objectivity. Its members are of unimpeachable integrity, and most of them are distinguished leaders in their field. They have least self-interest in the problem before them, yet they bring understanding of important group interests before a mediating chairman. The Royal Commission has impartial expert assistants. It taps all important sources of knowledge. Its cross-examination and other techniques embody due process. It is independent and relatively free of time limitations. It derives strength from its political linkage and can rise above the restrictions of that origin. It has a congenial matrix of other structures and norms. And it has a long history of service.

In the light of that character it certainly appears reasonable to ask what other persons, what better process, could a society use to arrive at a more trustworthy guide to decision?

Royal Commissioners are obviously fallible, unable to escape their prejudices or transcend their intellectual capacities. Hence a certain proportion of their judgments may be found inadequate or erroneous. But this would be true also of any creative genius, any inspired group, any other regularized process of decision. From experience with single rulers, democratic assemblies, and elites of all kinds, history combines with modern knowledge to point the superiority of the processes embodied in the Royal Commission to achieve year after year and generation after generation trustworthy solutions to difficult social problems.[1]

There is no conflict here with social science. This discipline seeks to develop a body of knowledge about social interaction which, presumably, might then be applied to practi-

---

[1] In this Conclusion the term "Royal Commission" may be taken not as an exclusively British mechanism but as a generic term for the ranking investigatory and advisory body, in any society, whose standards approximate those of the British Royal Commission.

cal problems to get an objectively valid solution. Where the knowledge so far accumulated in this pursuit applies to the problem of a Royal Commission, it will normally be communicated by social scientists serving as members, staff employees or consultants, or expert witnesses.

Since this knowledge rarely points to the unchallengeable solution but a decision must nevertheless be made, where is the society to find the most reliable judgment? If fallible human beings lacking objectively proved knowledge (though if this is obtainable the Royal Commission can get it) must still make portentous decisions, the safest guide for the society would appear to be the Royal Commission—despite the occasional, inevitable lapses from ranking performance.

If this is true, the more widely and the more thoroughly it is understood the better for the society. If this superiority is not recognized, and judgments are delivered, from any source, that conflict with those of a Royal Commission, on what principle do citizens and blocs and political leaders choose? On the basis of their own predilections? On the basis of their own particular interests? If the conclusions of a Royal Commission, a political party, a newspaper, a special-interest bloc, a well-known scholar, a private research group, a Parliamentary division, are all regarded as of the same character, there is no standard of reference, no principle of rank or choice, in the babel of conflicting judgments. No one knows what the operative facts are; no one knows how to evaluate the differing judgments. Policy and social direction are then usually at the mercy of the most vocal, the most politically and economically strong.

This is certainly not to suggest that criticism of a Royal Commission, or disagreement with it, always represents ignorance or fanaticism. If a Government violated the norms by appointing incompetent or biased members or by slanting their terms of reference, it would be a public duty to criticize the Government. If a Commission itself failed to handle its problem in a professionally competent manner it would certainly be open to just criticism.

The "truth" or validity of Royal Commission findings, in sum, is not to be taken as infallible but as presumptive and comparative. Its descriptions of the segments of the social and physical worlds relevant to a problem are more accurate than would be found elsewhere. Its evaluations of facts and judgments and its consequent prescriptions are, if implemented, more likely than evaluations and prescriptions from other sources to lead to an adjustment to some situation that would be to the best interests of the total society.

It follows that unless the norms have been violated, by the Government in appointment or by the Commission in procedure, anyone undertaking to dissent from the findings of a Commission has a heavy responsibility. He must clarify the relation of his dissent to the Royal Commission process. Otherwise he is in effect claiming that one viewpoint of a problem is closer to reality than the multi-perspective arrived at in the frame of the Royal Commission. It is precisely because the full import of the Royal Commission in its structural relationships is not understood that editorialists, commentators, and representatives of one or another group often address the public as if it should accept the individual critic as wiser than the collective Commission.

No one would advocate irrational reverence for any set of persons or any decisional process. No one would demand that those whose strongly held beliefs—moral, religious, political, or economic—are not confirmed by a Royal Commission should bow down in submission and forthwith abjure their beliefs. Let such advocates continue to press for broader acceptance; a free society is the better for competition in ideas.

But what can justifiably be urged is a careful comparison of the types of persons and the procedures that deliver the findings of the Royal Commission with the persons and methods and conclusions of political parties, the civil service, private blocs, newspapers, or any other organizations or individuals in the society. Then a rational judgment may be made as to which set of results is likely to be most accurate in terms of objective reality, or most valid in terms of most advantage for the largest number so far as it can be known at the given time.

In judging this mechanism it is important to see it not alone, in a vacuum, but as it is linked with other structures, particularly Parliament and the Government.

Royal Commissions stand apart from the body politic, whose members comprise the citizens affected by Commission recommendations and the agents for their implementation. Commissioners are not elected by citizens. They disband on completing their work. They are not held accountable for the results of their advice.

Herein lies the related function of Parliament and the Prime Minister. These elected leaders express the country's choices. They are responsive and responsible to all the citizens and, in a sense, to representatives of the many special-interest blocs into which citizens divide. They have final authority for action. It is they, therefore, who have the function of taking the balanced, longer-range, strategic directives of the Royal Commission and effecting them tactically as far and as fast as possible, while maintaining social order or ensuring orderly social change.

They must carry along all the extremist groups and individuals to whom the Royal Commission has no accountability. But the extremists are the fanatics, the half-blind of myopia. They are often able to prevent full immediate implementation of Commission directives. If Parliament and the cabinet (some of whose members may themselves be extremists) did not intervene between the Royal Commission and these groups, policy might get so far ahead of what these groups would accept that only force (stronger than Statute Law by itself) could gain their compliance.

But force, even for a right policy, has quickly reached limits in aiding orderly progress or stability or even speed in social change. There is, unhappily, too often a vital distinction between the sovereign intent that "Right be Done" and the timing of this doing via the legislative, executive, and judicial arms of that sovereign will.

Final policy must be set by persons accountable to those affected by it. The role of the Royal Commission, when called on, is to help ground that policy in reason and justice, to help point the strategic direction in which that policy will take the society in response to never-ending challenges of what ways to maintain, what changes to make, how to improve efficiency, or how to achieve greater equity.

The Royal Commission, of course, is hardly the only source of wise decision among all the writers, scholars, research agencies; the press; the civic, economic, social, and government organizations; and the political parties in any complex society. But when among all these voices there is uncertainty or controversy about what some final decision should be, experience holds up the Royal Commission (with counterpart committees) as the best and most reliable guide yet devised. The more fully this is recognized, the more quickly can the "Right" of Royal Commission directives actually "be Done" in policy.

Its functions do not end there. The Royal Commission is not a secret group furnishing its guide sights as confidential intelligence. By the character of its members and their methods of operation it helps induce voluntary acceptance of its directives. By enlisting the focused contributions of able citizens otherwise outside the decisional process it furthers the wise democratization of governance. By its public hearings and reports it widens social communication and increases the understanding of large numbers of citizens.

Utopian constructs are free from the perversities of human nature. The Royal Commission has operated for generations in the very intractable world of reality. Its achievement is therefore the more remarkable, and could be even greater were its rationale more clearly and widely understood.

The Royal Commission in the United States

No other country has produced anything comparable in effectiveness to the Royal Commission of Great Britain as an agency to which appeal can be made for a definitive determination of controversial facts and for a trustworthy judgment on a complex public problem. It would therefore make a most enlightening study in cultural borrowing to examine what countries have chosen to use the Royal Commission, what countries have not, and why not. In countries—in Africa, Asia, Latin America—that have not yet developed efficient administrative departments the mechanism should have the added usefulness of pacing emerging civil services, as it did in Britain in the 1832 reform era.

Such a survey of foreign experience is beyond our scope here. Some preliminary consideration is possible, however, of the situation in the United States.

Present American advisory bodies

As in Great Britain, individual departments in the United States Government have come increasingly to use advisory bodies, permanent and *ad hoc*. The Department of Agriculture, for one, had 50 in 1955 as against only four in 1938, when there were under 100 in the entire federal government.

These committees or boards range in size from two to several dozen members, most of them outside the government and usually representative of the various interests affected by the appointing department. They are used mainly to get outside advice, to test ideas, or to help secure public support. During the 1959 steel strike, for instance, Secretary of Labor Mitchell set up a group to study the labor troubles in this industry.

Investigatory and advisory bodies originating in the legislature have been used very extensively in the United States, but with nothing like the nice discriminating relation of tool to problem with which the British have used the Select Committee or Tribunal of Inquiry.

The Senate has 16 standing committees, each dealing with a major area of government, such as Foreign Relations, Armed Services, Government Operations. While these rarely conduct investigations themselves, they frequently appoint subcommittees for this purpose. The chairman will be a member of the parent committee, which will also furnish other members. These bodies are strictly bipartisan, membership being in proportion to the strength of the parties in Congress. The subcommittees then will hire outside personnel to help conduct the investigation.

If the problem does not fall easily under the jurisdiction of any of the standing committees, the Senate may appoint a Select Committee. Or if the problem is thought to be a short-range one, it may appoint a Special Committee, such as the well-known Kefauver Special Committee to Investigate Organized Crime in Interstate Commerce.

The House of Representatives also may appoint investigating bodies, of which in recent years perhaps the most publicized one has been the House Committee on Un-American Activities. Since the Second World War, however, the Senate has dominated the field of governmental inquiry, with the McCarthy Subcommittee on Investigations (of the Committee on Government Operations), the Subcommittee on Internal Security (of the Judiciary Committee) and the Kefauver Committee. All these committees and subcommittees have full subpoena powers.

There are two chief public purposes of Congressional Investigating Committees. One is to check the performance of executive agencies and the expenditure of government funds. The other is to determine if a problem exists which may call for legislation, and then to develop information about the problem necessary for proper legislation.

Congress originates other investigating and advisory bodies. Sometimes it collaborates with the executive branch, as in the Hoover Commission on Organization of the Executive Branch of the Government, the first one set up in 1947, the second in 1953. Congress passed the enabling legislation. President Truman appointed four of the twelve members, including the chairman, former President Hoover. The Speaker of the House of Representatives appointed four, and the President Pro Tem of the Senate appointed the other four.

Sometimes Congress collaborates with private groups. Thus

its Mental Health Study Act of 1955 authorized a non-governmental Joint Commission on Mental Illness and Health, created under the leadership of the American Psychiatric Association and the American Medical Association. The Commission was composed of 45 members representing 36 national organizations in the fields of medicine, hospitals, and education. Federal funds totaling $1,400,000 were granted, and private donors contributed another $132,000. The funds were administered by the National Institute for Mental Health.

The executive branch of the government also creates advisory bodies. Authorization may come from a general grant of power by Congress, such as the National Industrial Recovery Act, under which President Roosevelt set up, for instance, the Committee on Economic Security in 1934. Or the authorization may be specific, as when Congress in 1929 authorized the Wickersham National Commission on Law Observance and Enforcement and paid its costs, while the President named the members.

The President can also create advisory bodies by Executive Order alone, his authority for this deriving from his right to create cabinet committees, his emergency powers, his authority as Commander in Chief or as chief agent in foreign relations. So President Truman set up in 1951 a nine-member Commission on Internal Security and Individual Rights, with Fleet Admiral Chester W. Nimitz as chairman.

The chief difficulty with Presidential Commissions lies not so much in any lack of Presidential authority to create them as in finding a source of funds to pay their expenses. In 1909, in a rider to the Sundry Civil Act of that year, Congress, in reaction against President Theodore Roosevelt's commissions, prohibited the use of public funds for any commission, council, or similar body unless its creation was authorized by law. This law is still in effect, and, though it does not prevent the President and cabinet officers from creating such bodies, it does make them hesitate to ask Congress to meet the bill. The Roberts Commission on Pearl Harbor, for instance, was set up by Executive Order. Congress gave it subpoena powers; and it was paid for by Emergency War Funds. When President Eisenhower appointed his Commission on National Goals in 1960 the funds came from eight private foundations.

The chief public purposes of Presidential Commissions are to secure information on which the President can base policy or recommend legislation, to crystallize ideas and stimulate public interest, and to investigate administration of executive departments.

The United States also uses advisory bodies on the order of National Conferences, such as President Eisenhower's White House Conference on Aging. During his tenure President Eisenhower called sixteen of these Conferences. These publicize a problem but rarely have much influence. They are very large in membership, diffuse and mixed in responsibility, and their reports are very general. They have sometimes brought concrete results, however, such as the first of the decennial White House Conferences on Children and Youth, which led to the establishment in 1912 of the United States Children's Bureau and to enactment of child labor laws in several states.

In addition to all these bodies having their origin in one or another branch of the government, there are private investigating and advisory groups, which sometimes get wide publicity and even compete with governmental bodies. The 1956 Rockefeller Brothers Fund studies made recommendations in the same area of foreign policy and defense as did the Gaither Committee appointed in the spring of 1957 by President Eisenhower to make a study of defense efforts for the National Security Council. In April 1961 Robert M. Hutchins, President of the Center for the Study of Democratic Institutions, announced a two-year study of the character and moral and ethical attitudes of Americans.

Limitations of present structures

There is thus certainly no lack of variety in American advisory bodies. However, though some in each category have had beneficial results, none of these devices really approximates the British Royal Commission or has even established any priority in respect or effectiveness. Indeed, there are serious criticisms of all of them.

It is virtually impossible for private advisory bodies to match the prestige of public bodies. Departmental committees, Congressional Select and Special Committees all deal with minor or more specialized short-range problems and hence are of secondary rank even if they operate properly. There remain the Congressional Investigating Committees (or subcommittees), the Presidential Commissions, and the Commissions created by some joint effort of Congress and the President, as the chief American mechanisms for investigation and advice.[1]

Confusion and contradiction mark most Congressional Investigating Committees. The legitimate purpose of appointment—to determine if some problem requires remedial legislation and, if so, what kind, or to probe executive agencies—

---

[1] See for example: Alan Barth, *Government by Investigation* (New York: Viking Press, 1955); Telford Taylor, *Grand Inquest: The Story of Congressional Investigations* (New York: Simon and Schuster, 1955); *University of Chicago Law Review,* Spring 1951; Carl Marcy, *Presidential Commissions* (New York: Kings Crown Press, 1945); M. E. Dimock, *Congressional Investigating Committees* (Baltimore: Johns Hopkins Press, 1929); E. J. Eberling, *Congressional Investigations* (New York: Columbia University Press, 1928); M. N. McGeary, *The Development of Congressional Investigative Power* (New York: Columbia University Press, 1940); Edward T. Chase, "The Longest Way from Thought to Action," *The Reporter,* June 22, 1961.

is often mixed with the desire of Congressmen for public attention. This is no mere whim. The relative lack of solidarity of American political parties, the uncertainties of party support for individual senators or representatives, make headline-seeking almost a political necessity. And few opportunities for national attention equal the hearings of an investigating committee. Also, the legitimate purpose is often mixed with the partisan desire to damage political opponents. These influences invariably distort membership, procedure, and findings.

The membership of Congressional Investigating Committees, confined as it is to members of Congress, is hopelessly partisan and unbalanced. The members do not have the time to study problems adequately. They bring the single perspective of a party organization man, accustomed to look at problems in the light of political expediency and conditioned by the threat of elections. Absent are the perspectives of laymen, specialists, the impartial academic mind, and many others. The consequence is a structural incapacity to handle involved problems.

Criticism of the procedure of Congressional Investigating Committees has been very severe. Due process, constitutional and civil rights of witnesses, long-standing norms—such as the right not to incriminate oneself, the right of privacy, the presumption of innocence—have been repeatedly violated. Conduct in the hearings has sometimes been a national disgrace. The committees also frequently go on fishing expeditions outside their legitimate area of investigation. The consequence is that they tend to assume functions for which they are not fitted: the exposure of wrong-doing and the development of evidence for use in criminal prosecutions, which is the proper function of the police; and the punishment of wrong-doers, which is the proper function of the courts. Their paid counsel and staff, not being civil servants on loan, tend to develop a vested interest in prolonging the inquiry. Findings and recommendations are usually split, reflecting the partisanship of the members.

Many Congressional Investigating Committees have without doubt been useful in educating both Congress and the public on important societal problems. This could be done far more effectively, however, by another kind of structure and without the excesses, the corroding side-effects, the unsavory spectacles, the weakening of norms, the damage to respect for governmental processes which have also been the consequences of many of these committees. Even as they now stand, it would certainly be possible to correct these grossly improper procedures. There is no need to deny a legitimate place to these committees. But their unbalanced membership and their political party perspective make it quite impossible for them ever to achieve the competence and hence the prestige of the Royal Commission.

Presidential Commissions have no crippling inherent defects (except perhaps Congressional attitudes) that would prevent their approximating Royal Commissions. There have, however, been serious and persistent errors in their use, membership, and procedure.

At different periods, for example during President Hoover's tenure, they have been used so frequently, and unfruitfully, that the mechanism has almost been scorned. In far too many instances the terms of reference have been unconscionably broad, inviting recommendations so general as to be completely untranslatable into statutes or regulations. So, for instance, President Hoover's Committee on Social Trends in 1933 was asked "to inquire into social trends," which the Committee interpreted to mean, "to examine . . . recent social trends in the United States with a view to providing such a review as might supply a basis for the formulation of large national policies looking to the next phase in the nation's development." President Eisenhower's Commission on National Goals in 1960 had a similarly vague mandate.

Membership is usually bipartisan and has rarely been properly balanced. Where impartiality has been particularly sought, Commissions have often been over-weighted with persons from the academic world. Sometimes critics of the administration have been appointed in a clumsy effort to gain their support. Far too often, again, Commissions are characterized less by members willing to sacrifice time to the Commission's work than by those willing to accept the publicity of appointment in return for a minimum of effort.

Such memberships, as a consequence, tend to rely on their technical staffs to do most of the work, and the various studies by these staff members or consultants are published without any corporate responsibility. Rightly or wrongly, citizens have the feeling that the Commissioners just meet from time to time to frame their final and usually very general report—and the "bigger" the names of the Commissioners the stronger this impression. The President, moreover, has the right to keep the report secret if, for instance, its findings would be politically damaging to his administration.

Advisory bodies appointed in some collaborative effort of Congress and the President have probably been the most successful. Though too many of them are bipartisan in character, some have one or more independent members, for instance the Civil Rights Commission set up by the Civil Rights Act of 1957 to make recommendations in this field. The two Hoover Commissions on Organization of the Executive Branch of the Government have seen over half their recommendations implemented, and had the Commissions had more public attention there might be even more pressure to secure implementation of the rest.

It is these mixed Presidential-Congressional Commissions, then, that have most promise of development into American equivalents to the Royal Commission—if this mechanism were to be used in the United States.

Creation of American equivalent to the Royal Commission

There are several problems that must be overcome before this is possible, and the first and probably most serious relates to Congress. With the constitutional separation of powers between legislative and executive branches there is a built-in tension and rivalry between the two. Congress has the function of legislating, and to do that properly it must be informed on problems. And Congressmen are unable to rely on enough support in elections from their parties because of their loose structure; hence they take every possible chance to bring themselves to favorable public attention.

These facts of American political life form the basis for several attitudes of Congress. These attitudes need not follow, but as long as they persist they will be fatal to the development of any reasonable facsimile of the Royal Commission.

The first attitude is that Congress has the right, and need, to make its own investigations and that the best advice comes from its own members. The second is that unless any advisory body includes members of Congress its findings will probably be deficient or at least untrustworthy for legislative purposes. The third is that appointment by the President of advisory bodies on which Congress is not represented probably is an attempt to encroach on the legislative prerogative of Congress; that findings and recommendations by a genuinely impartial body somehow may impair Congressional responsibility for legislation—this last possibly inspired by some unspoken fear that their influence might be so great the public would demand implementation and Congress would then be just a rubber stamp. The fourth attitude is that investigations provide a legitimate (though never openly avowed) opportunity for building up individual Congressional reputations.

A second set of problems centers in the President. If Congress were willing to accept a Commission appointed by the President in place of one of its own investigating committees it would impose on the President a responsibility for understanding the nature of an effective advisory body and for meeting its standards. He must, first, use the device with discrimination, not too frequently and only on suitable occasions. It is no more possible to define a suitable occasion than to define due process. But there should be some element of controversy or uncertainty and a need for definitive findings on a subject of major importance—and a reasonable likelihood of action. The mechanism should never be used just to expose or punish wrong-doing.

The President must frame terms of reference that permit a sufficiently comprehensive inquiry but also call for recommendations specific enough to form the basis for legislative or administrative action. He must select members who are genuinely distinguished in intellect, sensibly balanced in their different perspectives, and willing to devote whatever time is necessary to make the Commission's findings *their* collaborative effort, not the work of a staff to which they merely lend their names. They must, in short, be able to inspire the confidence of citizens.

Any attempt by the President to use a Commission for political advantage, any attempt to slant its terms or to pack its members with biased or mediocre persons to secure a predesired end, would be fatal. An American President can never match the above-politics character of the British Monarch. But this does not mean that in creating a Commission he cannot subordinate partisanship to the standards of the structure, reserving exercise of his function as leader of his party to the disposition of the recommendations of the Commission. This is what a British Prime Minister does.

The President should also be willing to release on loan any administrative official or civil servant who would be capable of serving as the executive secretary of the Commission. If there is no one suitable from that source, he should be co-opted from among those already having an established position, so that the Commission does not have to hire someone who might benefit from prolonging the Commission.

Both the President and Congress should trust the discretion of the Commission as to the funds and time it needs, and not set limits on either. The Commission should report to the President and Congress co-equally (or to the President, who would in turn transmit to Congress), and, except for some situation clearly dangerous to the country's security, neither should be able to withhold a Commission's report from the public. Both these prescriptions apply also to any succeeding administration, which should not be able to dismiss or curtail the work of any already-existing Commission. A Commission, that is to say, for the length of its existence should be accorded a rank co-ordinate with the legislative, executive, and judicial branches of the government.

This is not to propose any constitutional changes. The act of creating the Commission and the right of final decision on implementation of any recommendations amply preserve the sovereignty of the legislative and executive branches. From this position of unchallenged supremacy Congress and the President could well afford to grant this temporary or acting equality to the Commission as an important element in its authority. If the President cannot be trusted to name competent persons of integrity to a Commission, he certainly cannot be trusted with the life-and-death powers he exercises, say

in military affairs. And if the best brains and balanced con-
sciences in the country cannot, as Commissioners, be trusted
not to squander time or money, who *could* be trusted?

The President should not ask Congress to give a Commission subpoena powers unless there is close to certainty that
information necessary for the Commission's work would not
be given except under compulsion. Commissions must rather
build up a prestige which will ensure voluntary co-operation.
Reliance on the genuine respect of blocs and public will also
help the Commission avoid any violation of due process.

A third set of problems centers in the public, the press, and
special-interest groups. The more understanding all three
have of the requirements for effective operation of a supreme
advisory body, the greater the likelihood of successful initia-
tion; and, once established, maintenance of its standards
should ensure its successful continuance.

It is on the President that the chief burden of initial education would rest. Citizens should give the first Commissions a
chance to prove the usefulness of the mechanism and not apply to them any sense of futility or disrespect engendered
from past experience with inadequately structured bodies.
The press should give maximum, nonpartisan coverage to the
hearings and reports of Commissions in news columns, and
should accept the responsibilities of segmental criticism in editorial columns.

There are two ways in which an American equivalent to
the Royal Commission might be created. Congress might pass
a single Enabling Act (something like the New York State
Moreland Act of 1909), which would permit the President to
set up a Commission at his discretion, to name its members,
and to frame its terms of reference. The Act would provide
funds for the operation of any Commission but would not
give it subpoena powers. These could be granted on request
of the President any time he was convinced a particular Commission needed them.

This method would oblige the President, as he ought in any event, to consult unofficially with Congressional leaders to avoid opposition to the creation, membership, or terms of any Commission.

A second possible method would involve creation of each Commission by Congressional statute. The Act would be initiated by Presidential request for a Commission. Again, the Act would provide funds but no subpoena powers unless specifically requested. The President would select the Commission members and frame their terms (again in informal consultation with Congressional and other leaders), and the Act would then include the terms but not necessarily the names. This method would oblige Congress to accede to Presidential request on the same presumptive basis that it presently accepts his choice of cabinet members. That is, it should approve except in the face of the very strongest opposition.

Neither single Enabling Act nor separate Act for each Commission should impose any restrictions on membership—for instance, that it be bipartisan or include members of Congress. Though the President might well include a senator or representative on any given Commission, his must be the responsibility for selecting the best persons regardless of source.

Neither method would remove Congressional right to create its own investigating committees, but where the President chose to create a Commission both methods would call for Congress to defer its own investigation at least until after the Commission reported. And both would require Congress to accord debate and serious attention to the Commission's findings. The fact that the findings would be entirely advisory and, even with Presidential endorsement if they secured it, would require Congressional approval for any legislative implementation would preserve the ultimate authority of Congress. Responsibility for creation, selection of members, and framing their terms of reference would, however, be centered in one person, the President, and criticism of any violations of standards could then home unerringly on him.

To mark out these Commissions, especially from the permanent executive or semi-judicial regulatory agencies, such as the Interstate Commerce Commission or the Federal Trade Commission, they should be given a distinguishing title, perhaps "The United States Commission on . . ." whatever the subject. The "United States" in the title should indicate acting equivalence in rank to the Senate, the House of Representatives, the President, or the Supreme Court of the United States.

It should be unnecessary to add one further requirement for the successful development of any American equivalent to the Royal Commission. All would be in vain if the national leadership, whether from inertia, intellectual incompetence, or inability to stand up to vested interests, were consistently to ignore its recommendations. The dismal record of disregard of the rare advisory groups that have really performed well is ominous. It may be that only some disaster can overcome this habit. But it would not seem unreasonable to regard the challenges that already face the country as sufficiently stimulating to muster the best possible attack. And not many improvements in problem-solving could match the development of an equivalent Royal Commission mechanism—if, then, its findings guide decision and action.

APPENDIX 1

Sample Royal Warrants of Appointment

The Royal Warrant of Appointment of the Royal Commission on Police Powers and Procedure:

George the Fifth, by the Grace of God, of Great Britain, Ireland and the British Dominions beyond the Seas King, Defender of the Faith, to

Our Right Trusty and Well-beloved Cousin and Counsellor Arthur Hamilton, Viscount Lee of Fareham, Knight Grand Commander of Our Most Exalted Order of the Star of India, Knight Grand Cross of Our Most Excellent Order of the British Empire, Knight Commander of Our Most Most Honourable Order of the Bath:

Our Right Trusty and Well-beloved George Rowland, Baron Ebbisham, Knight Grand Cross of Our Most Excellent Order of the British Empire;

Our Trusty and Well-beloved:—

Sir Howard George Frank, Baronet, Knight Grand Cross of Our Most Excellent Order of the British Empire, Knight Commander of Our Most Honourable Order of the Bath;

Dame Meriel Lucy Talbot, Dame Commander of Our Most Excellent Order of the British Empire;

Sir Reginald Ward Edward Lane Poole, Knight;

James Thomas Brownlie, Esquire, Commander of Our Most Excellent Order of the British Empire;

Margaret Beavan, Spinster, Lord Mayor of Liverpool; and

Frank Pick, Esquire;

Greeting!

Whereas We have deemed it expedient that a Commission should forthwith issue to consider the general powers and duties of police in England and Wales in the investigation of crimes and offences, including the functions of the Director of Public Prosecutions and the police respectively; to inquire into the practice followed in interrogating or taking statements from persons interviewed in the course of the investigation of crime; and to report whether, in their opinion, such powers and duties are properly exercised and discharged, with due regard to the rights and liberties of the subject, the interests of justice, and the observance of the Judges' Rules both in the letter and the spirit; and to make any recommendations necessary in respect of such powers and duties and their proper exercise and discharge:

Now know ye that We, reposing great trust and confidence in your knowledge and ability, have authorized and appointed, and do by these Presents authorise and appoint you, the said Arthur Hamilton, Viscount Lee of Fareham (Chairman); George Rowland, Baron Ebbisham; Sir Howard George Frank; Dame Meriel Lucy Talbot; Sir Reginald Ward Edward Lane Poole; James Thomas Brownlie; Margaret Beavan and Frank Pick to be Our Commissioners for the purposes of the said enquiry:

And for the better effecting the purposes of this Our Commission, We do by these Presents give and grant unto you, or any four or more of you, full power to call before you such persons as you shall judge likely to afford you any information upon the subject of this Our Commission; to call for information in writing; and also to call for, have access to and examine all such books, documents, registers and records as may afford you the fullest information on the subject, and to inquire of and concerning the premises by all other lawful ways and means whatsoever:

And We do by these Presents, authorise and empower you, or any of you, to visit and inspect personally such places as you may deem it expedient so to inspect for the more effectual carrying out of the purposes aforesaid:

And We do by these Presents will and ordain that this Our Commission shall continue in full force and virtue, and that you, Our said Commissioners, or any four or more of you, may from time to time proceed in the execution thereof, and of every matter and thing therein contained, although the same be not continued from time to time by adjournment:

And We do further ordain that you, or any four or more of you, have liberty to report your proceedings under this Our Commission from time to time if you shall judge it expedient so to do:

And Our further will and pleasure is that you do, with as little delay as possible, report to Us under your hands and seals, or under the hands and seals of any four or more of you, your opinion upon the matters herein submitted for your consideration.

Given at Our Court at Balmoral the twenty-second day of August, one thousand nine hundred and twenty-eight; in the Nineteenth Year of Our Reign.

By His Majesty's Command.
W. Joynson-Hicks.

The (Sankey) Coal Industry Commission is an illustration of a Royal Commission that also has a statutory origin. The Coal Industry Commission Act, 1919, reads: "Be it enacted . . . as follows: 1. His Majesty shall have power to appoint Commissioners, consisting of a chairman, who shall be a judge of the Supreme Court, a vice-chairman, and such other persons as His Majesty may think fit, for the purpose. . . ." There follow the terms of reference. The Act also gives the Commission the subpoena and other powers of a high court.

Then the Royal Warrant reads:

George the Fifth. . . . Greeting!

Whereas by an Act passed in the Ninth year of Our Reign . . . it is . . . enacted that We shall have power to appoint Commissioners for the purposes of the said Act. . . .

Now know ye that We, pursuant to the powers so vested in Us, have appointed, and do by these Presents, appoint you the said [there follow the names] to be Commissioners for the purposes of the said Act. . . .

APPENDIX 2

In the following list of all Royal Commissions appointed from 1900 to 1965, the date of appointment is the date of the Royal Warrant. The date of the final report is the date it was signed.[1] Though the list is in chronological order, when more than one Commission was appointed within a month they are listed alphabetically.

Occasionally the terms of reference or some of the members of a Commission are changed, and, technically, a new Commission is created—for instance that on British Horses, March 1906, continuing the original Commission of December 1887, or that on Defense of the Realm Losses, December 1918, continuing the original Commission of March 1915. The list does not include such "renewals" as separate or different Commissions unless (1) the Commission is the first one in the 20th century and is still in existence, as that on Historical Manuscripts, March 1919, continuing the Commission of December 1897 and the original Commission of April 1869; or (2) the "new" Commission has a different name, as that on Paper Supplies, June 1917, continuing the

[1] The reports of the Commissions on Motor Cars, 1906, on the St. Louis International Exhibition, 1906, on Electoral Systems, 1910, and on the International Exhibitions at Brussels, Rome, and Turin, 1913, are undated, and here the month reported is the month of issuance.

original Commission on Paper and Wood Pulp of February 1916.

The list does not include the Dardenelles and the Mesopotamia Commissions, 1916, or those on the Navigation Bill of Australia, 1904, on Old Age Pensions of Australia, 1905, and on the Meat Export Trade of Australia, 1914, all cited in the Cole and in the Clokie and Robinson lists (for which see below) as British Royal Commissions. The Dardanelles and Mesopotamia Commissions had no Royal Warrants, only statutory authority, and the last three were Australian Commissions, though their reports were printed as British Command Papers.

The sources of the list are these:

Original:

1. Parliamentary (or Sessional) Papers, House of Commons (London: H.M. Stationery Office). The Index, the last volume in each year's series of volumes, under subject title, shows in what volume for that year the report of a Royal Commission which has reported in that year, can be found. Each such report includes the Royal Warrant (which itself gives the date of appointment, the members, and the terms of reference) and the report itself, with the members signing and the date of signing.

Volume LXXIX of 1904 contains a Parliamentary Return showing the Royal Commissions appointed each year 1896-1903 inclusive. Volume LI of 1913 contains a Return showing the Commissions appointed each year 1904-11 inclusive. For the period 1914-16, see Vol. LV, Cd. 7855. For 1916, see Vol. XXIII, Cd. 8256. For 1917-18 see Vol. XXXVIII, Cd. 8741 & 8916.

For Royal Commissions appointed after 1917, see the *Consolidated List of Government Publications,* which is issued annually. Each List gives the title of each Royal Commission issuing a report in that year. Later lists also give the year of appointment. *Sectional List* 59 lists Royal Commissions from 1936.

2. *The London Gazette* (London: H.M. Stationery Office), under "State Intelligence," gives the Royal Warrant of Appointment for each Royal Commission when it is issued.

Secondary:

1. *A Finding List of British Royal Commission Reports 1860 to 1935* (Cambridge, Mass.: Harvard University Press, 1939). Prepared under the direction of A. H. Cole. The Commissions are listed in chronological order within problem areas.

2. H. M. Clokie and J. W. Robinson, *Royal Commissions of Inquiry* (Stanford: Stanford University Press, 1937). This volume lists Commissions from 1800 through 1936.

3. P. and G. Ford, *A Breviate of Parliamentary Papers, 1900-1916* (Basil Blackwell: Oxford, 1957); idem., *A Breviate of Parliamentary Papers, 1917-1939* (Basil Blackwell: Oxford, 1951); idem., *A Breviate of Parliamentary Papers, 1940-1954* (Basil Blackwell: Oxford, 1961). These volumes give, for the Commissions in the period covered, the date the Commission was appointed; the dates of reports; last names of the members signing the reports; and summary of conclusions of the reports. The Commissions are classified by problem areas.

4. *Catalogue of Parliamentary Papers, 1801-1900; 1901-1910; 1911-1920.* These are all published by P. S. King, London, no dates; they list the reports of Commissions with indication of contents. The reports are classified by subject title.

5. Whitaker's *Almanac,* London, annual. This now lists new Royal Commissions, giving title, date of appointment, terms of reference, and names of members.

6. The London *Times.*

Royal Commissions, 1900-1964

Appointed	Final report	Royal Commission on
Mar. 1900	July 1902	Salmon Fisheries
June 1900	June 1902	The Port of London (Administration)
July 1900	Jan. 1901	South African Hospitals (care of sick and wounded in South African campaign)
Feb. 1901	Nov. 1903	Arsenical Poisoning
July 1901	Feb. 1903	University Education in Ireland
Aug. 1901	June 1911	Tuberculosis (human and bovine)
Dec. 1901	Jan. 1905	Coal Supplies
Mar. 1902	Aug. 1903	Alien Immigration
Mar. 1902	Mar. 1903	Physical Training (Scotland)
Aug. 1902	Oct. 1902	Martial Law Sentences in South Africa
Sept. 1902	July 1903	The War in South Africa
Nov. 1902	Aug. 1903	Superannuation in the Civil Service
Feb. 1903	June 1905	London Traffic
Apr. 1903	May 1904	The Militia and Volunteers
Apr. 1903	? 1906	The St. Louis International Exhibition for 1904 [1]
Apr. 1903	Aug. 1905	Supply of Food & Raw Material in Time of War
June 1903	Jan. 1906	Trade Disputes and Trade Combinations
Apr. 1904	June 1906	Ecclesiastical Discipline
Sept. 1904	July 1908	Care and Control of the Feeble Minded
Dec. 1904	Apr. 1905	Churches (Scotland)
June 1905	July 1906	War Stores in South Africa
Aug. 1905	Dec. 1909	Allocation of Property between the Free Church & the United Free Church under the Churches (Scotland) Act, 1905 [1]
Sept. 1905	July 1906	Motor Cars
Dec. 1905	Oct. 1909	Poor Laws and Relief of Distress

[1] An operating Commission. The Allocation of Property Commission also had statutory authority. Incidentally, the Act provided there could be no appeal to the courts from the decisions of the Commission.

Appointed	Final report	Royal Commission on
Mar. 1906	Dec. 1909	Canals & Inland Navigation of United Kingdom
May 1906	June 1908	Duties of the Metropolitan Police
May 1906	July 1910	Registration of Title in Scotland
June 1906	Nov. 1910	Church of England & Other Religious Bodies in Wales & Monmouthshire
June 1906	Feb. 1911	Mines (Inquiry into questions relating to health & safety of miners & administration of mine acts)
June 1906	Jan. 1907	Trinity College, Dublin, & the University of Dublin
July 1906	May 1911	Coast Erosion and Afforestation
July 1906	May 1908	Congestion in Ireland
July 1906	Nov. 1906	Worcester Election (Inquiry into the existence of corrupt practices)
Aug. 1906	Jan. 1908	Lighthouse Administration
Sept. 1906	Mar. 1912	Vivisection
Nov. 1906	May 1909	Shipping "Rings"
Sept. 1907	Feb. 1909	Decentralization in India
Feb. 1908	1909ff.	Ancient & Historical Monuments & Constructions of Scotland [2]
Feb. 1908	July 1909	Whiskey and Other Potable Spirits
July 1908	Jan. 1911	The Land Transfer Acts
Aug. 1908	1909ff.	Ancient & Historical Monuments & Constructions of Wales & Monmouthshire[2]
Oct. 1908	1909ff.	Ancient & Historical Monuments & Constructions of England [2]
Dec. 1908	May 1910	Electoral Systems
Feb. 1909	Mar. 1913	University Education in London
Mar. 1909	Mar. 1913	The International Exhibitions at Brussels, Rome, & Turin, 1910 & 1911 [3]
May 1909	Apr. 1910	Mauritius
Aug. 1909	Aug. 1910	Trade Relations between Canada & West Indies
Nov. 1909	Nov. 1912	Divorce and Matrimonial Causes
Nov. 1909	July 1910	Selection of Justices of the Peace

[2] A semi-permanent Commission.
[3] An operating Commission.

Appointed	Final report	Royal Commission on
May 1910	June 1914	Metalliferous Mines & Quarries (health and safety of persons employed)
Oct. 1910	Apr. 1918	Public Records
Aug. 1911	Apr. 1912	Malta
Aug. 1911	Oct. 1911	The Railway Conciliation Scheme of 1907
Mar. 1912	Nov. 1915	Civil Service
Apr. 1912	Feb. 1917	The Natural Resources, Trade, & Legislation of Certain Portions of H.M. Dominions
Aug. 1912	Aug. 1915	Public Services in India
Oct. 1912	Sept. 1917	Housing in Scotland
Dec. 1912	Nov. 1913	Delay in the King's Bench Division
Apr. 1913	Feb. 1914	Indian Finance and Currency
Nov. 1913	Feb. 1916	Venereal Diseases
Aug. 1914	Sept. 1914	The Circumstances Connected with the Landing of Arms at Howth, July 26, 1914
Aug. 1914	Apr. 1921	Sugar Supply[4]
Mar. 1915	Nov. 1920	Defense of the Realm Losses[4]
Feb. 1916	(no R.publ.)	Paper and Wood Pulp[4]
Apr. 1916	Feb. 1918	University Education in Wales
May 1916	June 1916	The Rebellion in Ireland
Aug. 1916	Sept. 1916	The Arrest and . . . treatment of S. Skeffington, Thomas Dickson, and J. P. McIntyre
Oct. 1916	July 1925	Wheat Supplies[4]
Nov. 1916	Mar. 1917	The Allegations against Sir John Jackson, Ltd. (public works contractors)
June 1917	(no data avail.)	Paper Supplies[4]
Feb. 1918	Apr. 1918	Proportional Representation[5]
Aug. 1918	Feb. 1920	Decimal Coinage

[4] An operating Commission, administrative or judicial.
[5] Also had statutory authority.

Appointed	Final report	Royal Commission on
Feb. 1919	June 1919	The Coal Industry Commission[5]
Mar. 1919	Oct. 1937	Awards to Inventors[4]
Mar. 1919	1926ff.	Historical Manuscripts[6]
Apr. 1919	Mar. 1920	Income Tax
July 1919	Dec. 1919	The Economic Prospects of the Agricultural Industry in Great Britain
Nov. 1919	Mar. 1922	Oxford and Cambridge Universities
Mar. 1920	Nov. 1920	The University of Dublin (Trinity College)
Jan. 1921	July 1923	Fire Brigades and Fire Prevention
May 1921	Aug. 1921	The Importation of Store Cattle
Aug. 1921	Feb. 1924	Compensation for Suffering & Damage by Enemy Action[4]
Oct. 1921	Feb. 1923	Local Government of Greater London
Sept. 1922	Dec. 1922	Honours
Feb. 1923	Nov. 1929	Local Government
June 1923	June 1927	Mining Subsidence
June 1923	Mar. 1924	Superior Civil Services in India
May 1924	1924ff.	Fine Art [7]
July 1924	July 1926	Lunacy and Mental Disorder
July 1924	Feb. 1926	National Health Insurance
Nov. 1924	Apr. 1925	Food Prices
Aug. 1925	July 1926	Indian Currency and Finance
Sept. 1925	Mar. 1926	The Coal Industry
Jan. 1926	Jan. 1927	Court of Session (Scotland)
Apr. 1926	Apr. 1928	Agriculture in India
July 1926	Nov. 1926	Cross-River Traffic in London
Mar. 1927	Dec. 1927	Land Drainage in England and Wales
July 1927	Jan. 1930	National Museums and Art Galleries
Aug. 1927	1960ff.	Fine Art for Scotland [7]

[6] A semi-permanent Commission—in continuous existence since 1869.

[7] A semi-permanent Commission; technically called the Royal Fine Art Commission and the Royal Fine Art Commission for Scotland.

Appointed	Final report	Royal Commission on
Aug. 1927	Sept. 1928	London Squares
Nov. 1927	May 1930	The Indian Statutory Commission[8]
Aug. 1928	Mar. 1929	Police Powers and Procedure
Aug. 1928	Dec. 1930	Transport
July 1929	Mar. 1931	Labour in India
Sept. 1929	Dec. 1931	Licensing (England and Wales)
Oct. 1929	July 1931	Civil Service
Oct. 1929	May 1931	Licensing (Scotland)
Dec. 1930	Oct. 1932	Unemployment Insurance
Apr. 1931	Jan. 1932	Malta
June 1932	June 1933	Lotteries and Betting
Feb. 1933	Oct. 1933	Newfoundland
Mar. 1934	Jan. 1935	The University of Durham
Aug. 1934	Nov. 1935	Tithe Rentcharge in England and Wales
Dec. 1934	Jan. 1936	The Despatch of Business at Common Law
Feb. 1935	Sept. 1936	Private Manufacture of & Trading in Arms
May 1935	Feb. 1937	Local Government in the Tyneside Area
May 1935	Nov. 1935	Merthyr Tydfil
Dec. 1935	Dec. 1938	Safety in Coal Mines
Aug. 1936	June 1937	Palestine
July 1937	Dec. 1939	The Distribution of the Industrial Population
Mar. 1938	Mar. 1939	Rhodesia-Nyasaland
Aug. 1938	Dec. 1939	West India
Dec. 1938	Dec. 1944	Workmen's Compensation
Mar. 1944	Mar. 1949	Population
Oct. 1944	Oct. 1946	Equal Pay
May 1946	Apr. 1956	Awards to Inventors[9]
June 1946	May 1948	Justices of the Peace
Apr. 1947	June 1949	The Press

[8] Also had statutory authority.

[9] An operating Commission.

Appointed	Final report	Royal Commission on
Apr. 1949	Mar. 1951	Betting, Lotteries, and Gaming
May 1949	Sept. 1953	Capital Punishment
Jan. 1951	May 1955	Taxation of Profits and Income
May 1951	Apr. 1952	University Education in Dundee
Sept. 1951	Dec. 1955	Marriage and Divorce
July 1952	July 1954	Scottish Affairs
Jan. 1953	May 1955	East Africa
Nov. 1953	Nov. 1955	Civil Service
Feb. 1954	May 1957	The Law Relating to Mental Illness and Mental Deficiency
Dec. 1955	July 1958	Common Land
Mar. 1957	Feb. 1960	Doctors' and Dentists' Remuneration
Dec. 1957	Oct. 1960	Local Government in Greater London
Jan. 1960	May 1962	The Police
Mar. 1961	Sept. 1962	The Press
Aug. 1964	———	The Penal System in England and Wales

Royal Commissions 1900-1964
by type of problem handled

App't.	Composition	Number signing	Report[1]	Title
		GOVERNMENTAL PROBLEMS		
1902	Impartial	9	M-M	Superannuation in the Civil Service
1906	Impartial	4	Un	Duties of the Metropolitan Police
1906	Expert	8	Split	Registration of Title in Scotland
1906	Expert	3	Un	Worcester Election
1908	Impartial	8	Un-R	Electoral Systems
1909	Impartial	16	Un-R	Selection of Justices of Peace

[1] Un: Unanimous; Un-R: Unanimous but with some Reservations or Dissents, major or minor; M-M: Divided into Majority-

App't.	Composition	Number signing	Report[1]	Title
1910	Expert	9	Un	Public Records
1912	Impartial	19	M-M	Civil Service
1912	Impartial	11	Un-R	Delay in King's Bench Division
1914	Impartial	3	Un	Circumstances Connected with Landing of Arms at Howth, July 26, 1914
1916	Impartial	3	Un	Rebellion in Ireland
1916	Expert	3	Un	Arrest & . . . Treatment of S. Skeffington, Thomas Dickinson, & P. J. McIntyre
1918	Expert	5	Un	Proportional Representation
1921	Expert	14	Un-R	Fire Brigades and Fire Protection
1921	Impartial	8	Split	Local Government in Greater London
1922	Impartial	7	M-M	Honours
1923	Representative	11	Un	Local Government
1926	Expert	9	Un-R	Court of Session (Scotland)
1928	Impartial	8	Un	Police Powers and Procedure
1929	Impartial	16	Un	Civil Service
1934	Expert	7	Un-R	Despatch of Business at Common Law
1935	Impartial	5	M-M	Local Government in Tyneside Area
1935	Impartial	2	Un	Merthyr Tydfil
1946	Impartial	15	M-M	Justices of the Peace
1952	Impartial	15	Un	Scottish Affairs
1953	Impartial	12	Un-R	Civil Service
1957	Expert	7	Un	Local Government in Greater London
1960	Impartial	14	M-M	Police
1964	Impartial	16[2]	—	Penal System in England & Wales

Minority Reports; Split: Divided into three or more reports; (Op.):
An operating Commission.

[2] This is the number originally appointed.

App't.	Composition	Number signing	Report[1]	Title
		SOCIAL PROBLEMS		
1902	Impartial	7	Un-R	Alien Immigration
1904	Representative	14	Un	Ecclesiastical Discipline
1904	Impartial	3	Un	Churches (Scotland)
1905	Impartial	4	(Op.)	Allocation of Property between Free Church & United Free Church under the Churches (Scotland) Act 1905
1906	Impartial	9	Split	Church of England & Other Religious Bodies in Wales and Monmouthshire
1909	Representative	12	M-M	Divorce & Matrimonial Causes
1929	Representative	19	Split	Licensing (England & Wales)
1929	Representative	14	M-M	Licensing (Scotland)
1932	Impartial	12	Un	Lotteries and Betting
1944	Impartial	14	Un-R	Population
1947	Impartial	15	Un-R	Press
1949	Impartial	12	Un	Betting, Lotteries & Gaming
1949	Impartial	11	Un-R	Capital Punishment
1951	Impartial	19	Split	Marriage & Divorce
1961	Impartial	5	Un	Press
		ECONOMIC PROBLEMS		
1900	Expert	8	Un	Salmon Fisheries
1901	Representative	15	Un	Coal Supplies
1903	Expert	5	M-M	Trade Disputes & Trade Combinations
1905	Impartial	18	M-M	Poor Laws & Relief of Distress
1906	Impartial	15	Un-R	Coast Erosion & Afforestation
1908	Expert	8	Un	Whiskey & Other Potable Spirits
1908	Expert	10	Un	Land Transfer Acts
1911	Representative	5	Un	Railway Conciliation Scheme of 1907
1918	Representative	20	Split	Decimal Coinage

App't.	Composition	Number signing	Report[1]	Title
1919	Representative	13	Split	The Coal Industry Commission
1919	Expert	6	(Op.)	Awards to Inventors
1919	Representative	22	Un-R	Income Tax
1919	Representative	23	M-M	Economic Prospects of Agricultural Industry in Great Britain
1921	Impartial	5	Un	Importation of Store Cattle
1923	Expert	13	Un	Mining Subsidence
1924	Expert	16	Split	Food Prices
1925	Impartial	4	Un	Coal Industry
1930	Impartial	7	M-M	Unemployment Insurance
1934	Expert	4	M-M	Tithe Rentcharge in England & Wales
1935	Impartial	7	Un	Private Manufacture of & Trading in Arms
1938	Impartial	15	—	Workmen's Compensation (Never really functioned)
1944	Impartial	9	Un-R	Equal Pay
1946	Expert	8	(Op.)	Awards to Inventors
1951	Representative	13	M-M	Taxation of Profits & Income
1957	Impartial	9	Un-R	Doctors' & Dentists' Remuneration

HEALTH

App't.	Composition	Number signing	Report[1]	Title
1901	Expert	6	Un-R	Arsenical Poisoning
1901	Expert	5	Un	Tuberculosis
1904	Impartial	12	Un-R	Care & Control of Feeble Minded
1906	Expert	8	Un-R	Mines (Health & Safety of Persons)
1906	Representative	8	Un-R	Vivisection
1910	Expert	9	Un-R	Metalliferous Mines & Quarries (Health, etc.)
1913	Impartial	15	Un-R	Venereal Diseases
1924	Impartial	10	Un-R	Lunacy & Mental Disorder
1924	Impartial	13	M-M	National Health Insurance
1935	Expert	10	Un-R	Safety in Coal Mines
1954	Impartial	10	Un	Law Relating to Mental Illness & Deficiency

App't.	Composition	Number signing	Report[1]	Title
			EDUCATION	
1901	Expert	11	Un-R	University Education in Ireland
1902	Impartial	9	Un	Physical Training (Scotland)
1906	Expert	9	Split	Trinity College, Dublin, & Univ. of Dublin
1909	Expert	8	Un	University Education in London
1916	Expert	9	Un	University Education in Wales
1919	Expert	23	Un-R	Oxford & Cambridge Universities
1920	Expert	5	Un	University of Dublin (Trinity College)
1934	Expert	8	Un	University of Durham
1951	Expert	9	Un	University Education in Dundee
			DOMINION AND COLONIAL	
1907	Expert	6	Un-R	Decentralization in India
1909	Impartial	3	Un-R	Mauritius
1909	Representative	5	Un	Trade Relations between Canada & West Indies
1911	Impartial	3	Un	Malta
1912	Representative	10	Un	Natural Resources, Trade, & Legislation of Certain Portions of H.M. Dominions
1912	Impartial	11	M-M	Public Services in India
1913	Expert	10	Un-R	Indian Finance & Currency
1923	Impartial	9	Un	Superior Civil Services in India
1925	Expert	10	Un-R	Indian Currency & Finance
1926	Expert	9	Un	Agriculture in India
1927	Impartial	7	Un	Indian Statutory Commission
1929	Representative	11	Un-R	Labour in India
1931	Impartial	3	Un	Malta
1933	Representative	3	Un	Newfoundland

App't.	Composition	Number signing	Report[1]	Title
1936	Expert	6	Un	Palestine
1938	Impartial	6	Un-R	Rhodesia-Nyasaland
1938	Impartial	8	Un	West India
1953	Expert	8	Un	East Africa

CITY PLANNING, TRANSPORTATION, HOUSING

1900	Impartial	7	Un	Port of London
1903	Representative	12	M-M	London Traffic
1905	Impartial	7	Un-R	Motor Cars
1906	Representative	19	Split	Canals & Inland Navigation of U.K.
1906	Impartial	9	Un-R	Congestion in Ireland
1906	Impartial	5	Un-R	Lighthouse Administration
1906	Representative	16	M-M	Shipping "Rings"
1912	Impartial	12	M-M	Housing in Scotland
1926	Expert	6	Un	Cross-River Traffic in London
1927	Impartial	11	Un	Land Drainage in England & Wales
1927	Impartial	14	Un-R	London Squares
1928	Impartial	12	Un-R	Transport
1937	Impartial	13	M-M	Distribution of Industrial Population
1955	Expert	12	Un	Common Land

MILITARY

1900	Impartial	5	Un	South African Hospitals
1902	Expert	3	Un	Martial Law Sentences in South Africa
1902	Impartial	9	Un	War in South Africa
1903	Expert	11	Split	Militia & Volunteers
1903	Representative	17	Un-R	Supply of Food & Raw Material in Time of War
1905	Impartial	5	Un	War Stores in South Africa
1914	Expert	6	(Op.)	Sugar Supply
1915	Impartial	3	(Op.)	Defense of the Realm Losses
1916	Expert	11	(Op.)	Paper & Wood Pulp
1916	Expert	5	(Op.)	Wheat Supplies
1916	Impartial	3	Un	Allegations against Sir John Jackson, Ltd.

App't.	Composition	Number signing	Report[1]	Title
1917	Expert	11	(Op.)	Paper Supplies
1921	Expert	3	(Op.)	Compensation for Suffering & Damage by Enemy Action

ART, MONUMENTS, AND EXHIBITIONS

1903	Representative	36	(Op.)	St. Louis International Exhibition for 1904
1908	Expert	(Semi-Permanent)		Ancient Monuments etc., Scotland
1908	Expert	(Semi-Permanent)		Ancient Monuments etc., Wales & Monmouthshire
1908	Expert	(Semi-Permanent)		Ancient Monuments etc., England
1909	Representative	53	(Op.)	International Exhibitions at Brussels, Rome, & Turin, 1910 & 1911
1919	Expert	(Semi-Permanent)		Historical Manuscripts
1924	Expert	(Semi-Permanent)		Fine Art
1927	Expert	(Semi-Permanent)		Fine Art for Scotland
1927	Expert	11	Un	National Museums & Art Galleries

Governments and Prime Ministers, 1900-1964

Government	Largest party	Elected	Prime Minister, Party, Date
Conservative	Conservative	Oct. 1900	Salisbury, Conservative[1] Balfour, Conservative, July 1902
Liberal	Liberal	Jan. 1906	Campbell-Bannerman, Liberal Asquith, Liberal, April 1908
Liberal (Minority)	Liberal	Jan. 1910	Asquith

[1] The Conservative Salisbury Government came into power in 1895.

Government	Largest party	Elected	Prime Minister, Party, Date
Coalition	Liberal		Asquith, May 1915 Lloyd George, Liberal, Dec. 1916
Coalition	Conservative	Dec. 1918	Lloyd George
Conservative	Conservative	Nov. 1922	Bonar Law, Conservative Stanley Baldwin, Conservative, May 1923
Labour (Minority)	Conservative	Dec. 1923	MacDonald, Labour
Conservative	Conservative	Oct. 1924	Baldwin, Conservative
Labour (Minority)	Labour	May 1929	MacDonald, Labour
National	Conservative	Oct. 1931	MacDonald Baldwin, Conservative, June 1935
Conservative	Conservative	Nov. 1935	Baldwin Chamberlain, Conservative, May 1937
Coalition	Conservative		Churchill, Conservative, May 1940
Coalition (Without Labour)	Conservative		Churchill, May 1945
Labour	Labour	July 1945	Attlee, Labour
Labour	Labour	Feb. 1950	Attlee
Conservative	Conservative	Oct. 1951	Churchill, Conservative
Conservative	Conservative	May 1955	Eden, Conservative Macmillan, Conservative, Jan. 1957
Conservative	Conservative	Oct. 1959	Macmillan Douglas-Home, Conservative, Oct. 1963
Labour	Labour	Oct. 1964	Wilson, Labour

APPENDIX 3

Social, educational, and occupational backgrounds of members of every sixth Royal Commission, 1900-1964

TABLE 1

Number of members, with mean ages, of every sixth Royal Commission, 1900-1964

App't.	Royal Commission on	Total no. of members[1]	No. age not avail.	Mean age at app't.	Problem area	Type
1901	Tuberculosis	6		49	Health	Exp
1902	Superannuation, Civ. Serv.	9	1	60	Gov't.	Imp
1904	Ecclesiastical Discipline	15		59	Social	Rep
1905	Poor Laws, etc.	20	2	54	Econ.	Imp
1906	Trinity College, etc.	9	1	58	Educ.	Exp
1906	Shipping "Rings"	20	2	54	Transpt.	Rep
1908	Monu., etc. of England	11	1	55	Art	Exp
1909	Divorce, etc.	15	1	55	Social	Rep
1912	Civil Service	27	2	52	Gov't.	Imp
1913	Venereal Diseases	15	1	62	Health	Imp
1916	Rebellion in Ireland	3		62	Gov't.	Imp
1918	Decimal Coinage	22	3	57	Econ.	Rep
1919	Oxford & Cambridge	24	1	56	Educ.	Exp
1922	Honours	7		56	Gov't.	Imp
1924	National Health Insurance	14	2	54	Health	Imp
1926	Cross-River Traffic	6		57	City Plan	Exp
1928	Police Powers & Procedure	8	1	59	Gov't.	Imp
1930	Unemployment Insurance	7	1	50	Econ.	Imp
1934	Dispatch Bus. at Com. Law	7		57	Gov't.	Exp
1937	Distb. of Indus. Population	14	2	57	City Plan	Imp

Appt.	Royal Commission on	Total no. of members[1]	No. age not avail.	Mean age at app't.	Problem area	Type
1946	Awards to Inventors	8		62	Econ.	Exp
1951	Univ. Education, Dundee	9	2	57	Educ.	Exp
1955	Common Land	12	6	57	City Plan	Exp
	Total	288	29			
	Mean	12.5		56		

[1] The total number of members noted for each Commission includes all those who served on it—original members, even though they may not have signed the report because of death or resignation, and later additions. The one exception is the Commission on Ancient and Historical Monuments and Constructions of England. Here the members noted are only the original ones, since this is a semipermanent Commission in operation to the present day.

Of the total of 288 Commissioners, there are 11 who served on two Commissions, so the total number of different persons is 277.

Of the 277 Commissioners, 21 (or 7.6%) were women: 3—Poor Laws 1905; 2—Divorce 1909; 2—Civil Service 1912; 3—Venereal Diseases 1913; 2—Oxford and Cambridge 1919; 2—Health Insurance 1924; 2—Police Powers 1928; 1—Unemployment Insurance 1930; 2—Distribution of Industrial Population 1937; 1—University Education, Dundee 1951; 1—Common Land 1955.

The sources of the following material were *Who's Who* and *Who Was Who,* published by Charles Black, London, and the *Dictionary of National Biography,* published by Oxford University Press. These were supplemented by Dod's *Parliamentary Companion,* now published by Business Dictionaries, London; Whitaker's *Peerage, Baronetage, Knightage and Companionage,* London; the London *Times;* and individual biographies.

TABLE 2

Occupation of father of members of every sixth
Royal Commission, 1900-1964

Occupational field of father	Number
Church	36
Business (incl. banking, manufacturing, trade, etc.)	24
Peerage (i.e. no other occupation available)	15[1]
Law (judges, barristers, solicitors, etc.)	14
Labor (incl. farm & factory workers, mechanics, etc.)	11
Engineering (8), Architecture (1), & Surveying (1)	10

Occupational field of father	Number
Government (elected, appointed, or civil service)	8
Medicine	8
Baronetage (i.e. no other occupation available)	6[1]
Agriculture & land-owning	4
Military	4
Journalism and Publishing	3
Natural Science	3
Miscellaneous (Accountant 1; Manager, Widow's Fund 1; Museum official 1; Stores Superintendent 1)	4
Total	150
Father's Occupation Not Available	127[2]
Total	277

[1] In addition to these 21 there was one Commissioner whose mother was a Peer, and two who had uncles who were Peers, whom they succeeded.

[2] It is assumed that where the father's status was not given in the *Who's Who* sketches or was not otherwise available, (1) the father was not in the aristocracy; nor (2) in the professions, his own business, or the government except perhaps on a lower level in the civil service; and (3) probably came from a lower-middle- or working-class occupation.

TABLE 3

Secondary education of members of every sixth Royal Commission, 1900-1964

Place of education	Number
Ranking Public Schools (Eton 20; Harrow 16; Winchester 7; Charterhouse 6; Marlborough 6; Rugby 5; Shrewsbury 3; Haileybury 2)	65
Other Public Schools in Headmasters' Conference	47
Other Non-State Schools	59
State and Municipal Schools	17
Privately (17) and Abroad (1)	18
	206
Not Available	71[1]
Total	277

[1] Where secondary education was not listed in *Who's Who* sketches or was otherwise not available, it is assumed the Commissioner did not attend a public school in the Headmaster's Conference.

TABLE 4

*Collegiate education of members of every sixth
Royal Commission, 1900-1964*

Place of education	Number
Oxford	61
Cambridge	56
Other United Kingdom College	49
Abroad	12
Technical, Professional, or Military Schools	11
Privately	4
None	39
	232
Not Available	45[1]
Total	277

[1] Where place of collegiate education not given or available it is assumed the Commissioner did not attend Oxford or Cambridge and had scattered collegiate training elsewhere or none at all.

TABLE 5

*Primary occupation of members of every sixth
Royal Commission, 1900-1964*

Primary occupation or chief field of interest	Number
Government (Civil Service 28; Elected National 14; Appointed National 13; Local 7)	62
Business (incl. banking, industry, etc.)	41[1]
Law (judges, barristers, solicitors, other law officers)	39[1]
Social Science (scholars, writers, administrators, incl. 3 city planners—all mostly from universities)	36
Natural Science (scientists, teachers, etc., all mostly from universities)	20
Labor and Unions	17[2]
Church (ministers and priests)	12
Social Work	12
Architecture and Engineering (incl. 4 Surveyors)	11
Medicine (practicing physicians)	6
Agriculture (land agents and 1 landowner)	4
Journalism (3) and Publishing (1)	4

Primary occupation or chief field of interest	Number
Art and Antiquary	2
Military	1
	267
Not Available	10
Total	277

[1] Of these, 12 also served in Parliament, some over twenty years.
[2] Of these, ten also served in Parliament.

Comparative background of Royal Commissioners, Parliamentarians,
Cabinet Ministers and Civil Servants

	Royal Commissioners (1900-1964)	Members of Parliament	Cabinet Ministers	Civil Servants (adm. class)
SOCIAL ORIGINS				
Aristocratic	10%	13% (1918-35)[3] 8% (1945)[4]	23% (1918-35)[3] 31% (1902-35)[3] 38% (1906-24)[5]	37% (1851-1929)[1] for For. Office & Dipl. Serv.

FATHER'S OCCUPATION

Royal Commissioners:

Church	36	(13%)
Other Profs.	38	(14%)
Business	24	(9%)
Peers & Brts.	21	(8%)
Gov't. & Mil.	12	(4%)
Labor	11	(4%)
Misc.	8	(3%)
Not Available	127	(45%)
	277	(100%)

Cabinet Ministers 1801-1924[5]:

Nobility	182	(59%)
Business	36	(12%)
Other Profs.	24	(8%)
Rentiers	23	(8%)
Clergymen	20	(6%)
Workingmen	12	(4%)
Misc.	9	(3%)
	306	(100%)

Civil Servants:

	1929[2]		1950[2]	
Business	30	(25%)	73	(22%)
Oth. Profs.	26	(21%)	68	(20%)
Church	17	(14%)	32	(10%)
Civil Serv.	10	(8%)	35	(11%)
Gentry & Ind. Inc.	10	(8%)	10	(3%)
Labor	8	(7%)	55	(17%)
Misc.	20	(17%)	58	(17%)
	121	(100%)	331	(100%)

SECONDARY EDUCATION

	Royal Commissioners	Members of Parliament	Cabinet Ministers	Civil Servants
Public Schools: 40% 8 Top Public Schools: 23%		43% (1918-36)[6] 45% (1945)[4]	49% (1906-24)[5]	74% (1905-14)[7] 62% (1925-37)[7] 63% (1938)[8] 33% (1938)—9 top P.S.[8] 48% (1939)[9] 25% (1939)—10 top P.S.[9] 48% (1950)[2]

COLLEGIATE EDUCATION

	Royal Commissioners	Members of Parliament	Cabinet Ministers	Civil Servants
Oxford or Cambridge: 42%		29% (1918-36)[6] 28% (1945)[4]	61% (1906-24)[5]	88% (1931-36)[8] 69% (1939)[9] 47% (1950)[2]

Royal Commissioners (1900-1964)		Members of Parliament	Cabinet Ministers		Civil Servants (adm. class)
OCCUPATION			1801-1924[5]		
Government	23%	1918-36[6]	Rentiers	70%	
Universities	21%	Lawyers 23%	Lawyers	13.7%	
Business	15%	Company Dir. 23%	Business	7.5%	
Lawyers	14%	Tr. Unionists 13%	Men of Letters		
Other Profs.	8%	Other 41%	& Journalists	3%	
Trade Unions	6%		Trade Unions	2.6%	
Church	5%	1945 Election[4]	Soldiers & Sailors	2.6%	
Social Work	5%	Profs. 53.5%	Civil Servants	1%	
Other	3%	Workers 27.0%			
	100%	Emplrs. & Mgrs. 17.5%			
		Unocc. 2.0%	1916-35[3]		
(Not Available: 10 of 277)		(incl. 1 hswife.)	Lawyers & Prof.	44%	
			Rentiers &		
			Landowners	26%	
			Trade U. Officials	13%	
			Commerce & Ind.	11%	
			Other	6%	

[1] Robert T. Nightingale, "The Personnel of the British Foreign Office and Diplomatic Service, 1851-1929," *American Political Science Review*, May 1930, pp. 316, 319.

[2] R. K. Kelsall, *Higher Civil Servants in Britain* (London: Routledge and Kegan Paul, 1955), pp. 150-51, 125, 119, 137.

[3] W. L. Guttsman, "The Changing Social Structure of the British Political Elite, 1886-1935," *British Journal of Sociology*, June 1951, pp. 126, 125, and 131.

[4] Donald R. Matthews, *The Social Background of Political Decision-Makers* (Garden City, N.Y.: Doubleday, 1954), p. 46.

[5] Harold J. Laski, "The Personnel of the English Cabinet, 1801-1924," *American Political Science Review*, Feb. 1928, pp. 19-24, and 14-15.

[6] J. F. S. Ross, *Parliamentary Representation* (London: Eyre and Spottiswoode, 1948), pp. 43, 52, and 77.

[7] Herman Finer, *Governments of Greater European Powers* (New York: Henry Holt, 1956), p. 232.

[8] J. Donald Kingsley, *Representative Bureaucracy* (Yellow Springs, Ohio: Antioch Press, 1944), pp. 150-51, 149.

APPENDIX 4

List of Royal Commissions 1900-1964
having divided reports

Title	Remarks
GOVERNMENTAL PROBLEMS	
Superannuation in Civil Service, 1902	7 to 2, minority more "conservative," feeling no changes were needed
Registration of Title, Scotland, 1906	Split 3-2-2-1, technical differences on how to keep ownership records
Civil Service, 1912 (4th report)	16 to 3, minority more conservative
Local Government of Greater London, 1921	Split 4-2-2, minorities more "radical" in giving more comprehensive analysis and advocating more sweeping changes
Honours, 1922	6 to 1, minority more radical in recommending abolition of State honors for political (i.e. party) services
Local Government in Tyneside Area, 1935	4 to 1, technical differences on how best to administer the area
Justices of the Peace, 1946	14 (3 with more radical Memo of Dissent) to 1, minority advocating replacement of lay Justices
Police, 1960	13 to 1, minority more radical in recommending national police force
ECONOMIC PROBLEMS	
Trade Disputes and Combinations, 1903	Split 3-1-1, both minorities more conservative in wanting restrictions on trade unions
Poor Laws, etc. 1905	14 to 4, minority more radical in advocating more far-reaching reforms

Title	Remarks
Decimal Coinage, 1918	Split 13-4-3, the two minority groups being banking vs. retailer blocs
Coal Industry, 1919	Split 6-5-1-1, ranging in advice from minor changes to nationalization; two reports more conservative, two more radical
Economic Prospects of Agricultural Industry, 1919	12 to 11, minority (including Labour representatives) opposing continuance of government guarantee to farmers of minimum price of corn
Food Prices, 1924	Split 14-1-1, one minority more conservative, the other more radical in wanting more government intervention and more working-class consumer influence in proposed Food Council
Unemployment Insurance, 1930	5 to 2, minority more radical in wanting one contributory State unemployment scheme rather than dual system of insurance scheme & relief
Tithe Rentcharge, 1934	3 to 1, minority differing on rate of repayment of government stock to be used to compensate expropriated owners of the tithes
Taxation of Profits and Income, 1951	10 to 3, minority (in Dissent, not separate report) advocating more far-reaching changes in certain areas

SOCIAL PROBLEMS

Title	Remarks
Church of England, etc., 1906	Split, differences over definitions, procedure, statistics
Divorce, etc., 1909	9 to 3, minority more conservative in recommending adultery as sole cause of divorce
Licensing, England, 1929	Split 16-1-1-1, two minorities more conservative, one more radical in wanting immediate public ownership of the trade
Licensing, Scotland, 1929	10 to 4, minority being opposed to extension of permitted hours and recommending reduction in number of licenses
Marriage & Divorce, 1951	Split 9-9-(4)-1, minorities more radical on issue of divorce by consent

Title	Remarks

HEALTH

National Health Insurance, 1924 — 9 to 4, minority more radical in advocating abolition of Approved Societies & extension of benefits; Labour Government appointed but Labour Commissioners signed minority report

CITY PLANNING, ETC.

London Traffic, 1903 — 11 to 1, technical differences on traffic control

Canals and Inland Navigation, 1906 — Split 16-1-1-1, minorities more conservative in limitations on State aid; majority included conservatives, liberals, labourites, & socialists

Shipping "Rings," 1906 — 11 to 5, minority mostly colonial members, in U.K. *vs.* Empire business interests clash

Housing in Scotland, 1912 — 8 to 4, all recommending State assumption of full responsibility for housing, but minority judging local authorities could not carry such a burden without aid of private enterprise

Distribution of Industrial Population, 1937 — 10 to 3, minority more radical in recommending more authority and wider functions for State agency

EDUCATION

Trinity College & Univ. of Dublin, 1906 — Split, religious differences

COLONIAL AND DOMINION

Public Service in India, 1912 — 10 to 1, minority an Indian (one of several on the Commission)

MILITARY

Militia & Volunteers, 1903 — Split 8-2-1, all agreed on compulsory military service, but the minorities wanted limitations in application

Index